To Har

[handwritten inscription, partly illegible]

ALL THAT GLITTERED WAS NOT TOLD

A BEVERLY HILLS EXPOSÉ
BY
THE ILLEGITIMATE GRANDDAUGHTER OF
THE FOUNDER OF BEVERLY HILLS

[signature: Diane Hunt Stockmar]

DIANE HUNT STOCKMAR

Diane Hunt Stockmar
Scio, OR

Book Edits: Marsha Logan Campbell
Jean Kellogg

Printed in the United States of America

ISBN: 1475217414

This book is dedicated to my entire family. I think it only fair that they know the facts of my rather unusual heritage.

Unlike my previous books that are fictions drawn on embellished happenstances from our lives, this novel is instead a journal of the truth.

It took me over sixty years to gather the courage to write these facts. Many times I have faltered in the telling because revealing the truth is often far more challenging than the spinning of fictional tales.

Stephen, my wonderful husband was with me almost every step of the way. To him and our enduring love, I dedicate this journal.

Thank you for being there and believing in my abilities to be your life-long companion, and my abilities to write. You have been, are and always will be, my dearest and very best friend and truest love!

PROLOGUE

AN INTRODUCTION TO THIS FANTASTIC SAGA

Author's Notes:

Dolly Wellborn Green was my mother. She was the daughter of Burton Green, one of the primary founders of Beverly Hills. The world at large never knew that I existed within that family. It was widely perceived that Dolly was indeed childless all her life. I had been told by my adoptive parents that my true relationship to the Greens needed to be kept a secret for all time.

Long gone is the founding family. Long past is the apparent requisite need for concealment regarding these previously clandestine memoirs. I am committing them to this journal for anyone who wishes to read this story and finally be privy to these fascinating facts.

This book is an amazing history, one that all my life I have held close to my heart. Over the years I felt that my upbringing with the founding family of Beverly Hills was only extraordinary to me, myself and I.

However, after a lengthy conversation with bestselling author, Michael Gross, who was venturing that he would use some of my life story in his pending book, my perspective regarding my little 'secret' was completely revised. I never realized how small a part I would play in Michael's novel, Unreal Estate, nor how dispassionately my story would be treated.

When finally reading Michael's book, I was a bit surprised by the introduction where he actually admits that 'one of his greatest frustrations in researching his book was his difficulty in seeing the estates he was writing about in the Los Angeles, 'Platinum Triangle', all of which are hidden behind gates, fences, and foliage and visible, if at all, only in glimpses'. He then goes on to further relate, 'how he took commercial tours and went around with a real estate broker and repeatedly drove through the communities he'd decided to write about' and that 'he was invited into a few of the breathtaking houses described in the pages that followed'.

This was when I finally decided to compile my own revealing novel on the early days of Beverly Hills.

I have been in all the homes that I describe to the reader, long before the days of 'gates, fences and foliage'. They were all important Beverly Hills private homes. I was not on the outside looking into an unobtainable picture. The mansions and the inhabitants I describe in my novel, were simply a part of my early life.

I am not a figment of anyone's imagination, I have all the paperwork and proof of my place in Dolly Green's life in my possession . In my book, I am going to enlighten the reader as to exactly who I am today and the part I played in the illustrious life of the Icon, Dolly Green, a daughter of the founder of Beverly Hills.

My story about the Green family and my ties to it are not 'wished-for-illusions' of a life that could have been or something that I read in a newspaper clipping. They are revelations of actual happenstances.

Most of my entire life, I was a person who was allowed behind those hallowed gates. I only felt frustration and rejection when, as an adult, I returned to Los Angeles and sought to solve a mystery regarding challenging circumstances with my mother, Dolly Green. Only then did the gates of one 'Platinum Triangle' mansion shut on my life. I was exiled from my former gilded haven forever, once and for all.

So this is how the journey begins with the telling of my tale...All That Glittered Was Not Told.

CHAPTER ONE

EARLY DAYS

This story began many years ago in 1946 to be exact, in the fabled City of Beverly Hills. Dolly Wellborn Green Graves Walker became pregnant with me.

Dolly was having a long standing affair with my father, Neil McCarthy. Neil was a prominent attorney for many Hollywood stars. He represented the movie studio of Twentieth Century Fox, several stellar movie actors and in addition, he was often the trusted legal counsel of the illustrious, Howard Hughes. Neil was a very prestigious man.

Dolly and Neil had been lovers for some time and Dolly had divorced her second husband, William Walker, just to be with her current flame. 'The divine, Neil McCarthy'.

All Dollys' men had been, 'Divine'! Until they were not, then they conveniently disappeared from her life.

It was a small problem that Neil was married at the time of their liaison. His wife was fairly ill but Dolly knew full well how that went. Her own mother, Lilian, had been an invalid at the end of her life and her father, Burton, had several lovers in the wings while Lilian's life wound down. It was de rigueur in Beverly Hills to have a 'private partner' on the side.

But Dolly just knew that having Neil's child would sway him into divorcing his rather 'inconvenient' wife. The birth of a darling child would surely turn the tide.

Dolly became pregnant with me and off to Europe she fled while the so called 'baby bump' became noticeable. She slunk home a month before the birth and hid behind the cloistered walls of her 613 Mountain Drive château.

I was born at home with a mid-wife in attendance on June 11, 1947. She named me Beau because she thought me so beautiful and it seemed such a 'cute' name after all.

Once Dolly recovered from the birth ordeal, she showed me off to her friends and family with great motherly love and pride.

She dressed me in red and white outfits so she could show me off at parties and teas. Several friends came often to visit, and she adored showing me off again.

"Oh come see my darling little 'Beau-Beau'!" she would croon.

Dolly regularly took me with her when she visited her parents' home. The illustrious Burton Green adored me, held me and bounced me on his knees. Dolly routinely took me to her mother and father's, until I was almost two years old.

But the days, weeks, and months passed and 'the one' that Dolly wanted to impress *the most,* was her lover, Neil. He viewed the entire 'child' situation with chilly reserve. He refused to divorce his wife as he was of the Catholic faith, and Dolly never could sway him from that conviction. Even with the birth of 'their' adorable 'child', he would not put his wife aside.

So after one and a half years and an obviously failed turnaround of the situation, Dolly set upon a course to give her 'little indiscretion' away.

Dolly accomplished her goal with a vengeance as the reader will discover in the contents of this book. Dolly engaged Neil McCarthy as her legal representative. He was to place me in an orphanage called Maryvale.

Fortunately for me, a couple named Hunt, were seeking an additional child to privately adopt. So the experience at the orphanage was mercifully bypassed.

Maryvale, founded in 1856 by the Daughters of Charity, was then and is now, still considered the finest facility for orphaned children. I was not really qualified to go there, as Dolly was my mother. But she and Neil had been making quite the plea to the sisters to take me anyway. Though I was not an orphan, Dolly wished me to be placed at Maryvale--only if she could oversee the adoption. The sisters had flatly refused. So it was with great relief that Dolly's 'attorney' discovered this 'private' situation with the Ralph Hunts.

'The child' as I was so delicately referred to in the adoption papers, had become "a burden, an unnecessary expense, a bother, and (I) was causing Mrs. Walker undue distress". So Dolly wished for the Hunts to take the child, as quickly as possible off her 'overburdened' hands!

So they did!

The reader will be privy to my days, months and years of recollections regarding the 'hand-off' of me to the Hunts. The adjustment to the situation was a bit rocky...to say the least as this did not come to pass until I was at the formative age of two.

Then, the reintroduction into my life when I was six years old, as my 'godmother', was also an additionally interesting event!

Everyone believed that I had forgotten those early years with my mother, Dolly. I went along with the elaborate charade just to be allowed back into my former mother's life.

I did, however, recall everything from the past. I was bright enough to understand that any recognition of my new 'godmother' would put the reunion and future contact in severe jeopardy.

For all the years I was allowed to be back in Dolly's life, I never revealed my knowledge of my early life until I was eighteen years of age. Then and only then, did Dolly and I have a confrontation.

Many of the recollections of the early Green years were told to me by Dolly herself. Once she came back into my life as my 'godmother', she was quite proud of her own accomplishments.

She also kept a little red diary which she encouraged me to read whenever I visited her home. Dolly often loaned this journal to me so I could catch up on her own early years. She said that she thought I should have the memoirs to remember her by. She was very proud of her little log and suggested I keep one as well. Conveniently, I was not mentioned in her journal, or perhaps I had been jotted about at one time. There were a significant amount of pages torn away from the center of her book.

I have kept a journal all my life. But what Dolly's little log did for me, was provide me the ability to write the part of the legend of her amazing journey through her early years.

Dolly Green was an orchestrator beyond belief! The little red diary revealed how she manipulated people and perfected the use of her little white lies well beyond state of the art.

Dolly was a very turned inward woman. She was perhaps one of the most 'Narcissistic' of the early Beverly Hills 'Grand Dames'.

She would never hesitate to boast over her amazing prowess with men.

She was endlessly proud of how she was one of the guiding forces of fabulous galas and parties among the 'entertainment set' of greater L.A.

Dolly was great friends with Louis B. Mayer, head producer at MGM and had access to all the great celebrities through him and her lifelong amour, Neil McCarthy.

Her 'party lists' were the A-list of Hollywood, Beverly Hills, and Bel Air of the day.

Recollections regarding my parents handling of the difficult situation concerning my adjustment to my placement away from the Green household, are a culmination of my own amazing reminiscences.

Collaboration with my sister, Penny, and my continuous contact with Dolly's lifelong maid, Maria Rivera, also lends credibility to this story.

Once Dolly returned to my life when I was six, I was once again allowed to be alone with her in her home. She always treated me as if I were more of a confidant than a child or young woman. I guess for no other reason than she had very few woman friends…she saw all other women as her competition. So she treated me very much like a girlfriend…not like her daughter.

My parents, who were the saints that adopted me, would *never* discuss my adoption. To them, Penny and I were their 'chosen children' and the subject was simply not allowed.

Marie Hunt, our adoptive mother, died in 1972.

Neither Penny nor I together discussed our own adoptions' until after our adoptive father, Ralph Hunt died in 1981.

My sister, Penny, was my primary source of collaborations. She was interactive with the situation from the very beginning. She was present when first introduced to the 'Grand Dame', Dolly Green Graves Walker. Penny was actually five when the Hunts began negotiation with Dolly regarding my possible adoption. Penny recalled the events in amazing detail.

In later years, after Daddy died, Penny and I finally joined forces to recount our memories to bring this book to fruition.

Penny likened that first meeting with Dolly, as being a bit like going to pick out a puppy. If Penny liked me, she would eventually get to take me home.

I, myself, have compared my adoption as a bit that way. But the times were different then, than now. The supposed 'experts' on child psychology know a great deal more about a child's memory in this present day. That long ago, a psychiatrist advised that I would simply adjust to the 'switched situation'. Their belief was that young children recalled very little of their early childhood, if anything at all. So the late hand-off would certainly be eventually forgotten by me, the 'chosen child'.

Over the years, between 1982 through the year 1990 when Dolly finally died, Penny and I were able to piece this amazing journal together.

Many of the recollections that were shared with me over the years were from the ongoing litany told by the maid, Maria Rivera. Maria was unlike any of the Green servants, in that Dolly confided 'beyond the pale' in Maria. The Greens rarely confided in their staff. Servants were the help and they were not part of the inner sanctum's royalty.

Dolly had hired Maria Rivera to be her personal maid when the Puerto Rican woman was a very young girl. It was because of that long running association to Dolly's every private moment that Maria was treated like a confidant not a servant. To my knowledge, Maria was the 'only servant' who Dolly so closely confessed.

However, because Maria had been with Dolly practically since the woman was a child, Dolly held her in the strictest confidence.

Once reunited when I was six years old, Maria kept me in her confidence and told me all that had transpired after I was adopted by the Hunts. Because Maria knew of my true relationship with Dolly, she always kept me informed as to the happenings behind the castle Greens mysterious doors.

Maria and I were dearest friends. While I was in residence at Dolly's home, Maria would bring me up to speed as to the happenings in Dolly's life.

The reader may find this amazing that a servant and I could have this kind of bond, but Maria thought of me as her own child. More so than Dolly ever did.

Maria adored me and kept me informed about Dolly to her bitter end, and it is those confidences that she gave to me, that I believe cost her...her very life.

There are several people that talked to Maria toward the end of Maria's life, that all concur, that there were things going on in the 'Castle Green' that were very odd indeed.

But with Maria's unexpected death in 1989, Dolly's death in 1990, then my sister's tragic death in 1991, I put this true life journal on the back burner.

I then used portions of the dialogues to write my fictional book called the *Dark Side of a Fairy Tale.*

However, in 2010, certain circumstances reared their heads to slap me in the face, making me decide I needed to do this exposé now.

Primarily though, I am the one providing the facts. I was there first hand.

I was the one who was given away... *AND... I will never forget it to my dying day.*

CHAPTER TWO

Author's Notes:

Life is an interesting journey. However, some lives are more mundane than others. Perhaps the dull ones are easier to endure, less challenges, less wear and tear. Those who choose to exist that way must be content for their days to transpire thusly.

For myself, life has always been painted by several artists' brushes and I believe that was the best for me.

These vignettes of my past life I am sharing, in large part, because I believe they are amazing. I had an existence of wondrous experiences and if I never committed them to a journal, they would remain unshared. So readers...hold on to your hats!

The following revelation regarding a phone contact by the author, Michael Gross, is in large part, the reason I finally decided my 'real tale' needed to be revealed.

The emails from Michael Gross are verbatim. My suppositions regarding Michael's take on our conversations are conjectures on this author's part.

However, Michael was fully aware that I would exemplify him and his fate turning contact within the contents of my own book. I told him I intended to utilize him and he enthusiastically agreed. Michael is a very passionate writer. He was very interesting to work with during the two intensive weeks that he gleaned the facts he believed he needed regarding my relationship to his subject, Dolly Green. However, once he had what he required of me, little contact has been extended since. But that is perhaps all in the way he conducts his investigations of everyone. So here is my take on our brief email and phone relationship.

THE DECISION OF A LIFETIME

Monday, September 6, 2010

Email from Michael Gross:

Diane,
Your husband was kind enough to share this email address
when I just called him trying to reach you. I am an author
at work on a history of Beverly Hills and understand that
you may be related to one of my leading characters, Dolly
Green. I hope we might speak about this. I will be out of
town tonight through Sunday night but will call you
tomorrow if I possibly can as Stephen suggested. Should
you get this before that, I would be thrilled to hear from
you.
Best Wishes,
Michael Gross

That was the beginning of a two week intensive email
blitz and subsequent telephone conversations regarding
my 'relationship' to Dolly Green. Apparently Michael
had been doing research for a new book regarding the
early iconoclastic families of L.A. and had seen an article
regarding Stephen and my nuptials. The article reported
that Dolly Green and sisters Burtie and Lily attended our
wedding.

Michael is a very competent investigative reporter and
apparently had exhausted all leads to any 'skeletons' in
the Green 'closet', but got a bit of a tickle of interest at
this little piece of news regarding the Green sisters
attending our wedding.

It seemed his research had revealed that Dolly made
absolutely no appearances of this kind. It mentioned that
her sisters, Ms. William John Bettingen(Burtie) and Mrs.
William M. Rains(Lily) had attended, as well. Now this
seemed very odd to Michael Gross. He wondered what

tie this iconoclastic trio might have to this young girl, Diane Hunt?

The Green sisters were notoriously, socially reclusive, and it seemed quite odd that all three would attend such a seemingly 'low-key event'...as a private wedding in Beverly Hills.

In a preliminary conversation with my husband, Michael divulged that his latest endeavor was a book he was writing on the rich and legendary families of Beverly Hills called, *Unreal Estates*. Gross wanted to interview me for his upcoming book, as he believed he had unearthed some pertinent facts regarding my tie to the Burton Greens.

In Michael's usual investigative-reporter-style after the discovery of the obscure article, he had then spent the better part of a week and a half trying to track me down. He kept running up against brick after solid brick wall.

For a multitude of reasons, my husband and I have maintained an extremely low profile on contacts radar. We have an unlisted phone, do not expose ourselves on the multitude of internet Blogs or Twitter's, and live in a very remote, rural area of Oregon. Our family is very low key.

Michael, having already written the chapter on the reclusive Greens of Beverly Hills, had almost abandoned finding me. I was apparently as elusive as the rest of the entire Green flock. Burton Green was one of the co-founders of the fair town of Beverly Hills.

Admittedly, Gross had almost given up his search for me. But because of his frustrating lack of sterling sources regarding information on one of Beverly Hills founding families, he decided to try a few last ditch efforts. Michael felt he needed to get in contact with this secretive Diane Stockmar. He wanted to see if I could add an antidote or twelve to that particular chapter in his book.

Since *The Los Angeles Times* had reported that all three Green sisters attended the Hunt/Stockmar wedding, it continued to strike Michael as very odd. Something kept niggling at his inquiring mind. Gross decided on a lark to look up Stephen Stockmar and he was rewarded by finding the man listed as the COO of a company called North Star Investments.

Of course, it was de rigueur for most Hollywood couples to split, so Michael assumed that the Stockmars were probably divorced after the passage of all these years. But perhaps Stockmar could let him know a contact number for his wife, after all, he probably was sending her hefty alimony checks.

So Michael had chanced a call to Steve Stockmar. He actually had gotten the man himself on the horn. They began to visit.

Michael Gross introduced himself as a writer looking for Diane Hunt Stockmar. He needed her input for the book he was researching on Beverly Hills.

Steve had then advised that his wife of forty years, had a successful literary career herself. He himself had not heard of Gross before.

Michael explained to Steve exactly who he was and what he, as an author was doing in regard to writing his novel about Beverly Hills.

When Gross ventured the question about Dolly's relationship to me, Steve's surprising answer was, "You mean my wife's real mother? That Dolly Green?"

Michael later admitted to me, that at that point he almost dropped the phone along with his jaw, at Stockmar's startling admission.

Steve then explained, "I'd better let Diane relate this to you, herself." He then added that his wife was off for the day and could she get back with him later that afternoon?

Michael admitted that he was slotted to spend the Labor Day weekend in the Hamptons. The soonest he could return a call would be that Monday to finish this cliff hanging inquiry. He would email Diane an introduction of himself, alerting her that he would be in touch by Tuesday at the latest.

Michael later admitted he had been a skosh discouraged not to get a return email from me. This often happened because of his career as a notorious 'secrets revealer'. He was used to the old 'glacial shoulder' and the usual lines, 'I have absolutely no idea who on earth you are talking about. I have no relationship to that family at all'. Or the other completely alternate *fav*, 'Twenty years ago? Even if I had anything to do with those people, I have completely forgotten those facts and certainly would not be sharing them with you'!

It made him feel all warm and fuzzy, but hey, that was just part of his job that he did so well. Nothing discouraged Gross from a potential story. He was like the proverbial, 'dog on a bone'.

Michael could not know that the internet gobbled the intended etext. He'd been a bit discouraged that he received no subsequent response from his email to me at all. He would later learn from me, that it never came through.

I was equally frustrated by the lack of communication from him. Steve had briefed me regarding Michael's call and I was still running over in my mind the details of the conversation. One of which was an intended email. So everyone spent the weekend wondering what was going on.

When Steve relayed the news regarding Michael's initial contact, I had been thrilled to have heard from him. I knew full well who he was and had actually researched the man because I had read several of his colorful exposés. Michael reminded me a great deal of Dominick Dunne and that author's revealing Hollywood tales. So I was eager to talk to Michael Gross to see what he thought of my early life with the infamous, Dolly Green.

Some years ago, I had tried to contact Dominick Dunn to help me write my own story about Dolly Green. Dunne, famous for his 'buss and tattle' tales could have been the key element in getting my story out in a very well done manner. I felt I was too close to the matter and thought I could collaborate with Dunne and get a more comprehensive job regarding my own fascinating and novel-worthy tale.

Dominick never so much as sent a note advising me that he was not the slightest bit interested in my bizarre fairy tale. Unbeknownst to me, Dominick was actually gravely ill and could not have taken on my venture. He died of cancer in 2009.

Over the Labor Day weekend, neither Michael Gross nor I, realized that we both were anxiously awaiting calls from each other.

Later he revealed that he stewed the holiday away. This was because of no response from me regarding his email.

He fully expected my rebuff. He had no cell reception where they were staying and a land-line was out of the question. He wanted to be in his office to have his computer at hand to be able to pull up articles. Especially with the remote chance that I would have a few anecdotes to reveal regarding Dolly Green.

He later admitted that Monday had not come fast enough for him to pick up the phone and call for his expected, gelid response from me.

Given the fact that I would even admit having any relationship to Dolly, I would then still need to prove to him without a shadow of a doubt, that I was the professed 'pretermitted heiress'. Without very credible evidence, the chapter would be a wash regarding Diane Hunt Stockmar and her potential link to Dolly Wellborn Green.

'Pertinent facts withheld' were Michael's middle name. It would all hinge on my valid integrity which he would determine with his initial call. He was a miracle man at this part of the 'track and pounce' and had the instincts of a stalking jungle cat. He could spot a 'pretender' across a crowded room at a flashy New York Charity Ball and slice the fraud's integrity to the rotten core, with a few simple words! He was the top in his field at the 'nitpick' game that he and his fellow investigative authors, liked to refer to as 'Credibility's, Judgment Day'.

Yes, there had been whispers regarding a baby having been briefly spotted in Dolly's life. But it had reportedly been 'an adopted child' as an end to a means, which had ultimately, miserably failed.

Michael admittedly had some dirt on which he could base his chapter on the Green family, but oh how sweet it would be if there was a true 'unmentionable illegitimate heiress' out there after all.

His success at exposing titillating things with these prominent families was legendary and obvious to anyone who had read his books. He researched his sources to almost a catatonic state. By the time he finished with his subjects, they were borderline ready to put a contract hit out on his life, after so thoroughly grilling them to death.

His 'fav' line when calling a source he was interviewing was, "Hi, there it's your favorite bother, sweetheart!"

I later admitted that after several weeks of confiding in him, I felt as if I had just been grilled on the witness stand. My brain was completely fried by all his 'Torquemada' like inquisitions, but that was just his way.

Regarding the Green connection, Gross had talked to naught but a few former Green associates and a speckle of friends whose recollections were spotty at best. Plus, add in the reclusive factor of the entire family, he really had hit brick wall after stone edifice of abhorrently lackluster information. Much of it had come as the dreaded and damnably unusable 'third hand' whisper that there was a child missing from Dolly Green's domain.

This would *not* kindle the types of 'flames' that he adored to 'tattletale' in all his previous books.

One former acquaintance of Dolly's, suggested that Michael call the niece, Sandy Gray Nowicki, as she was the only remaining living relative of Dolly Green's.

Great idea, lousy results! When Michael began his tactful inquiry, 'dearest' Sandy slammed the phone down in his ear.

The other Bettingen sibling, Berry Anthony Gray, apparently was deceased. Michael got a chilly dismissal from dear Berry's wife, who's only comment when asked if there had been a love child was, "I have no clue what you are talking about! I never heard of any 'love child' of Dolly Green's!"

Michael had a slew of legitimate leads that he'd tracked down, regarding an illicit affair that Dolly supposedly had with a very prominent attorney to the celebrities. The man's name was Neil S. McCarthy, Esq. But what Michael really wanted and felt he desperately needed to make his book a blockbuster, beyond all his others, was for the illusive Green skeleton in the closet to walk out and say 'how-dy-do?' A love-child would be positively peachy. Throw in a woman that would admit the actual facts of that little indiscretion would be the very best of all.

So that Monday, Gross girded himself for the wall of silence that might just occur on Diane Hunt Stockmar's part. Just because her husband, Steve Stockmar was open regarding the relationship of Dolly Green to Diane, did not prove that 'where there was smoke there was fire'. This admission did not necessarily mean that there would be the slightest spark on Diane Hunt Stockmar's part to admit that Dolly Green was her mother!

What he needed were facts! What he needed was a woman who had the most remarkable memory on the planet to recall the minutia that happened all these years ago. He needed help putting together the facts on the chapter, 'Green'.

Chances of something that remote happening to him, were about as likely as his winning a bid for the Presidency of the United States. With that in mind, he'd grabbed the phone and called Diane and I picked up on first ring.

Michael would later admit that he had been absolutely amazed by my recollections.

What transpired during that hour long phone call had left him so breathless by the time he got off, it elicited tears of joy in his eyes.

He admitted openly that he'd been astounded to find me! He was amazed by my autobiographical memory. I had immediate and correct answers for every question he tossed my way. He could tell beyond a shadow of a doubt, that there was not a jot of fabrication on my part, just shoot from the hip straight and honest facts.

I promised to send him information regarding the adoption, photos of this and that. I would do some scanning of the longer documents of my adoption and then the kicker, my 'will contest'! Apparently, some secretary had embezzled the entire estate! There were even whispers of a possible murder that Michael, from other sources, had heard not long before. Those allegations were immediately confirmed by me.

We agreed to talk sometime at the end of the week.

Michael was on cloud nine when the conversation finally wound down. He could not believe his luck!

From our initial contact, Michael Gross and I spent a grueling fourteen days of communicating the 'nits and nats' of the Greens. I have a two inch stack of printed emails and records of several hours spent talking on the phone with 'my favorite bother'.

I admitted frankly that Dolly Green was my parent, I was tired of this fact being hidden for all this time. I was born a 'Green' and Dolly chose to give me away because I did not serve her purpose.

So as the unrecognized daughter of Dolly Green, I am penning this story in my own words.

When telling Michael the facts, I believe he was amazed at the clarity of my recollections, but I have always had a remarkable memory. If tested, I do believe I would have a near autobiographical memory, and sometimes it does not serve me well. It is often painful to look back on a particular series of recollections, because they really were pretty horrifying to a two-year-old child.

However, in this instance, it served me well in revealing the facts after they were so conveniently buried for all this time.

I am not writing this to harm the families that will be affected; such as the niece, Sandi Gray Nowicki, who refused to speak to Michael. Or the Berry Gray family, both who refused to discuss anything with Gross. Despite the fact that they went so far as to disavow any knowledge of me at all, I mean them no ill as time could have conveniently erased all memory of me for them.

Also, the man I believe that was my father, Neil McCarthy, has family, that I know. Sharon Gless is his granddaughter. I do not wish to offend her with this book.

I have legitimate proof of whom I was dealing with and also knowledge of the legal talent that expedited my 'hand-off' as an innocent child. I am in possession of my supposedly 'sealed' adoption papers. As well as the many correspondences between Neil McCarthy and the attorneys that represented my adoptive parents. Many of these documents are quoted in this book.

So, as in any exposé, the truths that will inflict hurt should have been considered long ago.

Perhaps with twenty-twenty hindsight, they should never have foisted me off at two years of age. Even though most children might not have recalled as much as I did, two is a very formidable age to 'adopt out' a child.

Alternately, if they wanted so badly to get rid of me, then why in the realm of sanity did Dolly return in a blaze of glory as my 'godmother' when I was six years old?

That was the most ludicrous thing of all!

I attribute it to a combination of Dolly's guilt and inconceivable selfishness. She did not want me to clutter her life, but did not want to be completely without me either, so she conceptualized the ludicrous 'godmother' role with my adoptive mother, Marie Hunt.

Dolly was to transform into my 'godmother', after several years of absence. This was only to be allowed if I showed no sign of recognition, once she re-appeared in my life.

My adoptive father, Ralph Hunt, was always adamantly against this reuniting!

When Dolly again chose to briefly disappear from my life when I was twelve, Ralph Hunt, was relieved. I was the one who would have nothing to do with that. I brought Dolly back into my life when I was sixteen and firmly resisted her removal after that.

This is a complex tale of highs and lows and good times and bad circumstances. All weave the fabric of this autobiography.

If you are reading this because you think it is about a wonderful fairy tale 'godmother' that helped her goddaughter lead a fairy tale life, this is *NOT* the book for you!

Dolly Green was a spoiled, turned-inward-woman, who built a house of cards with little white lies. If it did not suite her, she simply made you go away!

She did it to me, husbands, lovers and friends. She simply could not abide anything that got in her way.

If this interests you, then read on. It is full of intrigue, romance, Hollywood celebrities, and lives beyond most people's wildest dreams.

This was the time of the *REAL* Hollywood, and Dolly knew everyone that was anyone and entertained them lavishly.

It is about a family that was regarded as an iconoclastic dynasty, yet their darkest secret to date, was Dolly's illegitimate child!

But Dolly dearest, fixed her littlest mistake in a highly calculated manner.

She heartlessly gave her own tiny daughter...away!

CHAPTER THREE

Author's Notes:

There is very little written about the Burton Green family of Beverly Hills. In large part, the reason is that they were a very reclusive family, and meant it to stay that way.

Also, one must recall that in this early era of the famous Beverly Hills families, there was little media-hype in the way we are barraged with it today.

It is not to say that there was any less curiosity regarding the upper-strata-moneyed families. It was more a case that these select few were far more ferocious regarding their secrecy and their privacy. They stalwartly refused to allow anyone on the outside into their closed doors or cloistered walls.

They all had servants that remained discreet, even well after they left the employ or the families died off.

But there was none of the tattletale press such as we are overwhelmed with today.

Of course there was interest in the upper strata, but there was not the hounding paparazzi as there is in this day and age.

Those wealthy families kept much to themselves. They remained that way well into the sixties when the trend of nosy press and star magazines began to flood the scene.

So there is precious little regarding many of the founding families that actually had a big part in the creation of the 'Fairy Tale City' called Beverly Hills and Bel Air.

This chapter is a compilation of facts taken from two books: Early Beverly Hills by Marc Wannamaker and Beverly Hills, by Genevieve Davis.

TIME WINDOWS:

EARLY HISTORY OF THE BURTON GREENS

FROM THE IMAGES OF AMERICA EARLY BEVERLY HILLS: A REAL ESTATE ADVERTISEMENT of 1922:

THE FRANK MELINE COMPANY WAS ONE OF SEVERAL DEVELOPERS WHO SOLD PROPERTY IN BEVERLY HILLS AT ALL PRICE RANGES.

BEVERLY HILLS: PRIDE OF THE SOUTHLAND:

Developed along generous lines with wide deep lots-broad, gracefully curving boulevards-ample park and garden spaces; BEVERLY HILLS has all the attributes of the ideal home section, yet it is conveniently accessible to the busy city.

Out in the open, the freedom of the hills-the far reaches of the valley-call you to make your home in BEVERLY HILLS!

The man of average means is especially welcome. He will find prices of property in Beverly Hills far from prohibitive.

The Frank Meline Co.
Owners, Representatives
Los Angeles   Beverly Hills

FROM THE BOOK: BEVERLY HILLS, AN ILLUSTRATED HISTORY BY GENEVEVE DAVIS:

The driving force behind the new Rodeo Land and Water Company was Burton E. Green, who was born near Madison Wisconsin on September 6, 1868. He led the founders of Beverly Hills through the ups and downs of the development and finance of Beverly Hills.

An unspoiled paradise, it seems, could not last forever, and in 1900 oil fever hit once again. A group known as the Amalgamated Oil Company composed of such men as Burton Green, Max Whittier, W.G. Kerckhoff, Charles E. Canfield and other, purchased the old Hammel and Denker Ranch with the idea of exploring for oil. When the oil venture failed, the investors reorganized and in 1906 they developed the Rodeo Land and Water Company with the idea of building an ideal residential community.

Burton E. Green was the guiding genius in this venture and it was he who was instrumental in the overall design and layout of a community with parks and tree-lined streets...calling it Beverly Hills. The origin of the name Beverly Hills as recorded in Green's letter; was a newspaper article about President Taft's vacation in Beverly Farms, Massachusetts. "What a wonderful name for our new community!" he said to his wife Lilian. She replied, "I think Beverly Hills would sound much better." And thus the city was christened.

The first three streets to be laid out were Canon, Beverly and Rodeo drives, followed in 1911 by Rexford, Camden, and Crescent drives. Water, gas and electricity were provided and the gently winding streets were planted in palm, acacia and Arizona pepper trees. The

Arizona pepper trees did not survive and were later replaced by magnolia.

The first house was built by Henry C. Clark in 1907. But shortly after the tract opened, the panic of 1907-1908 prevented it from, becoming a success. The tract lay idle until 1910 when it sprang to life under Percy H. Clark, sales agent and general manager of the Rodeo Land and Water Company. Clark went to work with Wilbur Cook, a prominent New York landscape architect. Both Cook and Burton Green as well as Clark deserve credit for the beauty and design of Beverly Hills' lovely streets and parks.

In 1911, only a year later, there were still only half a dozen houses built. The houses, located north of Santa Monica Boulevard, were owned by Pierce Benedict, Henry C. Clarke, William B. Hunnewell, J.M. Huntner, R.M. Kedzie and a Mr. Peters. No one had any idea that in four years' time enough people would reside in Beverly Hills to incorporate it as a city. Nor did anyone then have the slightest notion that the one-acre lots along Sunset Boulevard selling for from $800 to $1,000 an acre would eventually be worth millions.

The lots nearest Santa Monica Boulevard were then selling for only $300 or $400 apiece with a 10 percent discount for cash and another 10 percent discount if construction was begun within six months after purchase. The additional discount was given to induce purchasers to build promptly so that the area would take on the appearance of a live in community and induce others to buy. Clearly something had to be done to promote the tract for it had a barren and forlorn look. The sight of rows of telephone poles, unwired for lack of customers, did nothing to enhance it. Whittier, Canfield and Green decided to enlist the services of horticulturist John C. Reeves. Waving aside the issue of cost, they commissioned him to plant trees where he saw fit. Reeves needed no further encouragement. After drawing up a plan, which the investors approved, he lined each street in a different variety of trees. Reeves was admittedly gifted but he brooked no opposition. When Burton Green objected to the use of pepper trees along Crescent Drive, he stubbornly refused to back down. The first year saw the construction of only a dozen or so houses north of Santa Monica Boulevard and some larger homes on Sunset. There would have been more houses built had it not been for the recession of 1907, which lasted for three years.

When the recovery came in 1910, the Los Angeles housing market became active, but not the Beverly Hills market. The feeling was that it was too far away from central Los Angeles. Something had to be done, and done quickly to give the project a boost. Whittier, Green and Canfield came up with an exciting idea. Why not build a hotel? Not and ordinary hotel, but a hotel so fabulous that it would draw visitors from the East and from Europe as well. The Easterners, they felt, would be glad for a chance to escape the bitter winters, and some of them might even decide to settle down and buy a home in the area. Whittier, Green and Canfield had only to look and see what the construction of the Hollywood Hotel had done for the community of Hollywood. There was no reason why the construction of a fine hotel in Beverly Hills would not work as well.

No time was lost and that same year saw the Beverly Hills Hotel rise from what had recently been nothing but tilled bean-fields. Whittier, Green and Canfield did not stop there. The hotel they decided, would have nothing but the best, both in fixtures and in management. They enticed Margaret J. Anderson away from the justly famous Hollywood Hotel and persuaded her to take over the managerial duties of the new hotel. Anderson not only took over, but brought with her many of the old-time residents of the Hollywood establishment, together with some of the staff and furnishings. Most of all, she brought with her innate talent and know-how.

The Beverly Hills Hotel opened its doors in 1912 and was an instantaneous success. Anderson had gambled and won. She had come to the hotel against the advice of her friends, who had warned that she was throwing over a sure-thing for something unproved. The hotel, they warned, was too far out of town, for one thing. Who would want to stay in the midst of a bean field? Anderson had weighed all their objections, but had found the offer too good to resist. The Rodeo Land and Water Company, in order to secure her services, made an outright gift to her of a $250,000 mortgage along with the land. For another $125,000, she was able to furnish the hotel to her taste.

Across from the hotel the Rodeo Land and Water Company constructed a park. Triangular in shape, it boasted a fountain and reflecting pool set in a bower of trees, flowers, and shrubs with benches and promenades. The hotel and park were an oasis of splendor set in the surrounding bean fields.

The Rodeo Land and Water Company had made an accurate prediction. Lured by curiosity and attracted by the promise of a temperate climate, people flocked from the east and many of them stayed on to become permanent residents of the hotel, while others returned to establish homes and business. The world famous Polo Lounge would not come into being for a number of years but on Saturday nights, there were "flickers" shown in the Venetian Room, and the hotel was justly famous for its fine dining rooms.

The real estate market was still sluggish however so Whittier and Green and Canfield decided that they themselves would establish large homes in Beverly Hills. Their decision prompted other prominent businessmen to do the same.

Burton Green's home was a showplace. Situated on three and a half acres of land on Lexington Road and Oxford Way, north of Sunset Boulevard, it was a splendid Tudor mansion surrounded by mature trees and lavish landscaping.

So the lovely little rural hamlet of Beverly Hills was born.

CHAPTER FOUR

Author's Notes:

The following narratives are mine. My first hand memories are many. In addition, they are recollections from Dolly's little journal and stories related to me by Maria Rivera, the life-long maid of Dolly Green. The reader must remember throughout this book that my memory is likened a great deal to a camera for a documentary. The developed film was there all along, but until the creation of this novel, it was in storage. I'm just brushing off the 'glitter-dust' for all of you readers, now.

IDYLLIC DAYS IN THE FABLED LAND

Burton Green built a magnificent estate on Lexington Road that became one of the first landmarks in the area. Mr. Green was married to Lilian Wellborn, the daughter of Judge Olin Wellborn and they had three daughters; Burton, named after her father and later was called Burtie, Lilior, and Dorothy who was always fondly called, Dolly.

Dolly was the youngest and was spoiled by her dotting parents almost beyond belief.

People said that Dolly was born with a silver spoon in her mouth. When Dolly grew old enough to understand the meaning of the saying, she was blatantly proud of the fact.

The Greens were in a rather unique monetary position that allowed them to coddle their three daughters far beyond most parents.

Burton Green was a millionaire.

He'd been a wild-cat-oil baron in the late 1800's. His company, Belridge Oil, that was situated near Bakersfield, California, garnered him a pretty penny.

But, in the early 1900's, Burton drilled three dry holes on a parcel of Los Angeles real estate that he owned with some pals. Frustrated by the lack of crude, he decided to sub-divide and sell the oil-poor parcels, to his chums.

The little slice of heaven in So Cal was dubbed by Burton, Beverly Hills. So named after his recollections of Beverly Farms in Massachusetts that he remembered fondly from his childhood for its beautiful landscaping.

He made a killing in real estate.

He went from the oil fields into real estate development. According to his wife, Lilian, it was far more socially acceptable and prestigious than the dirty oil business.

But his corporation, Belridge Oil, continued to pay the majority of the extravagant family bills.

He had all the money in the world, so he lavished gifts on all his girls.

All Burton's children were horribly spoiled, but his adorable, Dolly, he over-indulged the most.

When Dolly was young, she'd been very sick, so the Greens were thrilled she survived the odd illness. To improve their daughter's outlook on life, they gave her absolutely everything she asked for, fulfilling her every spoken wish.

When Dolly yearned for a cote full of snow white doves, because her friend, Saundra Belridge, had them at her home, Daddy Burton had a famous architect construct it for his precious little girl. He filled it with the most beautiful cooing birds that had ever flapped their snowy wings in Beverly Hills. The interest lasted a week. Dolly became disenchanted with the whole messy, smelly pen. Dutifully, the gardener assumed the care of the lovely things.

Dolly wanted a puppy, so Burton flew in a Boxer from the Westminster Kennel Club Show that had been the

Champion of top honors that year. Dolly loved the doggie for weeks, but soon became bored with him. He was far too much trouble to walk and bathe. One of the servants was required to take over the care of the then bothersome pooch.

Carol Bell, a close friend of Dolly's, had her own gray pony and cart that she drove around the Bell estate. Dolly threw a tantrum until she received the identical vehicle and dappled pony, delivered to the Green's door. Burton felt nothing was too good for his 'precious' little child. The fascination for the carriage lasted almost two weeks, before boredom set in. Burton decided he was on to something with horses because the pony-cart held Dolly's attention for the longest time of anything, so far.

Dolly's best friend, had a champion bay pony that Dolly coveted, so Burton bought it for her within the week the lust was expressed. Nothing was ever too grand or unreachable, Dolly simply needed to ask. She obtained top notch riding honors with the pony and Dolly actually succeeded in keeping her interest in the sport for many years, much to her parent's astonishment. Previously, they found it hard to entertain their easily distracted child.

So at a very young age, Dolly was instructed in the equestrian art, which proved to be the only diversion that held Dolly's interest for any length of time. She became so skilled at the sport, she began to win at every show.

When Dolly outgrew the need for her pony, Burton bought a gelding that was shipped from the Kingsford Hall in Devonshire, England because that was where all the English Royal mounts were procured.

Dolly took her ribbons on a seventeen hand black gelding that had been ridden by the Queen Mother, herself. How smart his beautiful Dolly looked in her red riding coat, black hard hat, jodhpur pants and gleaming boots. She sat a mount as if born to ride, her grace as an equestrian was state renowned.

Dolly became an expert horsewoman, taking to jumping like a bird to flight. Her legendary equestrian skills far surpassed her scholastic skills, so Burton was constantly forced to *insist* a teacher tutor his 'princess'.

In her early years, Dolly hated the routine of classes so much that her career of studies actually ended up with private tutoring at her parent's spacious home.

However, at twelve, despite Dolly's rather vocal disgruntlement over the matter, Burton felt she needed a normal schedule and relationships with other girls. So his 'princess' was enrolled in Marlborough School for Girls.

It was about then, that Dolly began her career of perfecting 'little white lies' to an art form. She justified her twists of truth by convincing herself she was *special* and deserved nothing but her own way.

So when she became hateful towards her mathematics teacher, Dolly told her father that the instructor was an incompetent fool. Her daddy arranged to have her coached in that class by another tutor. Soon the 'incompetent fool' disappeared and coincidentally was replaced with Dolly's charming tutor.

Dolly also abhorred her swimming instructor. She lied that she spied on the girls in the locker room. Burton had her fired and arranged for the coach to be replaced by a fine swimmer from UCLA.

The piano teacher was deemed a dud, fibbed Dolly, after she and the woman had a horrible tiff. Burton paid the lady to disappear and replaced her with an instructor from Julliard.

It seemed things were always like that for Dolly Green. If she did not like something, Daddy fixed it. This became a dependable routine.

"What Dolly wanted, Dolly got," was the chant about the school.

As she got older, the 'want lists' went from small requests to more important matters. The first of these were easy monetary obligations, but later, her requests became far more psychologically demanding for everyone involved!

Burton, without a falter in his stride, believed his 'princess' deserved every bit of his helpful parental doting, after all, he told his wife, what were fathers for?

Dolly admired a diamond choker owned by a special friend. Burton had Tiffany's copy it to the exact, last stone.

The Trousdale girls frequented the Gazebo Salon. So at Dolly's insistence, Burton hired the Trousdale girl's hairdresser to do Dolly's raven locks at their home, once a week.

When Dolly turned sweet sixteen, Burton bought Dolly her first car. It was a Dodge, shiny and sleek. She hated it. It was returned and her preference, a Cadillac, was delivered to her door.

But she hated driving.

Dolly told her daddy that Ginny Robinson had her own 'dreamy chauffeur'. So, Burton hired the 'dreamy chauffeur' at higher pay and bought the man a home down the way from the Greens. The driver, Brian, boasted he was the highest paid baby sitter in Beverly Hills.

Dolly had her first affair with the 'baby sitter' who drove her car. In fact, it was in the back seat of said 'Caddy', that Burton found his 'princess' with the driver...both naked as jays.

Without much of any fuss, Brian disappeared. The house he owned was sold to a couple from Santa Monica and his driving position was replaced by a lanky black man named Tom.

Nothing was said to scold Dolly. But, to Mrs. Green's extreme horror, she was forced to explain the consequences of Dolly's slight indiscretion.

Fortunately, nothing came of that liaison with her first, of many, 'dreamy men'.

CHAPTER FIVE

Author's Notes:

It was a time of experimentation on Dolly's part and her father simply could not bring himself to reel his willful daughter in from anything.

Dolly was amazingly beautiful and smart, but the word wanton comes to mind for a woman of that era. Dolly Green was the original 'Party Girl'!

TIME MARCHES ON

From an early age, Dolly really hated school work, but none of the girls she befriended believed studying did them any good. It was a status thing to achieve marginal grades and be 'tutored up' just to pass the final tests. All Dolly's cronies considered that practice, chic. However, no matter how they all tried to underachieve most of her compatriots actually earned degrees from Marlborough. As for Dolly, her diploma was pushed forward a bit by a generous grant from Mr. Green to re-build the library of the prestigious girl's school.

Lilian Green bought Dolly her senior prom dress. Pink, piped in lace. Perfect for her raven haired daughter who was always a tiny size. Dolly threw a fit! She tore the pink confection to shreds and demanded the chauffeur take her to Bullocks. She returned shortly after with a fire-engine red chiffon dress that made her look like a harlot, but the parents kept still, not daring to incur their precious girl's rage.

She went to the Senior Prom with a man no one approved of, mostly Burton, who could not stand the boy. Jack Graves was three years older than Dolly and a banker at that. Burton thought all bankers were crooks.

The couple eloped that night.

In less than five weeks, Dolly wanted an annulment. Graves beat her, she told her doting dad. It was a little white lie, but she had quickly grown to abhor the man, so he needed to be eliminated, fast.

She knew her father detested marital violence, so it was the strongest case she could make. The truth that her husband bored her to tears would hardly capture her daddy's sympathy. The little untruth about his beating her would hardly be noticed, and in Dolly's eyes, the man simply had to go.

Burton gladly made the arrangements and paid the man off for his silence about the fiasco. Graves was never heard from again.

That was only one of many of her escapades that Burton was forced to cover up. One man fell to his daughter's charms, after the other. But she always tired of them and Daddy had to *insist* that they leave his precious 'princess' alone.

To get his daughter away from the latest upset of parting with a man, Burton decided to take the whole family on a European grand tour.

That proved to be a monumental mistake. If Dolly had seen the American men as 'dreamy', she went crazy over the 'divine' European men. Unbeknownst to her parents, Dolly slept across Europe from Paris to Rome. She would feign exhaustion and troop off to bed at each given hotel. Then she'd sneak out the window or back door when her parents were secure in their own rooms.

Dolly Green painted 'rouge' the Casinos, Cabarets and bars the entire time they traveled Europe's highways and byways. She slept with the high-brow to the low. From artists, Counts to Earls, she hopped into their beds. She partied every night till dawn pinked the sky.

Unfortunately, for her fun, the power failed one evening at the hotel where the Greens resided while visiting Cologne. Father Green went to check on his daughters. Lily and Bertie were fast asleep in their respective suites.

Dolly was nowhere to be found in the entire hotel!

Burton sat in her room, waiting for his missing girl. Throughout the entire night into the hours of dawn, he waited for Dolly to reappear.

His 'princess' snuck in at six, reeking of booze and sex.

Burton had the family packed and back on an ocean liner before the ink on the tickets was even dry.

Once stateside, Dolly fell *madly* in love with a man by the name of William Walker. She swore to her father that he was 'the love of her life', and that there would never be another man more perfect for her.

They were married with great pomp, ceremony and all of the Green's influential friends attended the ceremony of the decade. All Saints Episcopal Church bulged with invited guests.

They had a fairy tale reception at the Beverly Hills Hotel.

Dolly and William Walker were whisked by chauffeured limo from the party to the airport where they flew to Hawaii on a private plane loaned by Douglas Aircraft. Doug was one of Burton's best pals.

They spent two glorious, love filled weeks on mainland Hawaii.

Then home to a palatial mansion Daddy and Mother had bought them, high above Beverly Hills, at 613 Mountain Drive.

Marital bliss lasted three years.

CHAPTER SIX

Author's Notes:

There was a real pattern being perfected by Dolly, one she would employ all her life... the perfection of little white lies!

There is some belief that the socio-economic situation helped her believe she was so privileged, that she was entitled to this right.

However, this is hardly anything new, look at celebrities today.

The more money you have, the more you can get away with. Just look at the recent cast of marital indiscretions.

The more you earn, the more you are allowed to lie and cheat and get away with it!

Wow, how exactly has it changed?

Need I say anymore?

ONE MORE LITTLE WHITE LIE

MAY 1945

One day, Dolly announced to Daddy Green, that she and Willy were incompatible, just another little white lie. As the years passed it seemed easier and easier to tell fibs. She was beginning to perfect 'white lying' to a form of art. Truth be known, she'd fallen hopelessly in love with Neil McCarthy, an attorney for MGM.

She *flung* Willy Walker out of their palatial home and began her hot pursuit of Neil.

There was a minor obstacle in Dolly's way with her 'dreamy' new friend.

He was married.

But, his wife was ill! She was an invalid.

41

Yet Dolly, with all her lust was certain that Neil would get rid of the 'inconvenient' wife.

Neil refused to divorce his wife, but, he seemed fine with them trying an affair. Once together, they were like sparks doused with kerosene.

They went everywhere together. Neil was heavily into breeding Thoroughbreds, so they were continuously at his ranch. The breeding of the stallions excited them both so much, they constantly had sex in the barns. Hard, plunging, pummeling one another just like a stallion servicing an eager mare. This copulation in the barns turned them on so much, they could hardly wait to get home to *her* bed to fornicate even more.

Nothing could quench their passion. Not even the chauffeur driving their car could keep them from having carnal, lascivious, sex in the back seat of the limousine. After all, he was just a servant. He was paid to be blind and keep his eyes front and drive the car.

The lovers were mad for one another...crazy, unbridled, hot.

It was a wild roller coaster ride of eroticism and lust that for Dolly, finally resulted in an overwhelming, unquenchable, obsession. No matter what they did or how often, she could not get enough hard-core sex with Neil.

With this in mind, Dolly decided to take matters into her own hands and force the issue of his divorce.

She became purposefully pregnant with Neil's child. Of course the baby was an '*accident*', she lied. Another falsity in the '*house of cards*' she was constructing. But Neil never knew the truth.

All throughout the pregnancy while she and Neil continued their wild erotic sex, Dolly cajoled him that he must divorce his wife or this passion could not go on.

She absolutely knew he would relent and divorce his wife the minute he saw his baby born. She always eventually got what she wanted; this matter was simply taking more planning than her usual, stalk and pounce, routine.

The darling child, Beau, was born June 11, 1947.

Dolly delivered the child at home, under the care of a registered nurse who was assisted by Dolly's faithful young servant, Maria Rivera. As in most home deliveries in those days, the child's birth was never recorded.

Dolly named her baby, Beau Melody Green. She proudly showed the baby off to Neil.

He was very happy the birth had proceeded easily, complimented Dolly on a beautiful child, but announced that it changed nothing. He stalwartly refused to divorce his wife, as he was faithful to the Catholic Church.

There began the campaign to win Neil over to the baby's side.

CHAPTER SEVEN

Author's Notes:

The narration of the book now progresses to my talking in the first person. I realize that the reader might find it hard to believe that I knew everything from the time of my birth. Obviously, I do not recall the very early months, but I do recall things far more vividly than most. I am able to reflect while writing and pulling these recollections to the surface. I have vibrant memories from the time I was barely one year of age. My first clearest recollections begin with the Christmas when I would have been eighteen months. I remember the white-flocked Christmas tree, the servants helping decorate it with all silver ornaments and the lights were the bubble kind in white. It was a shimmering image of the fairy-land that I lived within. There were masses of presents under the tree on Christmas day.

Sadly, it is also at eighteen months, that I recall the change in Dolly's attitude toward me. It was the beginning of the covert approach she affected when she and I were together. Our times with one another began also to dramatically decline and that seemed oddly sad to me.

Clearly things were afoot, however as always, she played the part to the hilt of motherhood. But children are so intuitive. I knew something was wrong as little by little, she began to draw away from me. Sensing that I had done something very wrong, I tried to be a very good little girl, but nothing seemed to avail.

As Dolly drew away from me, that is when Maria Rivera really came into play as my constant companion and dearest friend. Inadvertently, Maria became my surrogate mother, and she really remained in that position all my early life.

From the standpoint that I recall images that early, I begin from here to write often in the first person as the narrator of the tale.

Of course, some of the recollections obviously were relayed to me by Maria as told to her by Dolly Green. Dolly probably should never have confided so completely in that maid, as Maria eventually revealed all the amazing details of these happenings to me.

TAH DAH! HERE IS MY DARLING 'BEAU-BEAU'

Early in my life, my mommy, Dolly, took me absolutely everywhere to show me off to her admiring friends.

Her sisters "ohhed" and "aaahed". Mommy especially liked to get me dressed up like a little doll in red satin and white lace frills and take me to her mother and father's home on Lexington Road.

Burton was most attentive. We would go for tea and have all manner of jam sandwiches, and milk and cookies while my mommy had tea. Grandfather adored me and he would bounce me on his knee.

I would be taken out into the vast gardens and walked by one or two of the lady staff members. They all adored me and made much of me when I was there on the Lexington Road property. It was vast, and it seemed to me as if it were a castle, where my grandfather lived with his lady fair. My grandmother was always somewhere hidden away in a shadowed room.

By the time I was plunked into the elder Green's lives, grandmother Lilian had a type of dementia that had made her very vague. So she was very quiet and when Mommy brought me for the habitual bi-weekly visits and teas, Lilian was withdrawn and reserved. Very often she would not emerge from her rooms. I recall she was a beautiful woman in a tragic, mystical sort of way.

We visited them often and I always will recall going up the winding drive to be taken out of the car by Mommy and hustled into the atrium that lead into the enormous manse.

Mommy's home was palatial, but Grandee's home was beyond enormous and I was fearful that I might get lost in there and never find my way home. But I always looked forward immensely to the trip to my Grandee's home.

My house was beautiful as well. Mommy was very proud of her home and people were always visiting us to have tea.

At my home on Mountain Drive, I had the most beautiful room that was decorated just like the interior of a circus tent. It had red-striped wallpaper, and a circus-striped-canopy hung over my little bed. There were all varieties of stuffed toys about the room on shelves. My crib in my room where I used to sleep, had been converted into a cage for a huge Steiff tiger, stuffed toy horses, panda bears and all kinds of animals from every kingdom. I would play by the hour with the animals in their 'crib' cage.

My home life was filled with playing in the yard and chasing goldfish in a long pond. There were a lot of fan-tail ones that were multi-colored and so beautiful. At one point I decided that swimming in the pool with the fish was a good idea.

Unfortunately, Maria did not catch me in time and I was knee deep in the fish pond, covered with algae when Maria hauled me out herself. She was furious with me at that.

"You could have drowned," Maria had railed. She hauled me into the house, into the servant's quarters where she bathed me and got me dried and re-dressed. She told me that under no uncertain terms, was I to ever do that again. I also believe she never told Dolly, because I think she perceived that it had been an error in her judgment to let it happen at all.

Dolly was not known for being lenient with mistakes made by the help. Again, as with people that she did not like, she would eliminate the staff for the slightest error.

So my days continued...playing outdoors and generally having a lot of fun by myself with my doggy, Poncho and Charlie the beautiful, black cat.

When I was one, I developed an odd reaction to my pets. I would play with them and begin to sneeze.

Mommy was horribly alarmed and took me to a doctor who told her I might be allergic to the animals, so to keep me away from them for a while.

It seemed to me that every time Uncle Neil came over to our house, he and Mommy ended up in an argument over something I was not supposed to know about.

Somewhere along the line, I'd been instructed to call him 'Uncle Neil', but I thought of him as 'Uncle Meany'.

However, I had perfected a little 'unknown to Mommy' routine. I would allow myself to be put down for a nap, then when they thought I was asleep, I would tip-toe down the stairs and hide behind the Chinese lacquer screen. I would listen to 'Uncle Neil' and Mommy endlessly argue about me.

I could not fathom what on earth I had done wrong and I never truly figured it out!

For one year and a half, Mommy screamed at 'Uncle Neil', swore at him, threw things at him while she continuously flaunted me at him. She threatened anything and everything!

Finally, in a last ditch effort, she denied him her always willing body. Even that did not succeed.

He refused to divorce his wife. He was a staunch Catholic and divorce was not sanctioned by the Church.

After one and a half years of failure, Dolly told Maria that she had realized over the long haul that she had never been cut out to be a mother. Neil was not going to divorce his wife, so it was time to clean up one more little white lie. I was in her way and hampered her ability to continue her uninhibited relationship with, Neil.

It was Neil who suggested she put me up for adoption because I had become bothersome to their relationship...hampering their inhibitions when having sex on the throw rugs on the floor. He was certain he had seen 'the little waif' hiding, spying on them from behind the Chinese lacquer screen.

He advised Dolly to place me in a very fine orphanage, Maryvale. Because after all, 'the child' was a horrible bother and lately had developed some sniffy-wheezy thing when she was around Poncho, the Boxer, that Dolly adored.

Dolly drew the line at getting rid of the dog as her doctor recommended. Far preferring the pooch over me. After all, I had not accomplished my purpose so she concluded I needed to go.

One afternoon, she announced to her father, Burton, that as much as she had grown to adore her child, this was another one of her *'little indiscretions'* that she needed her daddy to help her clean up.

She revealed the idea of Maryvale. Burton thought her idea of the orphanage, a bit harsh, but he had no better plan. From years of dealing with spoiled Dolly, he knew when his daughter set her mind on something she was rarely ever crossed. This bit of failure with Neil was perhaps the first and last time Dolly intended to lose a conquest, and frankly she was not wearing this mantle of defeat any too graciously.

They were set to dispose of me, at Maryvale in the course of just a few weeks. They had finally struck an unprecedented bargain with the Sisters at the Orphanage to take me on with a hefty donation from the Greens. After all, I for all intent and purpose was not an orphaned child but the monetary donation offered to take me was impossible for the Sisters to refuse.

I was one and a half years old.

Some people had mentioned to Burton that it could be traumatic on the little tyke to be displaced at such a late age. Especially since my relationship with Dolly and the rest of the family had been very close-knit.

However, Burton knew, there simply was no other choice. He continuously assured himself that little Beau's wounds would mend. I was just a little child and children didn't remember their childhood's at all. He certainly did not recall a wisp of his own.

Burton Green had been working on my disposal for weeks with Neil. My own father had agreed to personally deliver me to the orphanage himself, so no one saw any involvement with the Greens. Burton wanted nothing to come back to haunt the family, once this slight indiscretion was cleared away.

Maryvale had a very high reputation and was the choice of adoptions of the movie stars. Neil advised that little 'Beau-Beau' would probably be far better off to be placed with a Hollywood family than remain with Dolly and her rising hatred of the infringement of the child into her life.

Neil and Burton would sit in his office for hours hashing over Dolly's latest problem. Burton had dodged bullet after bullet all his daughter's life. At some point, he knew she would have to do things on her own. However, till she really seemed to grow up, he would have to front for her. He needed to continue to help her, as she was so helpless on her own!

Even with all his diligent work, Burton found himself having a huge problem with the disposal of his grandchild. Actually he adored baby, Beau. If his wife had not been so ill, he might have considered taking her, himself. But Lilian with her mental illness was far too vague, indecisive and frail to take on a rambunctious grandchild.

Burton's darling little 'Beau-Beau'. What would become of his daughter's child? She was the precious black-eyed baby he had bounced on his knee. Someone would have a beauty on their hands. She was the spitting image of his own spoiled Dolly. And bright? Oh, Lord the child was brilliant. Quick of wit and smile. Playing with that baby, one would have to be a dim bulb not to realize what a bright little penny she was and could grow up to be. So what indeed was to become of grandbaby, 'Beau-Beau'?

Burton Green was overcome with remorse. He couldn't allow his grandchild to heartlessly be put in an orphanage. Not his little 'Beau-Beau'. Dolly would have to come to grips with this. This was absolutely heartless! He was through with Dolly discarding her mistakes. He was finished with paying lawyers, doctors and acquaintances to silence and preserve the Green name. There had to be a better way for that darling grandchild he adored, to remain in their lives. Dolly would just have to relent.

At this point in time, Neil McCarthy had lunch with a pal at Chassen's. Neil casually mentioned that Dolly was getting rid of her child, Beau. That admission turned the tide against my being placed in Maryvale.

Late that same afternoon, Burton Green was stewing about my placement when the phone rang. On the line was his crony, Bill McKesson who had just finished lunch with Neil McCarthy who was 'handling' the 'placement' of Dolly Green's child. Bill McKesson was the Los Angeles District Attorney at the time and certainly a man to be trusted.

McKesson told Green that frankly he was appalled at what was going on with the family and little, 'Beau-Beau'.

Bill then told Burton some rather startlingly news. He had some close friends by the name of Hunt. The couple was actively looking to adopt another girl to be a sister to their other adopted child. When Bill learned that afternoon of Dolly's *situation*, he immediately thought of the Hunts.

McKesson continued to background the Hunts. They were a middle-aged husband and wife who lived in a beautiful home at 360 Rockingham Dr. in Brentwood. Mr. Hunt was the Treasurer of Douglas Aircraft. Mrs. Hunt was a housewife devoted to the care of their adopted four year old child, Penny. They were very solid folks.

To Burton, this was sounding too good to be true. His response to Bill was that he would contact Dolly and get right back to him.

No sooner did he click off, when Dolly happened to call.

Burton laid out the proposal to her. Dolly thought the plan was 'positively divine' for reasons other than Burton could ever imagine and she agreed to proceed.

CHAPTER EIGHT

Author's Notes:

What's in a memory? The thread of a wisp of a secreted thought?

I recall that I was playing out on my little jungle gym set with Maria, when this little tiny person did appear. She was blond, she was little like me and she was dressed to play in jeans, a red-striped-shirt and Mary Jane's. I was scared, I hardly knew how to react, but suddenly she rushed to me and grabbed my hands. We were off to play and have an incredibly happy day.

I can see this particular scene as if it were only yesterday. Looking back on this occasion, the memories shimmer in clarity much as gazing into a crystal mountain lake, long ago. Then clearly seeing an agate on the bottom, I reached to retrieve the precious object. I can conjure these visions as easily as I grasped that precious stone.

What's in a memory? The thread of a wisp of a secreted thought? There it begins. Eventually it weaves from the entire skein, creating the totality of your concluded life?

In some respects, I think because Dolly was so accustomed to being around people in the movie industry, she looked upon this period of her life as an orchestration on a set.

Her life was so ridiculously pampered as were the other grand divas of her fortuned ilk, she hardly realized how the 'little people' lived.

So to allow the Hunts into her gilded castle, was a bit of a stretch. They were not exactly ordinary, as Mr. Hunt was the Treasurer of one of her pal's companies, Douglas Aircraft. But they were certainly not of her ultra, strata ilk, rich.

But then it was all for the good of finding her 'Beau-Beau' a good home. So she entertained the Hunts for the *end to the means and my adoption certainly was just that... the end to Dolly's means.*

STALK AND POUNCE

A meeting was set for the next day between Mrs. Hunt and Dolly at her residence at 613 Mountain Drive.

Mrs. Hunt arrived at eleven with her daughter, Penelope in tow.

They were shown to the rear of the house.

Dolly was reclining on a white chaise situated in the center of her spacious verandah. She was dressed in a red linen Chanel suit, black patent pumps, and her hair had just been coifed in her bedroom salon. She looked cool, calm and chic.

The beautiful open air patio opened out to the rolling lawns where I was playing on a red swing set. Silently Dolly observed the mother and daughter who were being ushered into the room by her Puerto Rican maid, Maria Rivera.

Introductions were conducted in a very polite manner. Dolly prided herself on Maria. Coming to her mistress when only twelve, she had taken the child and groomed her into a perfect little maid. Maria spoke English quite well and Dolly had learned fluent Spanish in return.

"Señora Green, may I introduce you to Mrs. Hunt and her daughter, Penny."

Mrs. Hunt was a beautiful blond, red cheeked woman. Very svelte, she could have been in the movies on looks alone. She was dressed in a pale turquoise jumper that flattered her tiny waist, white kid shoes were on her feet.

Her daughter, Penny, was blond as well with bouncy ringlets and a peaches and cream complexion. For an adopted child, she looked remarkably like Mrs. Hunt. Clad in blue jeans, a red-striped-shirt and Mary-Jane's, she looked ready to have a fun, play day.

They all exchanged pleasantries.

Once spying me, Penny charged for the kill.

At first I was terrified over the aggressive actions of Penny Hunt. I had been so sheltered all my life, I had never seen another person my size. Penny was the first child I had ever been exposed to and it scared me a great deal. I refused to look at Penny for some moments. I cast my eyes downward, horribly shy with the other child. But it was only moments and Penny pulling on my hands before I looked up and acknowledged the pretty blond youngster.

We stood sizing one another up. Penny put out her hand and I took it. It was friendship at first sight. Arm in arm, we went to my swings and jungle gym to play. The ice broken, the adults began to chat.

Hours passed as Dolly worked her wiles on Mrs. Hunt. By the end of the afternoon, we had lunched on cucumber sandwiches, lemonade and ice cream. Penny and I had napped together and a deal had been concluded between the two women that would seal my fate for life.

After the Hunts left, Dolly asked me, "Did you like that little girl?"

"Oh, yes, Mommy."I shook my head vehemently."I wish Penny could stay with me forever and we could play every day."

Dolly was thrilled by my response. If it was wonderful for me on the initial meeting, then it could indeed be the perfect home to place me with the Hunts.

The Hunts came again for lunch. This time, however, Mr. Hunt came along. He was a six foot tall, sandy-haired, blue-eyed man. He was quick to smile at me. He seemed very kind and had a soft quiet manner about him that belied his tough business guile.

Dolly was totally snowed by the attractive couple. This could not have been better if cast in Hollywood. The best of all worlds for her 'Beau-Beau'.

We all ate lunch together. I flirted with Mr. Hunt who charmed me back. He certainly was far nicer than that 'Meany', Uncle Neil.

It was clear to Dolly that the whole picture was going to work.

After the long day of us playing and all the adults talking, while putting me to bed, Dolly once again posed a question to me.

"Do you like that family, 'Beau-Beau'?

"Oh, yes, Mommy," I'd innocently replied. "If only we had a Mr. Hunt like Penny's Mommy has him. Maybe Uncle Neil could be your Mr. Hunt, Mommy." Then I drifted off to sleep.

Dolly tucked me into my bed, pushing away the black bangs from my brow.

The die was cast, Dolly mused to herself...*YES*, the die was definitely cast!

So from that day forward the negotiations for the transfer of me to my new home began in earnest.

No one could have predicted how complicated a private adoption could become.

CHAPTER NINE

Author's Notes:

Ralph Hunt retained attorneys named Elmo Conley and Frank Mallory who were senior partners at the firm of Gibson, Dunn and Crutcher, one of the most prestigious firms in Los Angeles. Ralph wanted no slip 'twix the cup and the lip' when arranging to adopt me 'out' from the family Green.

There are pages and pages of correspondences between the attorneys during the time between February of 1949 and June of 1949 when I was adopted. However, I have only included ones that example the growing restlessness and frustration on Dolly Green Walker's (her married name at the time) part to be rid of me as her 'bothersome' child. It should also be noted by the reader, that I was never mentioned by name in the correspondences that I quote. I was referred to as 'the child' in absolutely every correspondence, not 'Beau', or 'her daughter'. Dolly had come to a place in her mind that she had already displaced me when these correspondences began. Finally, when almost all is said and done, then I am referred to as Diane Melanie Hunt, my legally adopted name.

I think I do need to stress the possibility of fate interceding when Dolly got so frustrated. She started with serious ultimatums when the transfer of funds became a huge issue in the whole scheme of things. But perhaps fate's name was Marie Hunt. She was the one who was so adamant that she and Daddy proceed to adopt me, despite all odds. The reader will see that toward the end, many of the correspondences indeed were addressed to Mrs. Hunt. Marie held firm on the belief that I was to be their second little girl.

Is it not the way of the world? My adoptive mother, Marie, the woman I spent so much of my early life resenting, was the primary person at steering my helm. Had she not persisted with my being adopted into their fold, all could have been lost.

My guess is there was no other 'nice young couple' in the wings. My belief is that Dolly's threat was the old 'heave ho' to get the Hunts off the mark. Make a move or we have someone else who will. But my conviction is that Maryvale would have been my sudden home, had Marie Hunt not intervened. Who knows what the cards would have dealt then?

The entire deal was nipped together rather neatly in the end, when all the papers were 'sealed' away and it was with incredible difficulty when I finally obtained them.

However I did, and once I got them, I began to do my own detective work.

LETTERS FROM THE EDGE

January 18th, 1949

Memo to: Frank Mallory
IN RE: Ralph Hunt Adoption Matter
The birth certificate shows that the child was born in Los Angeles on June 11, 1947.

The Birth Certificate does not indicate whether this child is legitimate or illegitimate, but the Petition for the Change of name states that the whereabouts of the father of the child is unknown.

Robert S. Allen
RSA: bjo
January 24th,1949

From: Frank L. Mallory
RE: Ralph Hunt Adoption matter

To: Neil S. McCarthy, Esq.
620 West Sixth Street
Los Angeles, California

Dear Neil:

As per your telephone inquiry, Mr. Ralph V. Hunt of the accounting firm of Touch, Niven, Bailey and Smart, is an old friend of Mr. Conley, and has retained us to handle the adoption of the child by him and Mrs. Hunt.

Client to be charged: Ralph V. Hunt
360 North Rockingham Road
Los Angeles, 24, California
Tele: Arizona 3-9107
Bus. Tel: TR-7691

HANDWRITTEN NOTES:

1-24-49 March

Mr. Hunt called:

Child now in custody of Mrs. Dorothy Green Walker
613 Mountain Drive, Los Angeles.
Alleged father paid $1500 into ck. Act. Boy's family took care of bills and put $1500 into ck for emergency.
$3000 in all.
Mrs. Walker had to pay bills will get return from father and mother.
The child's name to be:
Diane Melanie Hunt.
Have Mrs. Morrison take the money out to reimburse Mrs. Walker for bills of $1460.26 she has incurred for child's care.

Balance of funds of $1539.74 to be transferred to Mr. Hunt as an estate for the child.

Hunt will buy Government bonds, full amount in her name. Series E.

No cash income.

Bonds to be to fund education at Westlake School for Girls

School and transportation to it $400-500.

Note from the Author: This monetary issue was another situation that almost brought the adoption to a halt. Dolly's insistence that the father pay for the child's expenses during the period of time the Hunts began the process almost caused the whole thing to fall apart. Read Mr. Hunt's letter following;

Feb. 15, 1949

Handwritten by Ralph V. Hunt:

From Ralph V. Hunt
902 Consolidated Building
Los Angeles, 14. California

To: Elmo Conley
Gibson, Dunn and Crutcher

Dear Elmo,

When we talked yesterday I did not mention again that we feel that there must be a complete severing of the mother as trustee for those funds. We discussed it before you know and you suggested a bank trust controlled by a court. As I remember it there is a release executed by the mother.

We can't go on negotiating with the mother over the years. I wish the money had never gotten into the picture or that we could somehow erase it. In any event we both feel strongly that we must stay far away from any arrangement even remotely resembling consideration. Again, as I said yesterday, if all parties proceed whole heartedly and willingly, we want to go ahead. Otherwise in the interest of our little girl and ourselves, we had better drop it.

Yours sincerely,

Ralph Hunt

Feb 16th 1949

Mr. Ralph Hunt
902 Consolidated Building
Los Angeles, 14. California

Dear Ralph:

This will acknowledge receipt of your letter of February 15th, 1949. Also, I assure you that I agree heartily with your conclusions.

We will do everything possible to straighten out the money situation.

Yours sincerely,

Elmo

March 3, 1949

Mrs. Ralph V. Hunt
360 North Rockingham Road
Los Angeles, California

Dear Mrs. Hunt:

After our conversation this morning I had a conference with Mr. Conley and he has written a letter to Mr. McCarthy to re-assure him that we are doing all we can to expedite the money matter. A copy of Mr. Conley's letter is enclosed.

Yours very truly,

Gibson Dunn and Crutcher
By Frank L. Mallory.
March 3, 1949

Neil S. McCarthy, Esq.
620 West Sixth Street
Los Angeles, California

Dear Neil:

As you know, we have filed a Petition for Adoption in connection with the adoption by Mr. and Mrs. Ralph Hunt of the child which your client, Mrs. Dorothy Walker, has in her custody. We understand that Mrs. Walker is increasingly restless and impatient about the carrying forward of the adoption proceedings so that she can be relieved of the responsibility for the child and it can be permanently place. The Petition for the Adoption was filed over two weeks ago on February 16th and a copy sent to the State Department of Social Welfare that same day. I can assure you that we will do all we can to carry this matter through as quickly and smoothly as possible.
We trust you will be able to explain this to Mrs. Walker and reassure her that we will handle the matter as expeditiously as possible.

Sincerely yours,
Elmo H. Conley
EHC:bjo
cc Mrs. Hunt

Neil S. McCarthy, Esq.
620 West Sixth Street
Los Angeles, California

Letter dated May 10, 1949

Dear Elmo,

What on earth is the hold up on this Walker adoption with the Hunts? We have been under the impression that things were going well but nothing seems to get expedited at all.

Mrs. Walker is becoming very impatient and has in addition been visiting with another nice younger couple who seem interested in adopting the child right away.

I would advise you to relay this message to the Hunts. If they do not get off the dime, they will lose the opportunity of having Mrs. Walker's child. Mrs. Walker is becoming increasingly dissatisfied with the current situation and has been preparing the child to go to be Penelope Hunt's sister. Those children have become very close.

Please advise me regarding the pending situation as I am standing firm on championing the Hunt adoption because of the Walker child going to a home with another little girl.

Please advise.

Sincerely,

Neil S. McCarthy, Esq.

May 18th 1949

Memo to Mr. Conley, Files
In RE: Ralph Hunt Adoption

Mr. McCarthy called me this afternoon to inquire about the progress of the child's adoption as a follow up to his letter earlier posted.

Neil reiterated the fact that Mrs. Walker was extremely anxious to get rid of the child, that she felt that the expense of maintaining the child for the past five months which she has borne, despite some small reimbursement, has been an imposition upon her. He also said that there was a very nice young couple who were willing to take the child right away and Mrs. Walker has been talking about giving them the child. I repeated that the Hunts were proceeding in good faith in the matter and our sympathy with Mrs. Walker's views.

Frank L. Mallory
Gibson, Dunn and Crutcher
June 2, 1949

Memo to Mr. E. H. Conley, Files.
In RE: Ralph V. Hunt adoption

An excerpt from a letter from Elmo Conley, in RE: Ralph V. Hunt Adoption:

  With the anxiety of Mrs. Walker and Mr. McCarthy in mind, it is my conclusion that it would now be advisable for the Hunts to take custody of the little girl. My interview with Mrs. Ohmart (the social worker) and my conclusion have been reported to Mr. Hunt over the telephone and he seems to be in accord with that conclusion.

Frank L. Mallory

May 30, 1949

Letter from:

Neil McCarthy
620 West Sixth Street
Los Angeles, California

Dear Elmo,

It is with great relief that I received your most recent transmission from you regarding the Hunt's acquiescence to the final hand over of the child.

However, in the interim, Mrs. Walker has arranged to stage a very elaborate birthday party for the child. A kind of farewell for her to the family and staff as it is the child's second birthday.

Mrs. Walker has arranged for entertainment in the form of darling pony rides and a famous clown, Bo-Bo and is unwilling to cancel as she has already paid for the services. So it will be the best for all concerned if Mrs. Walker hands the child over the day after said event.

We hope that this is not too much of an inconvenience but we will await your reply.

Sincerely yours,

Neil S. McCarthy, Esq.

c.c. Mrs. Ralph V. Hunt

Hand delivered letter to Neil:
June 9th, 1949

Letter to Neil McCarthy:

Dear Neil,

I have spoken with the Hunts and that is fine.

They are anxious to have the child come to them in the best of health and mental state and to deny the child a birthday party that she undoubtedly was looking anxiously forward to would be a very large mistake.

The Hunts are willing and able to accept the child after the twelfth of June and will look forward to the exchange.

Again, we apologize for any inconvenience financially and emotionally to Mrs. Walker's well being. We also thank Mrs. Walker for her patience, as for the Hunts, this was a big step to undertake legally as it was a private adoption not one through the Cradle as was their other child, Penny Hunt.

They will look forward to the arrival of their new child when it is convenient for Mrs. Walker.

They are willing to make arrangements for her to be picked up.

Please advise.

Sincerely yours,

Elmo H. Conley.

Memo TO: Mr. E.H. Conley
In Re: Ralph V. Hunt Adoption

Mr. McCarthy called this morning to say that Mrs. Hunt and Mrs. Walker have been discussing when to transfer custody of the baby. Mrs. Walker wishes to retain custody until after June 11th as she is planning a birthday party for the little one on that date. It appears that the Hunts are leaving on their vacation June 12th so Mrs. Walker will keep the child until the Hunts return and turn her over to them after their vacation.

Frank L. Mallory

June 6th, 1949

Dear Elmo,

Mrs. Hunt and Mrs. Walker have again discussed the transfer arrangements and both women believe that it would be best for the child to be transported to the Hunt's abode by Mrs. Walker's chauffeur, Tom.

Mrs. Walker wants the child to think this is just a normal day that she is going to play with Penny Hunt and thinks if the Hunts were to fetch the child, there might be some trauma there.

So the child will be delivered to the Hunt's home as if it is going there for a little play together.

Thank you for your concern but we have this completely under control.

The chauffeur will deliver the child sometime around eleven.

We will be in touch.

Sincerely yours,

Neil S. McCarthy, Esq.

November 5, 1949

Mr. Ralph V. Hunt
Touche, Niven, Baily and Smart
607 South Hill Street
Los Angeles, California

Dear Mr. Hunt:
Enclosed is a form "Certificate of Adoption" which will be sent to Sacramento by the Clerk of Judge Bullock's court after the decree has been entered, in order to obtain a new birth certificate for Diane Melanie showing you and Mrs. Hunt as her parents. If you find that all of the information contained on the form is correct, would you please sign the form on the bottom line where I have marked a penciled X and return it to me.

At the hearing before Judge Bullock you and Mrs. Hunt will each be require to sign a form of consent and agreement to the adoption. A copy of the form that will be used is enclosed for your information

As I have already mentioned by telephone the hearing is set for 2 P.M. Wednesday afternoon, November 16, in Department 2 of the Superior Court, which is on the 16th floor of the City Hall. I shall look forward to seeing you, Mrs. Hunt and Diane Melanie there at that time. Of course, if you have any questions in the meantime, Mr. Conley or I will be glad to discuss them with you.

Yours very truly,
Gibson, Dunn and Crutcher
By:
Frank L. Mallory

November 18, 1949

Memo To: Mr. Conley

IN RE: Ralph V. Hunt Adoption

This matter came on for hearing before Judge Georgia P. Bullock in Department 21 at 2 P.M. today, Wednesday November 16th. The petition was granted, the consent signed and a form of decree and adoption certificate was left with this Court.
Mr. and Mrs. Hunt expressed themselves as very pleased with the way in which this matter was handled.

Frank L. Mallory
 December 9, 1949

Mr. Ralph V. Hunt
360 Rockingham Road
Los Angeles, 24, California

Dear Mr. Hunt:

Enclosed is a certified copy of the new birth certificate for Diane.

Copies of the Decree of Adoption and other papers in the matter are on permanent file in our office and will always be available should you wish them. I understand that you prefer not to have copies among you own papers at this time.

I shall keep you advised of the progress of the matter of release of the funds in the bank account. It will probably be a couple of months before that is wound up. As I mentioned to you, that matter will be handled by an independent attorney, with the indirect assistance and supervision of their office.

Yours very Truly,

Gibson, Dunn and Cruthcher,
By Frank L. Mallory
December 16th 1949

Mr. Ralph V. Hunt
c/o Touche, Niven, Bailey and Smart

Dear Ralph:

Enclosed herewith please find statement for services rendered in connection with the adoption of Diane.

I regret very much that the expense has run so high, but as you know there have been many complications and it has taken a great deal of Mr. Mallory's time in order to secure the necessary consents, etc. The statement represents the exact cost to us of the time with Mr. Mallory and I have spent over a period of almost a year. If this is not entirely satisfactory, please let me know and I will adjust it accordingly

Yours sincerely,

Elmo

January 5, 1950

Mr. Ralph V. Hunt
360 Rockingham Road
Los Angeles, California

Dear Ralph:
  We have received your check in the amount of $512.90
in full payment of our statement of the December 16th for
the fees and your disbursements in the adoption matter.
Thank you for your promptness.
With best wishes for the New Years, I am,
Sincerely,

Elmo

February 23, 1950

Bank of America
National Trust and Savings Association
6333 Hollywood Boulevard
Hollywood, California
Attention Mr. Duenckel:
RE: savings Account No. 6908

Dear Mr. Duenckel:

  We are counsel for Mr. Ralph V. Hunt as guardian of
the estate of Diane Melanie Hunt, his minor daughter.
  In accordance with our recent telephone conversation, I
am enclosing certified copies of the order appointing Mr.
Hunt guardian of his daughter's estate and of his letter of
Guardianship.
  You will note that the order directs Mr. Hunt as
guardian to take possession of all the funds in the
account. For this purpose, he will open an account at the
Security First National Bank where he does his personal
banking and through that bank will present a draft on

your bank for the purpose of withdrawing those funds. It is expected that this will be done on Friday or Saturday, February 24 or 25.

As I explained to you in our conversation, Diane Melanie Hunt is an adopted daughter and your assistance in maintaining the confidential nature of your records pertaining to this matter will be greatly appreciated.

Yours very truly,

Gibson, Dunn and Crutcher by Frank L. Mallory

CHAPTER TEN

Author's Notes:

It had been an arduous trial for Dolly, as she anxiously awaited the baby's hand-off. She had never imagined that the monetary situation could have caused such an issue, but it did and the Hunts were stubborn to resolve that particular aspect of the contract.

Frankly, Dolly was furious with McCarthy for insisting that it be done that way in the first place. What was done was done and she had to settle for it finally resolving itself because of the Hunt's legal team.

Marie Hunt was the bull-dog in the end. She had seen the rapport established between Penny and me and was going to go down fighting to get her little 'Beau-Beau'. Again, I laude her tenacity. My father was a scrapper, but Marie Hunt was the one who would always go the final round.

THE HAND OFF OF 'BABY BEAU'

June of 1949

Everything had seemingly been arranged for the hand off between the Hunts and Dolly Green.

In the ongoing negotiations between Marie Hunt and Dolly, they came up with an amazing deception that both the women thought was 'positively divine'! When I was six, Dolly would come back into the darling child's life as the benevolent 'godmother'.

Marie agreed it sounded fine, never thinking of how Ralph's reaction would be when the time would roll around. He vehemently opposed the reuniting but as always, Marie prevailed.

Dolly chose the godmother route because she simply could not completely say good-bye to her adorable, 'Beau–Beau'.

Marie was thinking that it would be a good move down the line, to have someone of such an important and influential family to mentor their daughter. Marie was a very bright woman and always had the welfare of both her girls in mind.

They agreed that Ralph never needed to know that Dolly was my mother. The story from the beginning had been that Dolly was taking care of me for a friend who decided that she no longer could support the child.

Then the monetary glitch arose and almost stopped the adoption proceedings flat! It delayed the proceedings for another six months. Which meant that I was two years old before I was wrenched from my happy surroundings and flung aside by Dolly like an unwanted, baby doll.

Despite that, Dolly proceeded with my disposal like a driven woman. She was determined to eliminate me as soon as was humanly possible.

It was frustrating for Dolly because she thought everything had been so neatly arranged. When in fact, nothing seemed to progress very rapidly in the removal of her child. Once determining she could no longer tolerate me as a permanent fixture in her home, she was chomping at the bit to be relieved of my responsibility.

Tension filled the air at her home and the feeling of resentment affected her entire interaction with me.

Finally, Dolly began fabricating reasons to not be around me at all. I began to wonder if I had been so bad that she no longer wanted me and I recall feeling constantly sad and abandoned.

I lived for the days that Penny Hunt would come to play with me.

Dolly had thought that the 'arrangements' had been so neatly agreed upon with the adopting family, that she was frustrated that there was delay after legal delay.

But finally by June, all ends had been tightly tied. I was ready to go to my new home.

So signed, sealed and delivered, the documents were executed by the Hunts and Dolly Green Walker's attorneys.

The die was finally cast for good.

I was to celebrate my second birthday June 11, 1949. Dolly planned an elaborate party. These events were not to be altered because Dolly had made them some months previously and refused to relinquish me till the party had been celebrated.

There was Bo-Bo the clown, a multitude of presents and a huge cake. There were ponies that I was supposed to ride but getting near them caused me to wheeze and sneeze. So I was hurried away while Penny was led around on one of the adorable pinto horses. Both ponies were decked out in silver adorned bridles and saddles and festooned with all manner of red bows on manes and tails.

Poncho, the Boxer, and Charlie, the black cat, cavorted around in the sun amongst the adult guests.

Burton Green attended though his wife was too ill to come along. Both Dolly's sisters, Lily and Burtie, were there with lavish presents of dolls and clothing. The Hunts were there with their darling Penny, as was all of Dolly's staff.

It was a very busy day.

Penny helped me unwrap all my presents and we played with them all afternoon.

Dolly's present to me was a Steiff stuffed dog that looked just like her boxer Poncho and a silk coverlet for my bed that had my name printed on it in red ink, 'Beau-Beau'.

But most exciting, was a big blue plastic boat which Penny and I could play with the next time Penny came again to visit me.

I loved everything...but best of all I adored my stuffed doggie, because I could hug it and take it to bed without it making me sneeze.

So it was just a wonderful birthday! One that I would remember forever. My mother was so excited and charming that I wondered if things had not turned around? Dolly seemed so happy and elated over all the company and the party's success.

I remember that night when Dolly hugged and kissed me and put me to bed, I thought that things would be okay again.

As she was saying good-night, I recall thinking that perhaps if I was just a 'really good little soldier', as Uncle Neil was always asking me to be, maybe things would go along better for me.

How things were to change from then on, I could *never* in my wildest childhood dreams have imagined.

CHAPTER ELEVEN

Author's Notes:

My new home at the time of the adoption was 360 Rockingham. That 'Mansion' became famous in 1994 when Nicole Simpson and Ron Goldman were murdered. It was the O.J. Simpson home. An interesting side note, in 1995 my Westlake high school reunion was held at a private home down the street from the 'O.J. mansion'. The streets were barricaded yet traffic continued to parade nonstop down Rockingham for a glimpse of the famed 'Murder Manse'.

Several years later, the property was finally sold. However, the mansion was flattened to the ground by the people who bought the property, as they did not think it was possible to live in the defiled home.

I never saw the little Rockingham home as a mansion. Compared to all the Green domiciles, Rockingham was a small home. Funny how perceptions change over the years. When I viewed the home in 1995 as I too drove down the street with the other gawking drivers, little had changed but an enormous electric fence surrounded the entire lot. It still was not a mansion to me. It was just the little Rockingham home.

Then, looking back over the long years past to the day of my relocation, it always amazed me how cavalierly the adults orchestrated the actual hand-off. I mean, "honey you are going off to play with your little gal-pal. See you in about four years!"

Now that is just harsh!

But beliefs were so different in those days. I sure would like to meet the doctor who said I would forget my mother in six months.

I could tell him a thing or ten!

SURPRISE, SURPRISE, SURPRISE

Several days after my second birthday, I was unexpectedly packed up to go play with Penny Hunt. Mommy said it had been kept secret as a 'really big surprise'!

I had never been away from Mother, off on my own, alone.

When I was getting ready to go, all the servants acted odd. Alice, the cook, bolted from the dining room after serving me my morning cereal. She must have had a horrible cold because her eyes were red and she was sniffling. I hoped I would not get sick because Penny Hunt would hardly invite me to play if I had a cold.

The upstairs maid, Benta, was ill as well as she was runny-eyed and rushed off after packing a small day bag to take to Penny Hunt's home.

Maria was the only one who didn't seem sick as she fussed about my room. As I prepared to go to Penny's, the maid came down with the influenza as well, because her eyes streamed tears and her nose began to run.

When I was about to leave, Maria pulled me into her arms and said, "Beau-Beau, I love you my 'chiqua', I will always love you 'my baby'. Don't ever forget your Maria."

I thought this was pretty stupid for her to express since I was only going to be gone for the day.

The chauffeur, Tom, drove me over to the Hunt's 'little Rockingham house" in the big black Cadillac. He too seemed to have a cold, because he sniffled all the way to Penny's home.

I hugged my stuffed Poncho dog as we drove across Sunset down to 360 Rockingham Drive. It seemed to take forever to drive there from Beverly Hills. It was a long confusing trip down twisting streets. I hoped that Tom would not get lost when he had to come back for me that afternoon.

I was delivered with a promise to be picked up later. I had been given the big blue plastic boat to play with at my friend's. Tom carried it for me to the Hunt's door. I noticed that Tom did not look at me when he left. He must have felt pretty horrible from his cold, as there were tears flowing down his cheeks.

I am not entirely sure if being born with an almost autobiographical memory is a good or bad thing. Some say it is amazing, many regard it as remarkable. Others state they think that it is very odd indeed. I believe that the real bottom line is that it is quite handy for my chosen profession of novelizing, but in reality, in many instances it is painful. Certain happenstances across the course of my life, have been frozen in my mind. This is much like a dragonfly encased in an amber bead.

I have led a very interesting life from beginning until now, but honestly can admit that the most terrifying day of my life began in that normal way.

We had a very fun day of swings and toys and stories read. Lunch was peanut butter and jelly sandwiches. We had lemonade to drink and peppermint ice cream for dessert.

Mrs. Hunt made a big deal about us taking a nap which we did, but mostly we whispered together and giggled, and generally did not sleep at all. It was really wonderful having this new 'best' friend!

Sometime later, Mrs. Hunt came and got us up and said it would be a good thing for us to go out into the beautiful backyard to play, as I was staying a while. She needed to get dinner ready. She said that Mr. Hunt would soon be home and for us girls to just go out and play a little more.

I had not been *aware* that I was going to stay for dinner, so I was sure hoping that Mrs. Hunt knew what I liked. But she had given us a good lunch so she must have known how to cook for little girls. My own mommy did not cook, we had what mommy called a 'maid' who did that chore.

While we were playing, Penny and I got in a big fight over who was going to be the captain of the blue boat. It was mine. I was the rightful captain but Penny suddenly turned so mean that it made me really mad. I wanted to go home. If this Penny Hunt was going to be such a brat, then I wanted nothing more to do with her. I marched right into the kitchen and demanded that I go home. I did not want to stay for dinner, and I wanted nothing more to do with Penny Hunt!

By then Mr. Hunt had gotten there, he was a very nice, tall, elegant man. I had met him once before at Mommy's. He had come with Penny and Mrs. Hunt to meet Mommy and me.

He pulled me up into his arms and gently said, "Beau-Beau you are home now. We adopted you today!"

What was he telling me? I certainly was *not* home! I was stunned. I was frightened. I was bewildered, all in one. I simply could not understand what he was saying.

In my terror, I screamed at him, "I don't care if you 'dopted me today! I want to go home!" Thinking to myself, what was 'dopted anyway?

Mr. Hunt continued to hold me. "You are our little girl, now. Your mommy can't keep you anymore, she has given you away. So Mrs. Hunt and I are your parents now my dearest little child, and our little Penny is your sister."

I was shocked beyond belief! I had no idea what I had done to cause my mommy to give me away!

Mr. Hunt took Penny and me into a big wood-paneled room and got a book from a shelf. He said to both of us, "This book is from The Cradle Society, where we adopted your sister. It is called the '*Chosen Child*'."

He then sat down in a big chair with both of us on his lap and proceeded to read the book.

It talked about how we were *'chosen children'*. It told us how our other parents could not keep us anymore. But a new set of parents would come choose us instead. That we were far more special than just normal little babies because we were the *'chosen ones'*.

I listened to Mr. Hunt, because what else could I do?

That night after our dinner and baths, I cried myself to sleep.

Why should I be sent away from my mommy to be *'chosen'* by the Hunts! They meant nothing to me at all!

And still I did not get this 'dopted thing. It was a complete mystery to me.

Maybe I was like that little girl, Wendy that was captured by Peter Pan, the book that Mommy read to me night after night after night. I had been taken away by the Hunts and my mommy was now desperately trying to find where I had been hidden.

For the next many days, weeks, months and years, I tried to solve the puzzle.

Finally, after much time and circumstances, the pieces fell together and the mystery was eventually solved.

However, to this very day I don't ever recall being more terrified in my life, than when I was told that...I had just been given away.

CHAPTER TWELVE

Author's Notes:

The adjustment to the switch of families was agonizing to bear. I remember hiding in my closet for hours while I simply cried and cried. I could not fathom why I had been sent away. Days seemed to go by like molasses, while Mrs. Hunt tried to invent ways to bring out her petulant child.

There was a lady that came to visit to evaluate my placement in the home. I remember her coming and though I was dry-eyed and reserved, I did not like her and made little bones about it. However, I later found in my adoption papers that the same woman who visited was the Social Worker and reported that I was adjusting very well. I guess she was well paid to say that by Dolly Green.

So time just moved on and on.

THE DAYS AFTER THE DEED

Days went by as I awaited the arrival of Tom to whisk me off and away, back to my own home. It became almost the image of a rescue mission in my mind. I decided that I would not speak to anyone or eat anything until I was indeed saved from my captors. I determined that starving to death would be a far better choice than to be held prisoner, at the Hunts. And I told everyone just that.

However, I did get awfully hungry and in the end of a twenty-four hour period of time, changed my mind about the eating thing.

But I still refused to speak to my captors. Penny tried and tried to get me to talk. It became a challenge to the little, blond-haired girl to get her new sister to speak.

For a week, all I did was sulk. And I was very good at sulking, for such a little child.

The doctors that the Hunts had consulted, warned the new family that there were usually two reactions to displacement from a home. If the environment had been a fairly well adjusted one, the child would be violently objective to the new situation and carry on irrationally. Or, the child would be quiet and withdrawn; sulking for a fair period, but after a bit of adjustment and the passage of time, the child would completely forget the previous situation and embrace the new one with enthusiasm.

I defied the norm!

I sulked, and then out of the blue I would explode, screaming and crying at the top of my lungs demanding my mother back. Then I would hide in my room for hours at a time, surfacing only to eat a bite of food then I was back to my room again. Mostly, I hid in the closet for hours on end. Now this was becoming a very unhealthy routine.

Penny got fed up! This adoption stuff was supposed to have gotten her a fun playmate, not a sulky little brat. So on a campaign similar to the quest for the Holy Grail, Penny Hunt set out to break down the barriers of her new sister. Even if I was determined to ignore the parents, Penny was going to have no more of this teary-eyed child, garbage. She wanted us to play like we did before I had come into permanent residence.

After hours of badgering from my new sister, I finally agreed to come out and play. Once we were out in the yard on the swing set, I seemed to forget my dilemma, a bit. Penny had a wonderful dollhouse where we played for hours and the days slipped by a little easier.

I still refused to acknowledge my captors, the Hunts.

During those first early days I started calling Penny, my 'Penny Mama' stalwartly refusing to acknowledge Mrs. Hunt as anyone but my jailer. I knew in my heart that I was being held against my will and that any day,

Tom would come and rescue me from the horrible captors.

I even imagined that the entire Green family was desperately trying to find me. Tom just couldn't remember where he dropped me off the day he delivered me to play with Penny Hunt.

I watched and watched for a Cadillac circling the block so I could run outside and flag Tom down. But the chauffeur never found the home where the Hunts were sequestering me.

After a few weeks of stone-walling both the adults, I began to warm to Mr. Hunt. He really had little to do with the mean abduction away from my former mommy. So Mr. Hunt began to be a positive factor in my life. He would take us girls out into the ivy thickets that surrounded the house and we would help him weed the geraniums. All the while, I kept an eagle-eye out for Tom.

Mr. Hunt took us up the street to the Rose Garden that was planted in the center of the street. We would ride bikes as Mr. Hunt walked along behind to make sure cars did not come along and harm us girls. All the while, I watched for Tom.

Mr. Hunt set up a croquet set on the lawn at the Rockingham house. Penny and I giggled as we whacked the balls through the little wire hoops. I still held out hope for Tom. I watched for him out of the corner of my eye.

Mr. Hunt would take us out to the swing set and push us as high as the sky.

Finally, I just stopped watching for Tom. I decided he was never coming back for me, ever again.

It was many months before I spoke to Mrs. Hunt. She was the one who had plotted my horrendous fate. The one, who with my mommy, had conspired to place me in this detestable home situation that I abhorred. I wanted my real mommy. Mrs. Hunt was no substitution then and never could hope to be, not ever in this lifetime.

I could not figure out why no one had consulted with me and asked if I wanted to be sent away to this new home.

It was okay to go visit another kid, but why had I been sent away by my mommy? Was it because I had wheezed every time I touched Mommy's dog, Poncho or the black cat, Charlie? I would have promised to stay away from them if my mommy had only asked me to do just that. I was not a naughty child. Had I truly done something so horrible that my mommy sent me to live away from her with these *evil* people?

I would lie awake at night trying to think of a singular event that had triggered this abominable change in my life. Night after night, I tried to recall something specific. Was it when I jumped in the fish pond and tried to swim with the pretty fan-tailed fish? Maria had been pretty mad or maybe she had been more scared than mad. Was it when I let all my mommy's fan tailed-doves out of the cote at the back of the yard? It took our gardener, Yoshi, days to find all the silly birds. I had thought it was so much prettier to see them fly than to be cooped up in a cage. Mommy really scolded me for that event...maybe that was why she sent me away.

Or maybe Mommy had discovered my favorite pastime, the whisper game, where I listened from behind the Chinese lacquer screen to her and Uncle Neil when they hugged, kissed and then played leap frog on the white fur rugs. Maybe Mommy found out that Penny and I were doing the whisper game during our supposed naps and that had made her mad enough to send me away to Penny Hunt's home.

I always fell asleep before I came to any conclusions. Because obviously no matter what I came up with in my own child's mind, it would never be right. I could not seem to awaken from the nightmare. It just went on and on and on.

****

Days melted into weeks and weeks into months. On and on. And I could never seem to wake up from the displacement.

After a long time, I conceded to the hurt. I forgave the Hunt's their cruelty, began to accept my fate.

But I never forgot my mommy or my beloved, Maria. Every night I dreamed that I was back home with them again, and with my Boxer, Poncho, and Charlie, my beloved, black cat.

All children removed from their familial upbringing at that age, never really forget. Obviously some recall far more than others, such as I do. When relocated to a new situation, the children re-run the happy memories over and over in their minds. Whether it is in their dreams or waking day dreams, it becomes stronger than any usual routine recollection. It may become faded as a yellowed photograph, but it is virtually ingrained in the displaced child.

The events they so cherished with the other family are indelibly burned in their memories because they are re-played again and again because of the deprivation. No one can ever realize how much of an impact this can have on a juvenile.

However, in those days, people did not seem to believe children had this capability. So this relocation of babies was far more prevalent. And of course in those days, pregnancies whether planned or surprise, were not dealt with as they often are today, with an abortion.

Perhaps though, even more amazing than the fact that I was relocated at the formative age of two years old, was that the participating families never bargained on the fact that I was born with an autobiographical memory!

So nothing was ever forgotten, as they planned. It was forgiven, put to rest, placed on a back burner that might never have surfaced again, had the Hunts and Dolly Green not chosen such an unusual path to reunite.

CHAPTER THIRTEEN

Author's Notes:

This was not an easy time for anyone! I was overwrought by the displacement and constantly believing that I was in a revolving nightmare! I kept willing myself to awaken but nothing changed. My imprisonment with the Hunts continued day after endless day!

How could Tom have gotten so lost? I just could not fathom what sorrow my mother must have been going through.

Penny and the adults just were acting as if it were just a series of normal days linked together.

But all the while, I simply knew in my heart of hearts, that it would eventually turn around, and Tom would find his way back to rescue me.

This was nothing but my own childhood fantasy!

ADJUSTING TO THE HUNTS

In the weeks after I was adopted by the Hunts, I dreamt over and over of Maria chanting a lullaby at night. Constantly it went through my head. I would hide in my room and hug my stuffed Poncho and weep into my 'blanketie'. The only relics of the past that had seemingly traveled along with me on the horrible displacement day. Poncho and 'blanketie' were all that I had to show from my beloved former home. That and the remembrance of my missing life at Mountain Drive with my real mommy, whom I desperately loved.

I did nothing but long for being reunited with Dolly, Maria, Alice, the cook and Tom, the chauffeur. I even missed Yoshi, the gardener, who teased me mercilessly. I had not doggie nor cat to chase and it seemed that Mrs.

Hunt did nothing all day but sit and talk to people on the phone.

Continuously I watched for Tom. But as the months rolled by, I knew he too, had deserted me.

After weeks of pouting, Penny decided that enough was enough, and that I was going to have to come to grips with this 'adoption' thing. So she again pulled out the book that Mr. Hunt frequently read to her. She insisted that Mr. Hunt read it to me again.

The Chosen Child held more meaning for me that day than when Mr. Hunt had read it to us before. It talked about a Mommy and Daddy who were unable to have babies. So they went to places and picked babies up from people that could not keep their children for their own. It said that these adopted babies were 'specially chosen' and were far luckier than other babies who sometimes surprised their parents by coming along.

I *still* hated the story!

I said it had nothing to do with me. I knew that the Hunts were simply hiding me from my real mommy and I verbally declared that, 'someday my real mommy would come and rescue me'!

Penny made fun of me over that statement for weeks. But I needed someone to hold onto, so I began to call Penny, 'Penny-Mama', because I refused to acknowledge Mrs. Hunt as my mother.

Day after day, Penny refused to give into my bouts of pouts. She dragged me out to play with her friend, DuDu, who was Hume Cronin and Jessica Tandy's little boy. Why Penny called him, DuDu was a secret Penny and DuDu refused to share.

We all played with my blue boat and had a reasonably good time. But finally, DuDu would have to go home so it would be the close of just another miserable day away from my real mommy.

For months I would not quit asking to return to my real home. I begged, cried, complained and sobbed to no avail.

The days and weeks slowly went by while little by little, I began to accept my prison term as a lifetime ordeal.

One day, Penny and I made cookies with Mrs. Hunt and then had a tea party in the backyard with a new tea set Mr. Hunt had brought home to us. We poured real tea from the little china pot into cups and dipped our warm cookies into the brew.

Mr. Hunt had been home all day, as it was a Saturday. He and we girls weeded the geraniums that surrounded the corner lot on Rockingham. I had been afraid of the spiders in the weeds so 'Daddy' as he had asked me to call him, held me and sang a song, 'The Itsey Bitsey Spider going up a water spout'. It made me not so afraid of the leggy creatures.

All in all, it had been a good day.

That night the whole Hunt family was sitting on the back porch eating ice cream. It was May, a warm, muggy day, with a slow breeze occasionally puffing lazily from the Pacific. It had been a reasonably good day. Almost a year since I had come to live in my new home.

Cole Porter lived across the street from the Hunts and played the piano every night. He would open wide the patio doors and pound the ivory keys for everyone in the neighborhood to hear. When he started that evening with the haunting tune, 'Unchained Melody', no one imagined my reaction. It had been Dolly's favorite song and she played it on the phonograph all the time.

I threw my bowl of ice cream to the bricks, shattering the pleasantness of the evening into shards of pain.

I ran to my room sobbing and screaming for no apparent reason at all.

The Hunts, lulled into the false sense of security and peace of the evening, were unknowing as to what had set me off. Ralph came after me to try to calm me down.

They had been told to expect unpleasant outbursts, but this was far beyond what he was willing to tolerate. It was his firm belief that I had been allowed enough time to adjust by now, so he followed me to my room.

He found me sobbing uncontrollably on my bed. He asked me repeatedly why I was crying. My response was further howling and tears.

"Beau-Beau", his voice was very stern, "You have got to get hold of yourself and stop this right now!" he tried reasoning. "Look, you are going to have to stop this constant crying. Your mother and I have had it up to here with your complaining! This is coming to a point where these outbursts must be punished. I don't ever want to hurt you but you are leaving me little choice!"

I hissed at him with all the venom an almost three-year-old child could muster. "*You* are not my father and *she* is not my mother! My only mommy is Dolly! I will always hate you all. I hope you all die and leave me alone!"

With these words, Ralph stormed from my room slamming the bedroom door.

CHAPTER FOURTEEN

Author's Notes:

I was not adjusting and things were still often taking disastrous, dramatic turns. The doctors had forecast six months as being the outside time that it would take me to adjust...but I was simply defying the norm.

It was a horribly frustrating time for Mother and Dad, and an exasperating time for me.

Despite the wonderful things my adoptive parents were always trying to do, some small thing, a song, a mention of something that stirred a memory, and I would fly off the handle into a rage that made the eye of Hurricane Katrina look calm.

EYE OF THE STORM

Dolly was not in the slightest pleased with the reports she was receiving from the Hunts regarding my continuous digress in progress.

She spoke with Marie every week and even after all these many months, things were still not proceeding as well as everyone had planned.

Penny had been such a help, but was enrolled to go off to summer camp. This would leave me on my own with Marie, who was running out of ideas over what to do with such a stubborn child.

I would sulk around the house and pretend to not notice Mrs. Hunt. Marie had tried everything, but after all these months and my not even acknowledging her, she was completely at her wits ends.

Finally, one night, when I was almost three and a half, there was a monumental upset between me and Mr.

Hunt that left everyone at loose ends over which way to proceed to make things work for me.

Mr. Bailey, the head of Daddy's, firm came over and gave us children the gift of beautiful English play horses. They were fabulous. Fashioned on sturdy frames, covered with felt that seemed so real that they were soft and touchable. They had manes and tails of silk strands and they were completely tacked in English trappings. Penny's was a dapple grey and mine was coal black like the one in a picture of Dolly on her favorite jumping horse that hung in her front entry hall.

I managed to be polite while Mr. Bailey was there, but once he departed, I went into a complete melt down. I dissolved into tears and after screaming "I wanted my real mommy", I flew off again to my room, slamming the door with a resounding crash.

Mr. Hunt completely came apart. It seemed to him enough time had passed that I should have adjusted by now and I simply was not coming around. Brandishing Marie's silver hairbrush, he barged into my room. He grabbed me, sat on my bed with my wriggling form held firmly over his knees and whacked my bottom soundly, several times with the bristles of the brush.

I had been yelling at what everyone thought was the highest decibel, but with the lashing, howled so loudly the glass in the window panes shook.

Mr. Hunt took me from over his knees. Standing me on my feet, he shook me until I stopped screaming.

I stared at him wet-cheeked and spat, "I hate you! I never will love you! Any of you! I'm going to hold my breath till I die." I turned red in the face but did not accomplish mortality, so continued to uncontrollably sob on a level of hysteria.

Mr. Hunt spoke in a stern, commanding voice, "Beau-Beau, we have had enough of these tantrums! You are our daughter. All the screaming in the world will get you nowhere. The next time you carry on like this I will spank you, again. I will continue to punish you in this manner, and if you persist with this behavior, I'll spank you again and again! You need to learn that this is unacceptable in our home! We are your parents. You are our daughter. You will be living with us for a long, long time. You had better get used to it or you will be spending a lot of time in your room trying to work this out. These are my final words!"

He rose and stormed from my room, leaving me shaken with fear and grief. He had not really hurt me with his 'spanking' but my feelings had been deeply wounded.

I did not speak to Mr. Hunt for weeks.

CHAPTER FIFTEEN

Author's Notes:

For a mother who was so anxious to get rid of her child, Dolly certainly monitored my progress very actively. No matter what the situation, Dolly got a progress report. The past months seemingly had quite a few more downs that ups.

Both Marie and Dolly agreed that Penny going off to Brentwood Academy was the problem. With my sister absent, I simply was brooding even far more.

Something needed to be done and it came in the form of a very unexpected change.

ANOTHER 'DIVINE' IDEA WAS BORN

Marie Hunt had called Dolly for her weekly report and the news greatly alarmed Dolly. It seemed her strong-willed-child was making very little progress in the adjustment field. Her daughter took one step forward then a million back and there was seemingly no forgetting the past for her head-strong, 'Beau-Beau'.

Dolly was uncertain what on earth they were going to do. She and Marie had discussed several alternatives, doctors' consultations, more daytime activities, maybe even a governess. Each were willing to explore for help and distraction for the child but neither had the solution to my continued sadness. It seemed the doctors had been wrong. I was simply not adjusting at all.

So they decided to try a governess and that is when Ida Hecktlie came into our lives. Ida came highly recommended by the Huntington family who had long ago employed her for their own children.

Ida was a German war camp refugee. She was a kindly woman who had tattoos on her arm from being a prisoner of that recent, horrible war. She came to us and worked with us for many years. She was benevolent, understanding and frankly took the burden of weight off Marie Hunt. It seemed to be working to a certain extent, however all the adults concurred that something more needed to also dramatically change.

CHAPTER SIXTEEN

Author's Notes:

The reader must remember that recollections from Dolly's standpoint were relayed to me by Maria Rivera. Maria carefully documented Dolly's activities, as she had been privy to the knowledge that at some point, I would be allowed to come back into the 'Grand Misses' life as the godchild. In order to be able to inform me as to the progression of the early days after the handover, Maria documented all her daily encounters with the 'Grand Dame' in own meticulously kept journal, which she later shared with me once I was again allowed back into the 'Green fold'.

DISTURBING NEWS RESOLVED

Dolly was sitting in bed in her room, clad in a red-satin-dressing gown, when Maria entered with breakfast on a tray.

Maria noted her seeming agitation and asked, "Mrs. Green looks upset this morning. How come? You are usually on the phone with your broker by now and I have to interrupt you for your tray. You look as if you lose your best friend."

Dolly sighed and accepted the offered meal, saying, "I simply can't understand why our little 'Beau-Beau' is still so horribly upset. Marie says she pouts all the time and simply is not adjusting well. Oh, Maria, what are we going to do?"

Maria perfunctorily advised, "Maybe all she needs is a change of scene. Move that baby to a new house and she not fret near as much." Maria then went about tidying her mistress's room as if she had suggested the most obvious thing in the world.

Dolly seized upon her words as if they were delivered from Saint Peter, himself. "My, God, Maria! What a brilliant thought!"

Immediately, Dolly picked up the near-by phone. She dialed her father, who rapidly answered the call.

"Daddy? Don't you still have that divine little house over on Strathmore Drive, the one Tom Mix had until he moved to the Valley?"

There was a slight silence before Burton replied, "Well, yes."

"Oh, thank God," Dolly had then interrupted. "Call Mr. Hunt and see if they would like to trade Rockingham for Strathmore. Beau needs a change from that home. I think she will never adjust to the relocation unless we get her out of where she was sent away from me. Tell Ralph that you think that's so and that Marie is horribly worried about how badly Beau is adjusting. Hell, just tell him you'll give him the damn little home to help our little 'Beau-Beau' adjust to this family modification!"

There was a moment of resistance on the other line before Dolly disconnected. She knew her father would handle it.

Quickly, as an afterthought, she dialed him back again. "Daddy, since it is almost time for school to start again, register both the girls in Westlake School for Girls. It is right there up the street. Call Carol Mills and insist the girls be accepted. That should cinch it, getting the darlings into one of the best private schools in Los Angeles."

She clicked off again. Dolly was enormously pleased with what she'd accomplished for the latest re-adjustment of her little Beau-Beau.

Maria just shook her head with dismay at how easily Dolly *always got her way!*

96

And as usual, Dolly did!

The Hunts moved to the 'divine little' Strathmore house, within a week.

It was a complete surprise for the girls who were told they were moving to a new home, but did not see the 'little house' until the day they moved.

The mansion, 10360 Strathmore Drive, sat high on a rise of the lot. The entry was an enormous marble-floored foyer. The ceiling jutted thirty-five feet high where, from the center, hung a huge, pear-shaped crystal chandelier. Wrought iron banisters spiraled up a circular staircase to the three individual bedroom suites.

First, our family climbed the stairs to view the upstairs.

The pale, plum-colored master bedroom, harbored a large sleeping area and two enormous dressing rooms. A spacious mulberry and jade colored bathroom was complete with a huge marble shower stall and a sunken tub with gold faucets which were on the sinks and other fixtures.

Next they showed me my room. It was a pink suite in the middle. It had a main sleeping area, a dressing room and a bath done all in white marble. A porch opened over the garden that looked out at the azure pool.

Penny's designated room was to the rear of the domicile. A spacious blue bedroom that looked out over the greater Los Angeles area; her suite was complete with a dressing area, massive closets and her bathroom was done all in pink hues.

Downstairs, again we toured the rest of the home.

The main floor opened onto a into a huge formal living-room that jutted back to a den, which led out windowed doors, stepping outward into an authentic English Rose Garden.

The home had a massive, rose-wood paneled dining room with a sizable breakfast room that overlooked a covered patio. Behind the dining area was a long Butler's pantry filled with silver cupboards and counter-tops that served as preparatory areas when the owners entertained.

To the right of the pantry was a commercial-sized-kitchen.

The 'servants quarters' were at the rear of the house. Connected at the back of the home was a cavernous, three car garage.

An Olympic-size-swimming pool was on the northern portion of the property, and a greenhouse and orchard were at the back of the three-quarter-acre corner lot.

Ninety-five hundred square feet of interior space, the 'little' Strathmore residence boasted and it was a block away from Beverly Hills.

The first moment we children saw the imposing pink stucco structure, Penny asked Daddy if she had become a princess because the house looked like a castle to her.

It was palatial, compared to the smaller Rockingham home that we had previously occupied.

Once shown through the huge mansion, we girls could not wait to change and get into the pool.

I sat on the water's edge and watched Penny tread water, as we did not yet know to swim very well. We were promised by Daddy that a teacher was scheduled for tomorrow to work on swimming lessons with both of us. Dorothy Poynton, the Olympic diving champion had been engaged to instruct us first in aquatic prowess, then to teach us to dive.

Mr. Hunt, a strong swimmer himself, guarded over us as we frolicked and played in the water.

In the dark recesses of the butler's pantry, Mrs. Hunt was on the phone with Dolly, reporting the move.

She joyously advised, "I have never seen Beau so happy." Marie was shedding tears of joy. "She actually hugged me when I helped her change into her swimsuit. Dolly, this was positively brilliant! Ralph and I will never be able to thank you and your father enough for helping us make this change."

Dolly answered, "Marie, I am so thrilled, but I must go darling, I'll be late for my date. I've got a lunch appointment with my attorney, Neil. Bye dear, I'll call you next week for my update. Maybe it won't be as long as we thought that I can come back into her life."She was gone, leaving Marie staring at the suddenly silent phone.

But the curtness and lack of Dolly's interest about her child, was far overshadowed by Mother's joy over my sudden seeming zest for life. The sound of her children's joyous gales of laughter out at the pool was music to her ears. It seemed to be a sign of how things were going to change for the best.

The unexpected move of homes, the removal of me from the routine mundanities at Rockingham were exactly what the doctor ordered. And, although Dolly took credit for the brilliant move, Maria Rivera knew she alone had been the inspiration that had helped her precious, 'Beau-Beau' lead a new and happier life.

CHAPTER SEVENTEEN

Author's Notes:

Somewhere along the line, I finally decided to accept my fate and refer to and think of Mrs. Hunt and Mr. Hunt as Mom and Daddy. But I never called Mrs. Hunt...Mommy. Dolly was my mommy and Mrs. Hunt was simply, Mom.

FINALLY ADJUSTING TO THE NEW LIFE

Our family life proceeded from that day with leaps and bounds into fall, when Penny attended her first day at Westlake School for Girls. We all went with her that day.

Miss Carol Mills, the Headmistress, ushered the family around the sprawling campus and assured me that it would not be all that long before I joined Penny at classes there.

Penny was clad in a pale blue uniform and saddle shoes. I could not wait to have my own dresses that looked so crisp and starched.

We left Penny to attend her first day at school and on the way home we stopped at a wonderful toy store in Beverly Hills called Uncle Bernie's. In the center of the establishment was a huge tree that poured lemonade into a cup when you pushed a button. Daddy helped me get a glass of the sweet liquid. We browsed about the magical, toy store. I spotted a funny little doll and went right to it grabbing it and hugging it. It was a Humpty-Dumpty doll that had been handmade by Uncle Bernie's wife. She only made a few toys and I was attracted to this one. He was red and white and had been sitting on a wall surrounded by toy soldiers that apparently were waiting for him to fall. I loved the rhyme 'Humpty-Dumpty sat on a wall. Humpty Dumpty had a great fall. All the

King's horses and all the King's men, couldn't put Humpty together again'. So Humpty was my prize for that day.

We then went to Westwood and had lunch at Will Wright's ice cream parlor. For dessert I chose peppermint candy ice cream in a sugar cone.

It was a happy day.

A day completely alone with the Hunts. My first without Penny and it went unbelievably well.

We went home and I was told I had to wait an hour before I could swim in the pool for my lunch to settle.

I went out and sat on the lawn near the water and played with my new Humpty doll, placing him on my Steiff doggy, Poncho's back. I pretended that Poncho was Humpty's horse. I saw Mother and Daddy watching me from the living room window. Things were defiantly mellowing out for us all.

Because of the move, Daddy had taken some time off to re-group. It had given him an opportunity to be home more with us girls and really get to know us both, now that things were finally going so well. He was soon to be appointed a more senior partner of the accounting firm of Touche, Niven, Bailey and Smart. Things were really looking up.

He had to think of Penny's education and future. Even though his Beau was set for life with Dolly overseeing her financial future, Daddy had Penny to think of. Not to mention his eventual retirement and well-being. He could not work forever and after all, he was now in his fifties. He had to look ahead for Marie and his little girls. But what a wonderful life he had! He had a top notch job, a beautiful wife, and owned a more than fabulous home. I was finally adjusting, Penny was growing into a grand little child and things were coming up roses all over for the Hunts. It was a far cry from anything Daddy had ever imagined...after growing up delivering papers in Denver for the Post.

A far cry! Los Angeles was a going Jessie. His future looked bright. He'd made the right move in the early forties, when Marie had insisted they head West. Never in Daddy's wildest dreams could he have imagined all of this!

Best of all, after all the months of trial and error, it seemed I was going to adjust to their lives. It had been weeks since I had asked for Dolly Green.

In the months and years ahead, Dad suspected his 'special child' would forget the role Dolly originally played in her childhood rearing.

They had renamed me. On my birth certificate that the judge needed for the adoption papers, my name had been changed to Diane Melanie Hunt.

However, it was a long time before anyone called me by the name, Diane.

Daddy called me Beau, till the day he died. He always loved the endearment for his darling little girl.

CHAPTER EIGHTEEN

Author's Notes:

Yosemite days will remain in my mind as my very favorite time in my life. I would wait all winter then summer would come and we would spend it in Yosemite. It was like living in a whole different place and time. It was earthy, woodsy and I rode horseback every single day. There was no question that it was my idea of heaven on earth and a place I always wanted to be.

YOSEMITE DAYS

The summer of 1952 came and Dad announced that we were going on a grand adventure. We would leave very early in the morning and drive all the way to a place called Fresno. We would then spend the night in a motel.

Then, the next morning we would get up, go to breakfast, and go to a wonderful National Park called Yosemite.

This sounded like a grand adventure to us girls. We never went much further than to Grandma's over in Elysian Park or to Uncle Frank's who lived in Yucaipa. Those were always just day trips.

The morning of the designated 'grand adventure', we all got up very early. The car was already packed and we attached a cooler to the window putting ice in it as Dad said we were going through some *'mean'*, hot country through Bakersfield to Fresno. But by the time we would get to Yosemite National Park, it would be nice and cool. We were going to stay on the Valley floor at a place managed by the Yosemite Park and Curry Company. In tents!

Oh my gosh! I was so excited. It sounded to me as if we were going to be staying in the equivalent of our beloved tree house. Just on the ground.

Neither Penny nor I had slept well the night before, as we were both so excited to go on our 'grand adventure'.

It was still dark when we piled into the car.

It was indeed a long, hot trip. It took us almost eight hours to get to Fresno where we spent the night in a motel. That was a new adventure in itself, we had never done that before.

We had a wonderful dinner at a diner that had the best hamburgers ever and would become a favorite chosen spot over the years when we traveled to Yosemite.

We got to Yosemite and it was amazing. I fell in love with the towering Half Dome and all the other astonishing sights. The trees soared, the waterfalls plunged, and the air was pine-needle tinged and crisp to smell. Beautiful blue-jays darted all around and dove for bread crumbs when we picnicked on the Valley floor.

We went to a photographer's studio called Ansel Adams Gallery. Dad struck up a friendship with Adams that would last a lifetime and result in Dad pursuing an amateur photography passion that would take him to Japan to buy a Hasselblad. He took numerous courses with Ansel. However, unlike his amazingly talented instructor, Dad's photographic career remained forever lodged in mediocrity.

The time in Yosemite just flew!

Every night there was a fire-fall at the Awhanahee Hotel. There were stables and Penny and I rode to our hearts contents. Mom had discovered that if I wore gloves and did not pet the horses, my sneezing and wheezing did not come into play.

On our way home and out of the Valley, we chanced to stop at a junction called Wawona, where it pointed to a stable. We went down the little by-way to explore. There we found the Moore's Redwoods. They are still in business today renting the private cabins.

We found it, loved it and eventually bought a lot and built cabin #81. Jerry Moore helped orchestrate the building and we spent every summer there for years.

The trip to Yosemite was how we spent our entire August. We would build amazing rivers and canals in the dirt that was surrounding the house with dams and little play structures that we pretended were houses and small vessels that we imagined were boats.

When we got home we tried to do a similar channel system and that was shot down by our Gardner, Jack. I often wondered what people thought of the canal systems that were around the Yosemite house.

When we were older, there were other kids that were there from all over the Coastal area.

I met one of my first boyfriends there.

Even when I was in college, we spent the month of August in Yosemite.

I believe my absolute love of Yosemite and it's mountains, pines and rural environment played a paramount factor in my adult choice of where to eventually live.

CHAPTER NINETEEN

Author's Notes:

We really did normal things for us...just on a grander scale.

But the Hollywood birthday parties were simply a legend on their own. Someone could probably do a documentary on them, as they were as elaborately orchestrated as any movie production and perhaps enjoyed far more by the adults that their children.

SPINNING OF THE DAYS

Life had a way of sort of going on, day by day.

True to the doctor's forecasts, I accepted my fate more and more as the days melted in into weeks, the months into years.

Truly the most significant move had been the change of the domiciles. Left behind on Rockingham, were the haunting memories of the first days of my separation from my real mommy. There would be no return to that home or neighborhood, ever.

Though at first I resisted speaking to 'Mother', once Penny went to school it seemed dumb to be lonely and keep to myself. There was this really nice woman doing everything she could to be my friend, so what was the point in stonewalling her?

Furthermore, there were simply too many interesting things to do every day. My mother went out of her way to keep the hours that Penny was at school filled with exciting distractions.

There were swimming and diving lessons in our beautiful azure pool. There were excursions to the

Griffith Park Zoo where there was the carousel that played such pretty music. I rode the painted horses by the hour as Mother looked after at me as I rode.

People always stopped Mother to inquire about her beloved baby. I guess I was very pretty with my huge, doe, brown eyes, my black hair cut in a Dutch Boy and my dark flawless skin.

There were pony rides at the stables in a place called Bel Air. Around in a circle I would go on my special favorite, Buck. He was a beautiful tan and white pinto.

Uncle Bernie's Toy store was a regular stop when Mrs. Hunt and I went to Jorgensen's to market, in Beverly Hills. On the way home from marketing, she and I would stop at the little park at the bottom of the hill, and feed the ducks.

Then there were her Bridge Club luncheons that we attended. Other people had doggies. I seemed to sneeze and get stuffy whenever I was around dogs or cats, so I would sit and play with my stuffed Poncho and Humpty. I was unbelievably content unto myself. Marie's friends were astounded at what a good baby I was, always urging Marie to bring me the next time the ladies met.

So in this idyllic way, days melted to weeks and weeks to months.

I vividly recall the amazingly orchestrated birthday parties that both Penny and I attended in the early Westlake days. When we were five and eight, the extravaganzas were often combined and there were many celebrities children included.

Also there were boys.

Yikes! I was terrified of boys.

We had none at our school, so why did they need to be at the birthday parties? I began to dread those celebrations, despite the fact they were supposed to be such fun.

There were clowns, and all manner of things to delight little ones. But in reality, I think they were far more entertaining for the attending adults.

The Adlers and Cohens screened films in their projection room to entertain us little tykes.

The Getty's staged a party for their seven year old, Timmy. Penny and I were both invited along with several many other movie industry children. The Gettys staged a huge gathering, and the children attending were told to dress like pirates and there would be an actual treasure hunt. We swarmed over the lawn of the Getty home, seeking tiny treasure chests filled with chocolate coins.

It was an amazingly, unbelievable affair. There were fortune tellers, the atmosphere was circus-like and I believe the adults probably had far more fun that the children.

I was always shy at the parties and remember going to one at Kathy Cohen's home. Her father Harry was the President and Production Director of Columbia pictures.

I was just getting to the party and as always was unwilling to mingle with the other little kids, so I went to pet one of their Cocker Spaniels. He leapt up and bit me in the mouth right on my front lip. I was hurried into the house and the maid washed my mouth out with salt water and I was hurriedly sent to the doctor to see if stitches were needed. They were not, however to this day I have a lump from where the dog bit my lip. Mr. Cohen paid the doctor's bill. But that was long before the day of the 'drop of your hat' law suits, so Harry got off easy.

Years later my dad would kid how he really missed the boat not suing Harry Cohen for some of his millions. So that party did not linger in my mind as anything but a very unhappy day.

Others that come to mind were ones at our own home where Mother would orchestrate themes. It was all about the hype in the Hollywood town.

One theme was a Cowboy and Indian affair. There were Pinto ponies for the children to ride. Men and ladies rushed around tables serving cake and ice cream to the little tykes, dressed up like Cowboys and Indians. Roy Rogers came and sang. Everyone went home with a party favor of a little miniature guitar. It really was an amazing affair.

It was extravaganzas like this that were expected for all the birthdays growing up and all the parents complied. Nothing was too out of the ordinary for the children of the Hollywood upper strata.

Our parents lived in a world of make-believe and were tickled to death to create for their children a wonderland that was out of a fairy tale...if only for that golden afternoon.

After all, we were the privileged ones. We lived the Hollywood lives. We saw our friend's parents in movies on the silver screen. It was a part of our everyday life. All we knew was that it was their job to entertain. It was Mom or Daddy's place of work where they earned the money to pay the bills.

We were living in a bubble of shimmering, gossamer fabric, created by studios such as Fox, Columbia and Warner.

So to create a little birthday party for a group of children was as easy as waving a wand and the magic simply appeared.

We were the children of the fabled 'Tinsel Town', where nothing seemed beyond our grasp. Daydreams were effortless orchestrations of our expressed wishes.

Ask for the seemingly impossible, and yet we as the entitled, glibly received.

Movies, ponies, magicians with crystal balls, pirate hunts, Hawaiian hula parties, or Roy Rogers and Dale Evans materialized at the tip of the magicians hat. Just name your wished-for desire and it materialized before our widened eyes.

Our parents were the wizards behind the scenes.

To us, the astonishing was commonplace. Realism was a passing stranger, one that was far too obtuse to embrace.

So we lived in our diaphanous bubbles and were quite content to leave it exactly that magical way.

CHAPTER TWENTY

Author's Notes:

Our days were truly idyllic when you reflect, not compared to kids lives today. We were not shuttled endlessly to soccer matches, T-ball practice, on and on and on, like modern-day children.

My mother did not even learn to drive until Penny was twelve. Before that we had a chauffeur and he did all the driving. He was part of the live-in-help, phase of our lives. They were called Tela and Fred. They lived in the servants quarters' at the back of the house. Ida moved back to her home in Westwood and commuted to the Strathmore house and stayed with me till I went off to school. She became less of an influence in our lives then, but still was a constant factor till I was ten.

By then, Mother thought we had enough of the Governess stage.

'THE FORT'

Penny and I were growing up and doing all the stuff kids did. Rollers-skating, biking, and playing hide and seek.

There were no other children on our block, so we played mostly with one another. As children we developed a very strong bond and an ability to fabricate interesting things that were perhaps not the run of the mill with other children.

As a matter fact, we took the 'pretend game' to art form stages, fabricating situations from the purely mundane.

We played dress-up with our grandmother's old lacy dresses. Mrs. Hunt had saved her mother's vintage clothing for costumes. Never had she imagined what good use we girls would find in playing pretend with the outdated apparel. It was one of our greatest joys.

Penny always dressed up as a beautiful bride. Her fair hair and peaches and cream complexion were an amazing contrast to my dark skin. I had inherited my mother's olive-skinned-looks.

I, on the other hand, went for the more exotic and found a black lacy scarf, a red dress and a fan. I made myself up as a Spanish Grand Lady and marched about the house.

Mr. Hunt snapped pictures of both of us but when the negatives were developed, he was surprised at the image of his baby child. Me, with all the red lipstick and black eye paint, my face partially concealed by the red fan, the photograph revealed a glimpse of what a beautiful woman I would become.

But then, it was all in the game of pretty 'pretend'.

For instance our bikes were not bikes, they were horses. Penny named her's 'Blue Fire' and my horse was 'Buck'.

Penny was an Old West crime fighter, 'Billy Bob White', not unlike the Lone Ranger.

I was her faithful side-kick 'Niko', both names picked from a Gene Autry movie we had seen.

We played with plastic horses that 'pretend' made very real. We galloped them over hill and imaginary dale for hours at a time.

Our Flexie Flyer was a 'pretend' sled on snow. We plunged down the Strathmore hill much to Mrs. Hunt's horror, fabricating in our minds that we were sledding down a snowy slope on a mountain.

One weekend, Daddy announced that he thought it would be a really good idea if Penny and I had a special outdoor hideaway. Southern California had such a moderate climate in those days, that outdoor activities were almost doable year around.

So with boards and nails and ladders, Daddy picked out a large old oak tree and began the construction of what Penny and I would dub, 'The Fort.'

It took Dad no time at all to build it. He made a sturdy platform out of plywood, then hammered a series of boards that hooked together that formed a giant box.

It was huge! Maybe not to an adult but to us kids it seemed 'ginormous'!

We took our little outdoor kitchen and set it up out there, with a small table and chairs. A few pillows, some very special dolls, and games that we could hide in the little cupboard under the kitchen set and we were 'in business', as my dad would always say.

'The Fort' would be the equivalent of a hideaway that we kids would enjoy and use for many years.

We pretended to be international spies, or the Lone Ranger and Tonto, or any manner of crime solver.

We would eat our carefully packed lunches of peanut butter and jelly sandwiches, carrot sticks and Mom would put little bottles of juice in as well. Then there were always cookies that one of the maids would have baked. We always had homemade cookies in a big cookie jar.

We would mount our 'horses' and ride around to the 'Fort' and spend hours talking, reading, napping, just generally having a good time together.

It eventually became quite 'grand' because we took a little cupboard and sleeping bags and had dishes on which we ate our lunch. It was like a private little hideout for only us girls. Of course no adults were ever allowed.

Curiously, neither of us ever took friends there. It was our private little retreat that was never shared with the outside world of our other school chums.

The 'Fort' belonged to Penny and me. Our secret clubhouse, no one else was invited to join our exclusive sorority.

Often as an adult, I have compared my office to 'the Fort'. People need to have places that they can go and be surrounded by something comfortable and familiar. 'The Fort' was our haven as both of us were growing up.

CHAPTER TWENTY-ONE

Author's Notes:

Had someone told me that Dolly would come back into my life as my 'godmother', I would have told them to consult a shrink! She'd given me away, so she must never want to see me ever again. Of course, no one asked me if I wanted to be given away either, so I suppose it should have come as no little surprise that she would blast back into my life when I was six years old.

ENTRÉES THE 'DIVINE' DOLLY GREEN

The years passed without much of an eye blink and before anyone could believe, I was six years old and it was time for both of us girls to go to school in the fall.

My Kindergarten class had a pretty teacher named Mrs. Troxler. She was a dark-haired beauty that reminded me of my mommy from long ago. Mrs. Troxler rekindled my longing for my real mommy, however I said absolutely nothing about it. Long ago I decided that my fate was sealed. I would never see my real mommy again.

In my dreams and daydreams of 'pretend' I could remember my mommy and re-run the wonderful days lost. But to mention her was scary and I was incredibly bright. The saying 'once bitten twice shy' applied to me, twelve fold!

I had given up the quest for my real mommy the night of the hairbrush incident. I never wanted to be humiliated that way again. Ages ago I stopped hating Mr. Hunt for hitting me, but I never forgot the horrible spanking. It had scared me almost to death.

After a few weeks of my attending school, Mother announced that after my Kindergarten, she and a friend were picking me up to go to lunch. Penny had a full day of classes, so she would not be joining us. It would be just Mom, the friend and me.

I wondered who the friend was and asked Mother, who acknowledged, "She is going to be your 'godmother', Beau, darling. She's been a very close friend of mine for many years. She lives over in Beverly Hills. We'll be picking you up at noon."

So the morning went by slowly for me as I was anxious to meet Mother's friend who was soon to become my appointed 'Godmother'.

I was not sure what a godmother's duties were, but Melanie Adler's 'godmother' took her once a week to Blum's for ice cream. Susan Temple Black's 'godmother' took her to the Circus last week and the week before to the Venice Pier where she bought Susan cotton candy. So all in all, it sounded to me as if the 'godmother' was a very special person who was privileged to take their godchildren out only for elaborate treats.

Not that Penny and I were not taken often for treats, because in all honesty the Hunts lavished attention on both of us.

It was simply beyond a parent's normal spoiling duties, this 'godmother' thing. My little buddies and I talked at recess about my upcoming meeting with my soon to be appointed, 'godmother'.

At noon, I waited at the school's entrance for Mother to arrive. I was standing there, with Mrs. Troxler holding her hand when I saw a red and white Cadillac convertible pulling up to the entrance where we stood waiting for the ladies to arrive to pick me up.

Horror washed over me when I realized who was driving the car! Never in my wildest dreams had I ever expected it to be my former mommy, Dolly Green!

Momentarily, I did not know what to do. I was frozen to the spot. I simply could not believe this was happening to me. After all the years of day-dreaming about my missing mother, the tears shed over her foisting me off like some unwanted puppy, I'd still never come to terms as to the why's of the deal. Now there was Dolly Green in all her glory and she was beaming at me as was my adoptive mother.

Both women got out of the car and Mother walked over to me with her 'friend', introducing, "Beau darling, this is my good friend, Dolly Green. She is going to be your 'godmother', aren't you a lucky little girl?"

It took a snap decision on my part. In that split second I decided the best course of action was to have *my* cake and eat it too. If Mrs. Hunt and my mommy wanted to play their own game of 'pretend', I too could go along with the scheme.

After all, Penny and I had perfected the 'pretend' game to an art form, this was really no different. In my child's mind I made the decision of my life.

Had I acted oddly, pouted or reacted wildly that Dolly was my former mommy, I would have never seen Dolly Green again. That was the agreement with the Hunts. Dolly could return for visiting rights in person, but if I had reverted into the wailing child wanting her mommy, Mr. Hunt's bargain was that Dolly would disappear, for good. He'd not been all that keen on this bargain between the women, anyway. It had been a constant battle that they had waged since the day I came to live with them.

But all the doctors had agreed that in four magical years, I would have completely forgotten my former mother and that it would be safe for Mrs. Green to rejoin the fold. She could mentor me in person, not monitor progress weekly, only by telephone. This would only be allowed if I showed no recognition of Dolly at this reunion.

I offered my hand to my *'godmother'*, saying, "Pleased to meet you, Mrs. Green."

Immediately, Dolly gushed, "Oh, Beau, call me Aunt Dolly, darling. That is what I shall be to you. Now," she fussed over getting me into the car, "let's not be too late for lunch. I have reservations at Perino's and Jimmy the Maître D says I am always late for my reserved times."

We drove to Perino's in Beverly Hills where the adults had a lovely lunch.

I was strung too tight to eat much. I picked at my filet minion. I had my favorite, peppermint ice cream for dessert. I was relatively quiet throughout the meal but answered politely when spoken to by the women.

At the close of the meal, Dolly ventured that we go back to her house for a little tea party.

Mother seemed to hesitate.

I surmised that they were all treading on eggshells and Mother was concerned that a return to my former home might snap my memory.

It was then that I turned enthusiastic and urged them to go back to Dolly's home.

Dolly had the Maître D, wrap up my remaining, uneaten steak, saying we could take it to her doggie, Poncho, who loved scraps to come home from the restaurants she haunted.

I could tell the women were watching for any signs of reaction.

I gave them none, simply saying how much I loved dogs, and what kind of 'doggie' was Dolly's 'darling Poncho'?

"A beautiful Boxer," she batted her long black eyelashes, a trademark of Dolly Green's.

CHAPTER TWENTY-TWO

Author's Notes:

If the women could have read my mind as we were traveling toward the Mountain Drive home, they would have been perplexed. In both their minds, I was still the little girl who had been switched to another home.

Obviously, they were convinced that I had no recollection of my former life.

I'd forgotten nothing! I dreaded going to the Green home and having to pretend to all the servants that I did not recognize them.

But when we arrived and I was ushered into the home, I was in for a huge shock!

A LITTLE CASE OF DÉJÀ VU

We went to the Mountain Drive mansion. Dolly talked all the way there of how she was trying to buy a house in Bel Air. The house was 'dreamy' she said. She'd loved it since she saw it when her Daddy's friend Howard Hughes owned it. Now the owner, Elvis Presley had horribly abused the house because he let his chimpanzees have the run of the home. She prattled on about, 'how the monkeys swung from the crystal chandeliers. She was going to have to revamp the entire house, but she did not care because she wanted it so badly'.

We arrived at the Mountain Drive residence and exiting the car, we all went into the palatial estate.

I could sense the tension as we situated ourselves in the solarium for tea. Both women were vigilant for signs of recognition of the home, on my part.

I displayed no sign that would give my feelings away.

The women began to relax as tea and cakes were served by a maid that I did not recognize.

After a half an hour, I excused myself to go to the bathroom. The women were so engaged in talking, they hardly looked up except when Dolly directed me to the powder room, as if I did not know where it could possibly be.

Stealthily, I crept to my former room.

The circus-tent-decor was gone. It was nothing but a plain, guest room. Nothing remained to show that there had ever been a child occupying the airy room. I stood in the door for a few moments with tears of sadness trickling down my cheeks.

I suddenly became aware of a presence behind me.

Turning slowly, I came face to face with Maria who also had tears staining her cheeks. She tried to brush them aside before I saw her standing there crying.

Wordlessly we hugged. Unspoken recognition was transmitted in that heartfelt embrace. We knew we shared a secret so precious that it must always silently be sequestered among the two of us. A bond that had always been strong, was only strengthened on that day.

I put my finger to my mouth urging Maria to be still. There would be another time soon for us to talk.

Maria nodded, hugging me tightly. Relieved that now her little 'Beau-Beau' would be allowed back into the 'Green fold' on these odd terms. But she was content with anything to at least have her little 'Chiquita' back.

This was a wonderful day in both our lives because we had been so incredibly close.

Maria told me later that our separation had been almost as if her own baby had been given away.

I returned to the tea party and continued to sit and listen, attentively. I was so relieved that things were going this well. Dolly was back in my life and Maria had not been replaced like apparently all the rest of the servants had disappeared.

This was a banner day for me!

I had the Hunts. I had my mommy back and my dearest Maria as well.

In my lifetime, I'd never expected this to pass. Things from now on were going to be all up the hill.

CHAPTER TWENTY-THREE

Author's Notes:

These times were so precious I look back on them as if I was allowed to lead two lives, which of course I did.

I had a normal, for Hollywood, life with the Hunts, then my fairy tale world with Dolly Green.

Everything about Dolly was so luxurious. Her home was furnished with museum pieces, Louis Quatorze divans and dressers. She had a Louis Quatorze piano that came from Versailles. Titians hung on the walls as did all manner of photos of her and the sisters. Sevres vases were crammed with her beloved orchids, while white mink throws were casually flung on the 'Louis' divans. She had statuary that could have graced the Louvre, first edition books that belonged at the Huntington. My God! It was like going to a museum every time I walked through the hallowed doors.

I never returned to the Mountain Drive home. Dolly bought Bellagio Road early during the time I was allowed back into her life, so I recall my visits with her there very vividly.

EARLY BEL AIR REFLECTIONS

'The Godmother' role established, Dolly was allowed to have visiting privileges with me one day a week.

Often after school, but more frequently on a Saturday, we could have the whole day together to do wonderful things that we did. It was amazing how she treated me not unlike a girlfriend even when I was still very young.

Some adults never really treat children like they are little or uncomprehending. This is the way Dolly treated me from the moment I returned to her life. It was as if I was a miniature girl-friend.

Sometimes, because the Hunts were beginning to travel a great deal on Daddy's business, I spent several days with Dolly.

Penny was old enough to spend the nights with friends and she was a frequent house-guest at her best friend Karla Kirkeby's huge Bel Air mansion.

I was in heaven when I was allowed to stay at Dolly's but never once did I blow my cover of recalling my early childhood days.

It was amazing how during this early period, the years flew by. The contentment I felt with this unnatural arrangement was unfathomable. The only explanation was that I had always been an adaptable child and once over the initial trauma, I had molded very nicely to whatever the parents had wanted me to do. The parental group just had no idea of who molded whom. It became a pleasant routine where I felt as if I simply had two families.

Naturally, I preferred the glamour life of Dolly Green to the rather stayed routine of my life with the Hunts. But that was what made it so special between Dolly and me.

We had our days together that were like golden bubbles frozen in time. It became even easier to not recall former 'early life' situations when Dolly actually procured the Presley home and moved into her 'dreamy' new manse. It was a twelve-thousand square foot palace with a beautiful pool, formal gardens and great sloping lawns that rolled over a two acre corner in Bel Air at the intersection of Bellagio and Stone Canyon Road. The address was 10539 Bellagio Rd.

It was much closer to Westlake School for Girls, so my godmother's move made access to the Bel Air mansion, much easier. The school bus would often drop me at her door as it traveled to deposit other little Bel Air residents.

I would take the proper bus with Mary McCulloch, and Brookie Anderson, and the other girls who were delivered to that part of town.

When I spent the night, we had a wonderful routine.

Dolly always took what she called an afternoon 'siesta' to regroup after her usual frantic day of luncheons, shopping, fashion shows and soirees. When I arrived after school, Dolly would still be napping.

I would rush to my beautiful upstairs room to change. The 'back guest bedroom' was done in white moirés piped in gold. The ottoman was upholstered in gold and white as were the billowing drapes that during the day were drawn back with golden, tasseled cords.

The bathroom was massive, with a large white marble shower and deep soaking tub. All fixtures were of gleaming brass, a grape colored toilet and bidet were the only contrast against the white.

The huge bed was stacked with down pillows with crisp, white, linen cases and lace-trimmed sheets. A fluffy down comforter puffed the bed making it seem so huge and high it reminded me of the Princess in the fairy tale, the Princess and the Pea.

The decor hardly impressed me, nor was I phased by the fact that the entire house had been done by some amazing interior designer from Beverly Hills. The look had always been what Dolly chose for her homes. She always used as her pallet, gold's and whites and her favorite personal color, red.

I would change into my bathing suit in my palatial suite and then race down the stairs for an afternoon of swimming.

I would leave my room and fly by the cherry paneled library where Dolly told me that Elvis had played the piano. "He played to his chimps in what he called the 'monkey's room. This beautiful library!" Dolly would scoff, "for a bunch of filthy baboons!"

That room was draped in deep burgundy material that swaged from massive golden rods. There were large impressive mahogany furnishings, a desk piled with letters, invitations and bills. A Pope's bench positioned against the wall and several deep cranberry high backed chairs placed about were wonderful for reading. They would wrap their velvet wings about a reader who could become lost on a journey into another literary land for hours at a time.

Books lined the shelves. Rare collectibles, a Gutenberg Bible Dolly had shared with me, books by Thoreau, first editions of some man named Hemmingway, who Dolly said she knew. There were Keats, Walden, Browning, Helen Hunt Jackson, to name a of few other authors she collected.

Rounding the corner by Dolly's vast suite, I would tiptoe by the door, never wanting to awaken my sleeping 'godmother'. That had always been the code. Even as a little child I was cautioned not to wake the 'Mrs.', by my dear Maria. I would envision my beautiful mother with her sleep shades on her eyes. Dreaming of all her glorious parties, resting up for our enjoyable evening together. Dolly required her afternoon siesta!

Dolly's room was the largest of the three upstairs bedrooms. It was entered through a door into a narrow corridor off which jutted to the left a dressing room. Dolly had her hair dressing equipment set up there. Every evening, a personal stylist from Elizabeth Arden came to fix her hair. Everything necessary was already there.

On the right of that corridor were more closets. The hall led into a sitting area where Dolly had day couches and chairs artfully positioned; all were upholstered in reds and gold piping. The windows looked over the gardens and all the way to the coast, were draped with white and gold-piped, moiré. End tables and coffee tables were of gold gilt from the Louis V period and always were strewn with various magazines. The carpet was thick white shag.

Behind this sitting chamber was her bedroom and bath chamber. The dark colored bath was enormous. Fixtures all in burgundy and brass, it housed a huge shower, a deep tub with jets, a long two sink counter and a dressing table that was overloaded with cosmetics and perfumes. She collected rare fragrances but only wore, Diorissimo, by designer, Christian Dior.

In Dolly's bedroom was a large four poster with a red and gold draped canopy that enclosed her and kept her from draughts. Above her bed hung a crucifix, she had become very religious it seemed. Most of her pals had taken up one form of religion or the other. It seemed that Dolly's crew thought Catholicism was the current chique, religious affiliation, to join.

Dolly's bedroom was furnished mostly with gold and white dressers and tables. French curved back chairs surrounded a lovely gaming table where Dolly and I played cards.

"It was a George V." Dolly told me, she wanted me to be educated in everything from literature to fine antiques.

Passive education. Hands on, in a sense that I was surrounded by the most priceless antiques in the world and grew up with them. It did not seem apparent at the time, but I grew to have an incredible eye for everything from fine furniture, to books and jewelry. All the things Dolly always surround herself with that seemed taken for granted by both Dolly and me, did not go unobserved. I simply took for granted that this was the way everyone lived. All my friends lives were this way, so naturally, everyone must be this well healed. Or so I supposed.

Once past Dolly's room, I skipped down the curved marble staircase into the entry hall. I always marveled at the table that was there. The top surface was comprised of chips of lapis, garnet, jade and malachite in a random manner of a stony collage. For some reason, it always fascinated me more than any other piece in the house.

Most often an enormous bowl of cymbidiums rested on the surface that was completely inlaid with semiprecious stones.

I, loving horses, always paused to look at the pictures of the Lipizzaner's that hung on the halls, circular walls.

Dolly said someday she would take me to Spain to see these beautiful white horses. I hoped it would be sometime soon as I loved horses and could not get enough of the animals, even though they still seemed to make me sneeze.

Through the living room I would skip to where Maria sat waiting for me to arrive. Some days I would sneak up on Maria who often stood in the far solarium overlooking the pool. The maid would gaze out over the water while she waited for me to appear.

I would creep past the Louis Quatorze piano, past the Empire period divans and couches. So uninviting in their red and gold water silk, they were almost always covered with sheets so the dogs could lie on them and not harm the upholstery.

I would tip-toe quietly by the orchid laden Sevres vases at the end of the room and sneak behind Maria and poke her in the back.

Maria would feign a horrible scare whether or not she was surprised. She'd then hurry me off to the pool cautioning me not to make too much noise because 'the Mrs.' was still sleeping, as if I did not already know that fact.

Maria was ever vigilant as I splashed away the waning afternoon hours...waiting for Dolly to appear.

CHAPTER TWENTY-FOUR

Author's Notes:

In the winter, when darkness descended sooner and swimming was not an option due to the chilly air, Maria would have 'Cook Alice' fix us hot chocolate and she and I would play cards. My favorite game was 'Go Fish'. It was during our time together, that Maria and I whispered about our remembrances. I stunned Maria when I revealed all that I recalled.

At one point, Maria found herself involuntarily crying over the tales of horrible adjustment that I revealed.

Maria was further shocked at how philosophical I was about my current situation of 'having my cake and eating it, too'.

We agreed it was for the best, because in all truth Dolly did not lead the most motherly of lives.

When I was not in residence, Dolly was mostly off carousing with men until all hours of the night. She was never home except for my visits.

Maria admitted as gently as she could to me, that Dolly was in all reality, quite loose with her favors toward the men in her life.

So with Maria and my secret bond re-established, we rarely discussed the past. Only what was currently going on in our lives, while we happily wiled the afternoon away waiting for the lady of the house to arise.

LITTLE GIRL FOUND

In the evenings, Dolly always descended the winding marble staircase with a grand flourish and with her two Boxers nipping at her heals. She usually was clad in a flowing dressing gown of water silk red, piped with ostrich feathers or some other 'divine' concoction of her latest choice.

Her hairdresser would have coifed her hair and departed down the back stairs to leave unnoticed. Her nails were always perfectly shaped and painted bright red.

She would appear in the kitchen, cajoling, "Di, darling, let's go have out little drink. Maria, has 'Cook' fixed Poncho and Pixie their dinner?"

Then with Maria's usual positive confirmation of the fact that her dogs had been fed, Dolly and I would head for the solarium to have our evening time together.

Julio, her Puerto Rican butler, would collect himself to attention and fuss about pouring drinks in the sitting room as soon as Mrs. Green and I arrived. Julio spent most of his time polishing the multitude of antiques that were positioned throughout the house.

Dolly always had a cocktail of Champagne over the rocks. She would allow me only a little sip. I would then drink my Shirley Temple.

Our dinner was always served in the beautiful dining room. The same chamber that could easily accommodate seating for twenty-four, was set for just the two of us.

We would sit and talk for hours about my school, my riding lessons, and my friends while being served course after course of the meal.

Dolly always served my favorites.

Usually, the first course was cold lobster with Béarnaise. Next a baby Bib was drizzled with lime vinaigrette and small croutons. Onion soup with wonderful Gruyere cheese was served, then tender filets of beef au jus, asparagus and baby new potatoes drizzled with butter completed the meal. Dessert was Baba Rum.

As I said earlier, Dolly never talked down to me. From the time my visits began when I was six, Dolly treated me as an adult. I was never treated as a child by Dolly Green. Instead, I was treated as a peer.

Dolly Green had very few women friends. She was simply too jealous to have competition, however, in the looks department, she had little to worry about. Had she wanted a career in pictures, she probably could have had one. She was a woman of unequivocal good looks. She'd thought about the movies, but it simply did not fit her routine. So, with me happily back on the scene, she gave up thought of any career and decided her life goal was to enjoy herself and her 'godchild'.

It was in the evenings together that I began to seriously explore the library and became addicted to books. I adored the Gothic's and read them voraciously. Dolly, also an aggressive reader, would finish several works and give them to me to take home. Eventually, I had an enormous collection of literary works.

It was also in the evenings after dinner that endlessly, Dolly and I talked. We had such a terrific bond. It was not like mother and daughter, it was as if we were best friends.

Dolly told me everything there was to tell about her exciting life. We would talk till we were hoarse and then wander off to our separate rooms for a good night's sleep.

It was always after our visits that I committed notes to my ever growing journal. Dolly's life was so fascinating that I felt compelled to write everything down.

On the weekends, when there was no school, I would rise early and read until nine-thirty when habitually Dolly arose.

I would go to Dolly's room and knock on the door.

"Entrées!" was always her happily chirped reply.

I would go in and sit on Dolly's bed and wish her a good morning.

Weekdays, she would be on the phone with her broker. She had a separate line other than her Crestview number. Bradshaw 4-7251 was her private line where stocks and bonds were reviewed by her broker every morning at nine-thirty, sharp.

During the conversation, Maria would bring a bed tray for Dolly and a plate for me. Daily, Dolly had two eggs over easy, two slices of bacon, dry white toast and a glass of fresh squeezed orange juice.

I had the same but buttered my bread.

Dolly would leave the phone and we would eat our breakfast together while we planned our day.

When I was younger, it was a trip to the circus, or the Griffith Park Zoo, a stop at Uncle Bernie's toy store and Blum's on the way home for ice-cream.

By the time I was nearly twelve, we were doing adult excursions, shopping for clothing, lunching, going to matinees or ballets.

It was also at twelve, that I first met one of Dolly's gentlemen friends, Enrique Schondube. In Dolly's words, the "divine Spaniard". He was quite tall and very good-looking in the dark Latino way. His family owned a vast cattle ranch in Guadalajara. Dolly had him for dinner one evening, which was so contrary to our usual time together.

At first, I was really annoyed. However, he charmed me. He made me feel so very grown up, telling Dolly what a beautiful girl I was, and that was something I rarely heard.

According to Maria, Mrs. Green had been seeing Mr. Schondube a great deal. She had even been to his home in Guadalajara and out for a romantic cruise on his seventy-foot yacht. Maria suspected that Enrique would ask the Mrs. to marry him.

I was not particularly surprised. My mother was so beautiful, she deserved to be married to this handsome man.

Dolly told me that her great friend, Hernando Courtwright had introduced them. Hernando owned the Beverly Wilshire Hotel and his children were godchildren of Dolly's as well.

However, I never anticipated how both our lives would change once 'Heinie' was introduce into the equation.

CHAPTER TWENTY-FIVE

Author's Notes:

Westlake School for Girls was a institution of learning that was overseen by an amazing group of teachers and people who genuinely cared about all their girls.

Of course, it is now co-ed, but in our day, the dreaded boys were in Harvard Academy, over the hill and far away.

Never in a million years would I think that Harvard and Westlake would combine.

Penny and I were destined to go to Westlake, as Dolly wanted us there. I am quite certain that like the Strathmore house, Westlake was chosen by Dolly to educate Penny and me. I am also certain that Dolly subsidized our education. Though it is nowhere as expensive then as it is now, it was still a considerable expense to send us both.

I do recall Daddy saying how much money it cost. But compared to today's lofty tuition, it was a drop in the bucket. Of course things that were so little money then compared to now are amazing to me. In our day the tuition was $1700 a year, and now the tuition is over $29,000. I don't believe that even includes books.

EARLY WESTLAKE DAYS

I remember Miss Troxler who was my Kindergarten teacher. I recall her being by my side when Mother and Dolly came to pick me up for that fated godmother-godchild meeting.

I think Mrs. Troxler had been clued in, to the pending circumstances because she seemed nervous when the time came for her to take me out to meet with my mom and the 'godmother friend'.

It was pretty clear to me that Dolly had put the fear of God in the school for watching out for the Hunt girls. I do think that Dolly had warned them to be very careful, especially with me, as I was never allowed to go anywhere unless it was with an approved chaperone or a written note from my folks.

I did not learn until later in life, Dolly had quite the 'kidnapping scare' and was horribly frightened over anyone putting two and two together about me being from her former life. There was so much subterfuge between Dolly and everyone in those very early days.

As it turned out, I was not a good student. I was very slow in math and I was constantly tutored after school.

Penny was absolutely brilliant and I was always being compared to her and put down.

Every grade I went into I was measured up to Penny Hunt. They would say, "My, you certainly are not as bright as your sister was!" That was the bane of my existence.

Early on I had real trouble with my grades. Mother wondered if I was what they called 'dyslexic' and had me tested for that.

Dolly thought that perhaps I was still having psychological problems, so suggested Mother take me to a shrink. Mother subsequently scheduled all sorts of tests at UCLA. I was taken several times, given a Rorschach test and several counseling sessions.

That resulted in the doctor saying that under the circumstances, I seemed perfectly sound. The psychiatrist admitted that I was fairly well adjusted considering the trauma I had experienced when relocated as a child. Perhaps I just needed tutoring. So I was tutored with a vengeance for the rest of my Westlake days.

I had absolutely no self-confidence! My sister was the stunning beauty and I was just a little waif that my dad often referred to as, 'Shrimp'.

In the early days of lower school, I had a couple of good friends. Melanie Adler, whose parents were Buddy Adler and Anita Louise, was very much one of my best friends.

Buddy was the head producer of Twentieth Century Fox and Anita was a noted actress, who at the time, was the star in *My Friend Flicka*.

Buddy was a wonderful father figure. You would never have guessed that he was the head of a studio of the magnitude of Twentieth Century Fox.

He would come home like any normal daddy and Melanie and I would go into the library before dinner. He would sit us on his knees and read new movie scripts that were age appropriate, or Walt Disney books.

Buddy Adler took Melanie and me on the Twentieth set of *South Pacific*. He was the head producer for the movie studio and we were always with him on the back-lots.

My most vivid memory of Anita Louise was of her always running around the house in shorts and barefoot with her beautiful blond hair high in a ponytail on her head.

They were the most unassuming of couples.
Hollywood in those days was nothing like it is today.

It was a far simpler time.

The Adler's lived at 100 Delfern Drive. The home was a spacious rambling two story that was beautifully decorated and has lots of windows. I remember it as always being sunny and warm.

They had a glassed-in breakfast room where we would eat breakfast and lunch. Dinner was always served in the long formal dining room.

The color scheme was predominantly white, which I thought was amazing in a home with two children and two Dalmatian dogs. But Anita loved white, so white it was throughout most of the house. They had the carpets and furniture cleaned all the time.

Melanie had a brother, Tony, who we both detested as he was younger and was always teasing us and trying to pull tricks on us.

Melanie was a budding tennis star and we played a lot on the tennis court or swam away endless afternoons in their Olympic size pool.

Every birthday, Melanie had the most wonderful parties of all, as her dad always had access to any movie he could desire.

Bambi was loaned by Walt Disney to Buddy for one of Melanie's early parties and then I recall a later film being *Gigi*, when Melanie turned twelve.

I remember one Halloween going off to trick-or-treat. Now only in Hollywood did the chauffeur take you from block to block in a stretch limo, for goodness sake.

We were driving down Sunset Boulevard when we were sideswiped by another car that just literally ran into us, then drove off. The chauffeur said he thought it was a drunk.

That was of course before the days of cell phones, so a bystander who had witnessed the accident, rushed off to summon the police. They took an accident report and then we went on to trick-or-treat up and down the blocks of Beverly Hills' mansions. I recall I was dressed as a big, black cat. I guess I was Charlie and did not even realize the association...but oh well.

Saturdays, I would be delivered to Melanie's for a sleep over. I would be excited about that. I had no trouble with her dogs Pokie and Dot, two beautiful Dalmatians, as they were short-haired dogs. It seemed that I was growing out of my allergies. However, I still reacted badly to cats.

Melanie and I really had a very good relationship, but it ended suddenly one summer with a tragedy.

The summer of 1960, Buddy died of lung cancer leaving Melanie and Tony devastated and Anita Louise in a state of shock.

I heard of his death when sunning on the rocks at the 'Old Swimming Hole' in Yosemite. It was headline news in L.A. and was broadcast from a Fresno station. We were listening to the radio to the current tunes and the newscast related the crushing news. I cried my eyes out for Melanie that day! Not one of my friends parent's had died, so it really was a shock and he was so horribly young.

It was not very long after that the Adler's moved to New York for a change of pace. Anita had taken a role in a Broadway play.

Anita then met Henry Berger and marred him in New York and they lived between New York and Los Angeles.

I only saw Melanie once after the New York move when she came out to visit and stayed with us at the Strathmore house.

She had completely changed. She was very mature and had some kind of a liaison with a producer out in L.A.

She would disappear late in the evenings with this man, then arrive back late in the mornings.

Mom and Dad were distressed, but there was little they could seem to do.

Melanie was a very different girl and I have never heard from her again after that summer trip.

Melanie Adler's home sold in the high hundred thousands after Anita Louise died at the early age of fifty-five of an aneurism.

Eventually, the mansion was sold for millions in the nineties. My how things have changed!

Another very close friend when I was young was Ginger Hyland. The Hyland Estate was enormous. It rambled over several acres of land just down from Westlake School. As young children, Ginger and I shared a common love of horses and she and I played with plastic horses instead of dolls.

136

We went to Walker Lake to stay at some beautiful cabins and fish. It was amazing and so secluded. We flew there in a D-C3. Mr. Hyland had unlimited access to planes as he worked for Howard Hughes. We went there during Easter break and had the time of our lives. I think I discovered very young that the mountains and rural seclusions were something that really appealed to me. It was the grandeur of the mountains, the peace of the towering fir trees, the closeness to nature. That is not to mention the awe I found when encountering deer, elk and the ever soaring hawks. Like Yosemite, the stay at Walker Lake reinforced my love of rural solitude and peace.

So those two little girls were my primary, early, growing-up friends. I was a painfully shy child and two friends were about all I could manage to handle.

However, when I hit my teens, I began to seriously branch out with other girls in the school.

Melanie and her mother moved to New York after Buddy's death. Ginger was removed from Westlake as well, so I began to develop other friendships.

CHAPTER TWENTY-SIX

Author's Notes:

There were times in my life that I look back upon and realize that compartmentalized in my brain are little scenarios that are more brilliant than the overall picture of this amazing tale. This glance to the past is a paramount example. I can almost feel the sun on my back and the bracing water of our pool as I paint this scene for the reader. The light was shimmering, the air was blissfully warm and Penny and I were cavorting in the water when this event shattered the idyllic scene. Seems a little like the story of my entire life.

HOT AUGUST DAYS

One simmering August afternoon, Penny and I were swimming in the pool when unannounced, Dolly and Enrique Schondube were ushered out to see us as we swam.

Penny was introduced to Enrique who said he was "charmed to make the acquaintance."

As usual, he was dressed in an unbelievably suave manner. He was attired in a white silk sport coat and navy pants. His shoes were black patent and he sported a Panama hat on his head.

Dolly and Enrique tossed pennies into the shimmering waters of the pool for us to dive for and retrieve.

Enrique said to Dolly, "You know, I did not notice this the other evening, how much your niece looks like you, my love. She could be your daughter, not your niece."

Dolly said nothing.

Marie coughed.

Ralph walked away offering to bring out ice tea for everyone.

I chirped, "It's not the first time someone has said that about you and I, Aunt Dolly."

Dolly laughed and Enrique threw more coins for us girls to dive and retrieve.

The uncomfortable moment passed unnoticed, but I felt really alarmed. I was starting to look more and more like Dolly and several people had actually commented on that. What would then become of our relationship if I became the mirror image of my mother?

At the end of their visit, Dolly announced that she and Enrique were going to Santa Barbara to be married. They had bought a home on Edgecliff Lane in Montecito and were going to live there the better part of each year.

I thought little of this news as frankly, I had expected her to marry 'Heine' as she affectionately referred to the handsome Latino. They had been spending an inordinate amount of time together, so it seemed fated by the stars.

However, as the days passed and the weeks faded into months, I heard nothing further from Dolly.

I asked Mother about it and she responded that Dolly was busy with her new life. At the moment, her godchild just didn't fit into the social whirl.

Dolly called several times to actually talk to me, but her excuse of not seeing me was that she and Enrique were so busy with their social life in Santa Barbara. Between keeping the house in Guadalajara and Montecito, they were never in L.A. at all.

I was crushed. I actually decided I hated Enrique! Despised the suave Mexican for taking my real mother away. I had been so secure in my relationship with Dolly, so set in my routine of the weekly visits and constant phone calls, that I could not get her off my mind.

I blamed it on the fact that Enrique had so outright spoken of our resemblance. If a total stranger could see it, I wondered why people who were more familiar with the Greens, had never mentioned the resemblance before that day.

Perhaps, with my hair slicked back from the water of the pool, my high cheekbones, black hair and olive skin had provided a flash to Enrique that I looked like Dolly.

It haunted me that Dolly had again disappeared from my life. This time, fury was my tormentor and goaded me to gain her attention...once again.

I did not see Dolly until I was sixteen years old.

Only when I took matters into my own hands, did a reunion again occur.

CHAPTER TWENTY-SEVEN

Author's Notes:

Life of course went on for me, but without Dolly, I felt adrift. Things that I had overlooked seemed far more paramount and I had much more time to reflect on me and how I was turning out. It really bothered me a great deal that I was looking so similar to Dolly, that it had apparently driven her away.

So I consciously set upon making changes and I think they were all mistakes. I asked mother if I could get curly hair, some of my friends had permanents so we agreed that curls might be a good thing. What a disaster that turned out to be! I look back at some of the photos taken during my frizzy-haired period and think I look more like a Cocker Spaniel with a bad hair day than Dolly Green. But I was convinced if I disguised the 'Green' looks, perhaps she would eventually come back to be with me.

THE UGLY DUCKLING AND THE SWAN

After Dolly disappeared to Santa Barbara, I was forced to adjust to the fact that my fairy godmother, had washed her hands of me for a life more exciting than spending time with a mere child.

The routine of growing up with nothing but a normal life to fall back on, was at first a difficult transition for me.

I missed the weekly visits to the Bel Air mansion. I longed for my time with Dolly and also Maria's loss of contact was a huge void.

But I was maturing and the teen years were not easy ones for me to endure.

Once the initial shock of losing Dolly had passed, I had more important things to deal with, like the coping of day-to-day life. Mainly, because I had to deal with the strong personality of my sister, who frankly was the family star.

It had not seemed nearly as evident that Penny was so important until I was no longer off on my weekly visits with Dolly.

With those sojourns on the back burner, daily life was more intensified. I had nowhere to hide from Penny's overpowering center stage. My sister, Penny, was a stellar pupil at Westlake School for Girls. She was always an A student, so the instructors would compare me to my brilliant sister.

In my early years, school was very difficult for me. Eventually, I managed to achieve a method of studying that would carry me through college as an exceptional student by learning to take good class notes.

As well as scholastic pressures, there were heavy peer stresses, as well.

Penny was a magnet of popularity and hung around with girls like Karla Kirkeby, Candice Bergen and Sandra Keck.

All the girls' parents were the top business men, oil men, or leading studio personalities.

The Kirkebys owned a mansion situated on several acres in Bel Air. It was a huge home where Penny would go to play and when I was dropped off to go get my sister to come home, I would always get lost in the catacombs of the twenty-seven thousand square foot mansion. Mr. Kirkeby was the owner of large hotels.

The Bergens had a lovely Tudor in Beverly Hills where Edgar entertained Candy and Penny with Charlie McCarthy on his knee.

The Kecks lived in Holmby Hills and he was old California oil who dabbled, as well, in real estate.

So the pressure of being a popular child was also expected of me. To me, friendships did not come as easily as they did for my beautiful sister. I had to work very hard at relationships with other girls. Where Penny was outgoing, self-assured and poised, I was insecure, uncertain of my worth and crushingly shy. Things that came naturally to Penny, I had to strive hard to have fall into place.

In the end, I had no less the contacts than my popular sister, but had far more work invested in the relationships and they were more strongly bound.

It was like that all along.

Everything fell into Penny's lap.

I had to work for every goal I ever accomplished in my life. Because of this, early on, I think I developed a tenacious nature. I would target the most popular girls in my class.

I became front row with several stellar girls in my class that seemed important to me then. However, in retrospect, given the lack of contact in later years, I obviously made no lasting bonds. It was a time of shallow friendships, but they were what they were and I was satisfied to have what I had at the time. My choices were not as glorious as my sister's, probably because there were not as many movie or moneyed families in my particular class. But they were fine for me.

There was no doubt that both our choices of friends were quite a cross hatching of kids that attended Westlake School for Girls.

Mother and Dad reveled in our contacts as those connections led to invitations to parties and soirees at various mansions. Our parents were always royally entertained when grand bashes were thrown by several of the parents known to us.

Though it seemed that I was as popular as Penny, I secretly hated myself and despised living in the shadow of my beautiful popular sister. But I kept my sadness to myself. I watched as my father fawned over Penny, showing off his beautiful daughter to all his friends.

Then, almost as an afterthought, he would introduce me as, "his little Shrimp, Beau."

Compared to Penny, at twelve, I was very slight.

Penny, at fifteen, was a statuesque beauty, planning a modeling career with Elizabeth Arden.

I was pig-tailed, had shiny rail-road-track braces, and was my father's lanky five foot, 'SHRIMP'.

Dolly always told me that in the looks department she too had been a late bloomer.

Penny, was an early beauty, but those were not the ones that were so beautiful in later life.

Mother said basically the same thing, "Give it time Beau. You're just a little girl. You'll be beautiful someday."

I had long ago given up on the idea that I was going to be pretty. At some point, I simply quit looking for the promised metamorphosis. I knew it would never happen, so why bother to hope.

I hated myself. I disliked Penny to a certain extent and to worsen it, Penny started seeing boys. I hated boys, absolutely loathed them! This, because they made me feel even uglier than I knew I actually was. So I simply ignored them.

When I turned fifteen, my parents gave me a horse. She was a beautiful, liver-chestnut, quarter-horse mare. I named her Missy and began a career of riding with a vengeance. All I thought about was horses and how soon my dad could drive me out to the stables in the Valley.

Horses were my only love! I planned never to be married! I could not fathom what made women so crazy over men.

CHAPTER TWENTY-EIGHT

Author's Notes:

As a young girl, my own self image was unbelievably poor due to the dazzling beauty of my sister. Penny really was gorgeous, but she, compared to the other beauties that graced the school, was fairly ambivalent about that fact.

She was a pretty face among many and she never saw it as much of a big deal. I was overshadowed by the whole thing as I perceived myself as such a mess. Then there were circumstances that happened that simply confirmed my insecurities.

People can be so cruel and never realize the fact!

THE PRINCESS AND THE TROLL

By the time Penny turned sixteen, she was more than involved with the pursuit of boys. And, as beautiful as she was, she collected a bevy of handsome suitors.

But Penny was always protective of me as her little 'Sis'. Always standing up for me in any situation.

Penny loved me foremost of all and was always making sure I was watched after. She worried for me. She knew I was so self-conscious of my less than pretty looks, so Penny tried to always run interference if she sensed a hurtful situation could arise.

But she could not always intervene.

One day, Penny and several other Westlake Juniors were sitting in the parking lot bantering with a group of Harvard Military School boys.

I rushed up to my sister to ask for a ride home. My tutor had canceled due to illness and rather than have our chauffeur pick me up at the designated hour, I preferred to ride home with Penny in her 'cool', little red convertible. Being with my gorgeous sister in the snappy little car made me feel so grown up. It made me feel important to be seen with my popular sister. I almost felt like I too, looked pretty sharp.

Penny hugged me and said, "Sure 'Shrimp', I'll be right there. Hop in the car."

I got into the little Dodge Dart and waited for Penny to ditch the boys.

Penny was walking to the car when one of the gorgeous blond hunks followed her. The rest of the crew remained bantering with Candy Bergen, who was perched coquettishly on her purple Thunderbird.

The blond god grabbed Penny's arm and asked, "What's your hurry? I wanted to ask you out for Saturday night's dance."

Penny agreed, "That's cool, but for now, my 'Sis' and I have to take off. I'll talk to you later about the dance. Call me at home after seven, tonight." She started to come to the car.

I watched as puzzlement washed the young man's face. He voiced amazement, saying, "That's your kid sister? Boy, she sure got caught behind the ugly side of the door."

He knew the second his words were out of his mouth, his foot had lodged firmly down his throat. Back pedaling frantically he added, "I mean compared to you, she could be considered a real troll. I mean," he gulped. "You're such a princess and she is so," gulp, "nondescript."

There was no way out of his mess now and from the look on Penny's face and the tears in my eyes, he was doomed.

Penny turned to see if I had caught all the cruel words and it took her not a second to realize how deeply the boy's words stung her beloved baby sister.

Rushing to the car she jumped in and yelled at the boy, as she revved the motor, "You stupid dick! Forget

Saturday night or any other time, for that matter. Don't ever bother to give me a call."

Screeching out of the school driveway, Penny consoled me all the way home, saying how the boy was a creep. He had no taste. He was a horrid jerk. He needed glasses if he thought I was 'nondescript'.

But I sat weeping the whole way home. No amount of consolation on Penny's part could deter me from the affirmation that I was the ugliest person in the whole world.

That unpleasant scene would haunt me all my teen-age years.

CHAPTER TWENTY-NINE

Authors Note:

Growing up we had a series of hired help who worked for us and this is an interesting part of the story as well.

For every ethnic staff that mom and dad hired, I would end up learning a bit of their way of cooking.

I learned German cooking from a couple called Tela and Fred.

Then there was Mrs. Kerrick, who was just a generally good American cook.

Then Toshko who was Japanese.

Lupe was Mexican and she was the last of the live-in-help.

Hired staff became more and more impossible to retain, so by the time Lupe left, I was sixteen and dad and I took over kitchen duties on Strathmore Drive. We both loved to cook, so as long as Mother had cleaning help, we saw no reason to have live-in-staff.

BORN TO COOK

Our grandmother, Ada Sowers, was a cook and a baker. She taught me all I know today about canning and baking. By the time Grandma and I were making our magic in the Strathmore kitchen, we needed to sneak in because we had Mrs. Kerrick, who really did not like anyone in her domain.

So on maid's day off, Grandmother Ada and I would sneak in the kitchen and make something unbelievable for dinner. Then we would all enjoy our creative efforts.

I was very fond of grandmother Ada. She was what my dad called a wild hair. I later found out that he meant 'wild hare'. But for years I thought he meant she had wild hair.

Grandma was always going against the norm especially when it came to opposing what my father thought was right, so she did deserve his moniker of being a wild hare!

She decided that we needed to grow tomatoes in the formal rose garden and to hell with our Gardner, Jack.

So we grew a garden anyway. I believe much of my defiant nature was derived from my close affiliation with my grandmother Ada.

I recall her very fondly to this day for a variety of things that she taught me to do.

CHAPTER THIRTY

Author's Notes:

Upper class brought different issues. As a young girl, I never thought at all about boys. Well it was like some magic transformation over the jump from lower school to upper class-women. Without warning, suddenly there were boys to worry about.

WESTLAKE HIGH SCHOOL DAYS

Amazingly, considering the star studded community, there really were not all that many families from Hollywood that sent their kids to Westlake School for Girls. Along the way there were a quite few, but considering how many luminaries could have chosen the girl's school, I guess the balance went to Beverly Hills High School in Beverly Hills.

Industry kids in my class were Mila Malden who was Karl Malden's daughter. Susan Andrews who was Dana Andrew's daughter, and Brook Anderson, who was Gloria Swanson's granddaughter.

Darleen Rodenberry who was Gene Rodenberry's daughter, was in a lower grade.

Karla Kirkeby was of the Hotel fame.

Mrs. Lloyd Bridges was the president of the Mothers' club for several years while their girls attended there.

Jack Palance's kids, Brooke and Holly, were both there also.

Harry James and Betty Grable had a daughter there named Jessica James that was in Penny's grade and was her friend. Victoria James was in a grade below me.

Stephanie Zimbalist, whose father was Efram Jr., briefly attended as well.

Victoria Francesca Milland, Ray Milland's daughter was in attendance.

Edger Bergen's daughter, Candice was two classes above me.

There was something called Slave Days. As an underclassman, you bought a Senior for the day.

All Seniors were dressed up in ridiculous costumes. Candy Bergen was dressed, of all things, as a football player. She had put eye pencil on her legs to look like hair and was in a padded jersey and shorts. Candy was notoriously flat. She had huge thighs. To this day in movies you don't ever see her legs. You can't change that. I found out recently that like me, she was an avid horseman, ergo the large thighs. But on that day it was so funny to see her dressed that way.

I bought her for a song. I can't recall what all we had them do except carry our books to class and bring our lunch to us in the lunch hall. It was a really funny idea. I don't have a clue if they still practice this inane day anymore. I'm certain that they don't because it would be looked upon as having no practical purpose, however it was hilarious at the given time.

When Candy Bergan was our May Queen, the quote from the 1963 year book reported: "Westlake's May Fete opened with the procession of our May Queen, Candy Bergen: "Divinely tall, and most divinely fair." Followed by her attendants, Gay Lamont, and Josalee Douglas; Juniors Karen Manulis and Sue Lamont; Sophomores Edina Mommaerts and Donna Riorden; Freshmen, Melinda Miles and Cindy Rea; Eighth Grade, Leslie Sherf and Sue Noerdlinger.

A Dance of Spring composed by Mrs. Jane Ervin and her dance groups, tennis exhibitions under Mr. Tanasescu, Miss Perrine's aquacade in the pool building decorated by Miss Lamson's Art classes and flowers everywhere contributed to one of Westlake's most lovely ceremonies."

I remember when Candice was our May Queen. She was beautiful.

Little did any of us realize that she would go on to do so many movies and be such an enormous Hollywood star. To us she was just Candy B. She always was a bit of a class clown even before being cast so many years later as Murphy Brown.

In the 1963 Vox Puellarum yearbook, Candice Patricia Bergen was quoted as saying, "nothing can bring back the hour of splendor in the grass." Seen driving a purple T-Bird- "The Easter Egg"...Hobbies-water skiing, riding, painting...to be a starving artist and winter on the Left Bank."

In high school I chose to hang with a fairly forward thinking group of girls who were notorious for slipping off to Palm Springs for the weekend. We would tell our respective parents that we were staying at Sandy Dunbar's dad's house. Then we would go down to the Springs and hang out with a plethora of guys.

Yikes, we were all out of control and did not really see it that way!

I look back at the entire Westlake deal and it sort of mills around weird situations of friendships that really were not true friendships at all. This has always been an enigma to me.

It seems that in a class of thirty-three girls, someone would have kept better in touch with me. However, amazingly enough, no one has even ever tried.

I am not that unapproachable, although I did move quite far away.

It seems that some of the class has remained a bit in touch, but every reunion I go to seems fun, but a bit stilted and posed.

The women I was closest to, I have never been in touch with since graduation day.

It was as if once you left, you abandoned all recollection that you had even been part of the hallowed halls of Westlake School for Girls.

Molly Hughes was a very close friend. Yet I have never heard from her since graduation day.

But what I find paramount is that those friendships at Westlake were so seemingly disposable.

We were buddies. We did things like sneak down on the nature trial to have a smoke. We ditched with the best of them. We had cliques and I was with the 'in-crowd' but I really never felt they were my pals.

It just was never a true friendship and I cannot explain, even to this day, why it was that way.

A lot perhaps was that down deep I was a loner. I always loved being by myself and with my horse. I early got involved with riding and had absolutely no interest in boys until about the tenth grade when the peer pressure to date became overwhelming.

But until college, I really never got all that hung up on guys. I seriously dated a Harvard kid to keep up appearances that I was cool. But that relationship fizzled once I was off to college and found some real substantial guys.

Westlake was an education beyond compare. I have often said that the thing I liked the most, was that it gave a fantastic education and failure was not in our vocabulary.

In my class there have been some gals with brilliant careers. There have also been some who have not been so successful. There was one who actually committed suicide during college. Our class was a very mixed bag of ladies and remains that way today.

But in large part, all of us view our stints at Westlake, as a very upbeat, positive experiences in all our lives.

I continue to go to the reunions because we were fellow classmates and I think it is interesting to keep up. But as far as touching base in between, there is little or no communication.

Occasional emails, come now that emailing is so prevalent. Otherwise, it is a complete surprise when we get together every five years.

Is it something that keeps me awake at night? No. But I do find it curious that when thirty-three girls are together for as many years as we all were, that we care so little about one another now.

So perhaps that has a little to do with the dysfunctional life of growing up in Hollywood.

Sad but true!

Oddly enough, one girl who I never would have thought I would ever call a friend, has turned out to be the most wonderful contact. BJ Stuppy now Pike, offered her Malibu home to anyone traveling to the class reunion. I had never taken her up on it, as I had the ability to stay at a private home in San Marino.

However, for the forty-fifth reunion, in 2010, I did take her up on her kind offer. And we have been fast friends since then. It is amazing how your perception of someone when you are so young, can be altered when you mature. BJ is a wonderful woman and I only wish I'd gotten to know her long ago.

Hollywood lives really were not normal, no matter what anyone ever says. They were stilted even in the 'olden days'.

CHAPTER THIRTY-ONE

Author's Notes:

By the time I was fifteen, I had developed into a stunning, dark-eyed beauty. I could not for the life of me, seem to see the loveliness reflected in a mirror on the rare occasion when I viewed myself.

The girl that periodically returned my stare was nothing but an ugly 'troll'.

God I hated myself!

I became thoroughly involved with horses and made friends only with girls with the same likes. Most of them could not be considered dazzling, or even if they were, like me, they had horrible self-images of themselves.

One of my particular friends, Molly Hughes, had horses in the Valley. I spent all my weekends riding and hanging out with Molly. We became really good friends.

I positively refused to get involved with boys.

The only time I was happy was when I was riding my horse. Then it didn't seem to matter how unattractive I was, my mare, Missy didn't care.

So life went on in a routine way. School at Westlake, every week day, weekends at the barn.

I was coming up on my sixteenth birthday the eleventh of June. I was just planning my summer activities at fairs and Gymkhanas, when my parents announced that we were going to Europe, instead of being home for the early part of the vacation.

THE GRAND EUROPEAN TOUR

I had no interest in seeing a foreign country and certainly little interest in leaving my horse. But early June, we were Europe bound.

My sixteenth birthday was celebrated in Paris, France.

The Hunts had chosen to take us on a whirlwind tour of Europe, a la 'if it is Tuesday, it is Belgium'.

Paris was the first stop. We spent my sixteenth birthday shopping. Mom bought a petit point bag for me as her special 'sweet sixteen' present. My dad purchased a diamond heart necklace and a pair of two-caret-earrings at Cartier.

We dined at Tour Jardin, where everyone toasted my turning of age, with a bottle of Dom Perignon.

Penny was angry because she had left a boyfriend behind to travel to Europe with our folks. So she was generally unpleasant the entire length of the trip.

I was not terribly pleased to give up three weeks without my horse. But I bore my traveling with my parents with a higher measure of pleasant endurance then my pouty sister.

During the tours of libraries and castles, I saw paintings and furnishings that reminded me vividly of my surrounds when I had been with Dolly.

I determined during the trip that no matter what, I was going to re-establish a relationship with Dolly Green.

While in France at the Louvre, I saw a Monet that was no grander than the one that hung in Dolly's upstairs day room.

At Chateau de Chenonceau, the furnishings were all from many periods of "Louis" from Louis V to Louis IV, reminding me of Dolly's living room.

From our hotel in Paris, I sent Dolly a letter that described our trip to Europe. I pleaded with my godmother, that we re-unite.

As we traveled through Venice in a gondola along a canal, I wondered if my mother would respond to my letter or ignore the whole thing?

In Belgium, I posted another note. Telling Dolly how much I thought of her all the time, I related that every castle we visited reminded me of her home and of all her beautiful things. I thanked Dolly for giving me such wonderful exposure to the beauty of art and antiques.

When we reached Spain, Daddy took us to a show at the Spanish Riding School. I bought a post card that looked remarkably like one of the photographs in Dolly's front hall. Sending it to my godmother, I reminded her of how she had promised to take me there. Instead my parents were sharing in the adventure, not Dolly. That was my final jab. I rationalized to myself, if Dolly was not goaded by that, nothing else would move Mohammed back to the mountain. That the cause was probably a dead issue if the postcard of the Lipizzaner's did not throw salt on Dolly's open wounds of guilt, nothing would.

CHAPTER THIRTY-TWO

Author's Notes:

The European escapade was a whirlwind of events that were so crammed into the days and weeks that we were there, it almost made my head spin. It is on that grand adventure that I began to journal in earnest and have kept one ever since.

Once I discovered how much I loved to keep one, I did a reflective log that looked back on my growing up. Many of these reflections came from that very book that I religiously kept from the European trip.

DANCING OUT OF THE DARK

After three exhaustive weeks, we returned home. We all slept many hours to recover from the jet lag. I was slumbering deeply in my room dreaming about standing, throwing pennies in a fountain in Italy, when Mother called to me.

"Diane, your godmother is on the phone. Do you want to talk to her?"

This jolted me from my dreams. Want to talk to Dolly? Lord yes!

I picked up the pink princess phone and talked to my godmother for quite a long time.

It seemed Dolly had been so impressed by my maturity in my letters from Europe, she was just dying to see me again.

She wondered if Penny and I could motor up to Santa Barbara next week for lunch?

Excitedly, I agreed. I jotted explicit directions on a pad by my bedside.

Just barely sixteen, I was already driving, but an excursion up an unfamiliar major highway in all certainty, would be nixed by the Hunts. So regardless of Penny's wants, I intended to get to Montecito if I had to take the car myself against my parent's wishes. I simply had to see Dolly again! I was determined to re-kindle the relationship that had become so cold.

Penny, not at all true to form for those days, actually voiced excitement over the planned excursion. She had always enjoyed Dolly's favors, though not in quite the same intensity as me. But it was good for a lunch and a look at some new boys.

Dolly had instructed us to meet her at the Santa Barbara Polo field where the Mexican Polo Team was playing. She'd mentioned that the fellows playing for the Mexican Team were all charmingly, handsome men.

At that revelation, Penny was ready in a flash for the jaunt, especially since she'd had a tiff with her current boyfriend shortly after arriving back in the States.

The days seemed to drag by to the time we were to travel to Santa Barbara.

So because I thought I needed to impress Dolly with my sophisticated attitude, I felt I needed to spiff up my rather stodgy looks. Dolly was such a glamour queen that I felt I needed some kind of beauty help.

I made the great effort to go to Elizabeth Arden Salon to get my hair done and enlisted my mother's stylist.

I drove to 'Arden's' early in the morning and Dorothy was waiting for me at the door.

My hair was severely pulled back in a pony tail, which Dorothy announced, "Needed to go, Diane! You've been hiding your lovely looks under a barrel. It is time you came out and danced in the light. How are you ever going to get the boys if you look like one yourself? How about we shag your hair so you look pretty and soft?"

I had never had anyone ask me if I wanted to look 'pretty and soft'. It sounded fine, but I wasn't placing any money on the bet.

The last time I had gone in for a 'new do', the solution was a perm that left me feeling even more ugly under a cap of frizz. I had feigned illness from school for several weeks until I could manage to control the mass of frizz into a ponytail. It had left my salon experiences with a bitter taste in my mouth.

But Dorothy had convinced me that a miracle was pending, so I was willing to give it one last shot with this woman who seemed to be able to make Mrs. Hunt look like she stepped off a movie set.

Dorothy was the best Arden had ever hired. She did all the big network stars as well as Betty Grable, Marilyn Monroe, and Anita Louise to name a few of her star-studded following.

She had a mission with little Miss Hunt. Dorothy had long seen the beauty potential that I made such an enormous effort to hide. She almost had her chance to work with me before we were Europe bound. But I chickened out and canceled at the last minute.

Now Dorothy had her golden opportunity and intended to do her damnedest to surprise me by showing me what a smash I had become.

I had very large brown eyes. My lashes were long and black. My complexion was at sixteen, flawless, tanned the color of chocolate with cream. My usually smiling lips were perfectly shaped and my teeth were straight from years of braces and were white as pearls. My hair was a deep dark chestnut laced with strands of red-gold from exposure to the sun. I was pencil thin as Twiggy and 'athlete-hard' were my curves.

A large part of my own perception problem was because I'd endured such an ugly period when I was in my early teens. I'd avidly avoided looking very carefully in the mirror and had not seen the transformation happen before my very eyes.

Dorothy vowed to put an end to the ugly duckling phase and give flight to the beautiful swan she had finally captured, sitting in her stylist's chair.

Dorothy had a habit of working with someone like me by starting the cut with the client's back to the mirror. When she finished the hair-do and make-up application, she would whirl the client around and give them the full impact of the transformation. She was quite a showman, herself.

When she turned me to the mirror, I did not know what to say. So metamorphosed by the shaped fringe of bangs and shaggy layered hair, I was almost unbelieving that it was me.

My black eyes were accented with liner and mascara. A hint of blush was brushed on my California browned cheeks and a subtle pink gloss was on my lips. Truly I'd been transformed into a beauty! Before me in the glass, was a remarkably beautiful reflection.

The thought passed through my mind. Who are you and what have you done with Diane?

And in those confidence boosting hours with Dorothy, telling me how beautiful I was, I saw a glimmer of hope. Maybe Penny was not going to be the 'only show-stopping Hunt', after all.

When I arrived home, the reactions to my dramatically changed looks were mixed reviews.

Dad muttered something about a photograph from long ago when I was a dressed up as a Spanish lady. He'd seen my potential beauty then and he was seeing it for the first time that day. He was stunned by what a difference a haircut and a little make-up could make.

Mother complained that Dorothy had used too much rouge and paint.

Penny cheered at my evolution, saying, "It was about time Diane stopped playing 'Tom Boy' and became the beautiful girl she is! Thank heavens Dorothy had finally done the deed."

With that Penny urged us to depart for our Santa Barbara jaunt.

CHAPTER THIRTY-THREE

Author's Notes:

I was excited beyond belief to be getting a chance to be back with Dolly and willed everything to go well.

Penny was in a rare fine mood and I had not seen her that enthused for quite a long time.

It was as if the two sisters were off on a grand adventure and finally now that I looked more like a movie star than a troll, she was ecstatic to be going to such an exciting event.

A Polo field with a boodle of dreamy Latin men! Wow! Bring it on!

SMILE, BEAU! I PROMISE YOUR FACE WON'T BREAK

On the heels of our parent's warning us to be careful, we left for Santa Barbara with the top down on the shiny, red Dodge Dart. Free spirits on our way to an unknown adventure with the divine, Dolly Green.

Not knowing Santa Barbara at all, it took us a little while to find the Polo Field, which was located on the outskirts of the town. It was foggy and relatively hard to see. Usually the mists should have burned off by then, but it was not happening. We finally found the field by twelve o'clock after driving in circles for quite some time.

Penny parked the Dart and we spotted Dolly and Enrique standing apart from the crowd.

Dolly was holding onto the reigns of a beautiful black Polo pony, controlling it expertly as it pranced about.

Enrique was attempting to mount with some difficulty, distracted from the task at hand, because he was speaking rapidly in Spanish to his wife. It appeared the couple was heatedly arguing.

Enrique shouted something we could not hear as he gained control of the mount and spurred the animal away. It was clear that anger goaded his hasty departure.

Dolly spied us approaching and beamed a wide signature smile."Diane, Penny, darlings!"She cajoled and hugged us both. "Look at you two beautiful girls!"

Penny, under her breath, hissed, "Smile, Beau! I promise your face won't break!"

We chatted for some moments before we walked to the sidelines to watch the contestants play.

The Mexican Team clearly was far superior to the Santa Barbara players. They were thundering down the field with the Chucker having already score ten points to Santa Barbara's one.

Dolly seemed excited by the action but I, knowing Dolly well, knew there was fury behind the smile.

Something was amiss in paradise. I could feel it in my intuitive bones.

Abruptly, Dolly announced that because we girls had arrived so late, we needed to all go home.

Enrique could follow with his cronies, she needed to be home to supervise lunch. Did we girls want to stay or go home with her?

I wanted to be with Dolly but Penny chose to ogle the gorgeous riding men and come over later. Perhaps one of the charming Latinos would ride to Edgecliff with her in the nifty little top-down-Dart. The riders had already been hanging around, flirting with us, when a pause in the action allowed.

So Dolly and I departed in her signature, red Cadillac.

On the way to Edgecliff Lane, my godmother began to reveal her troubles to me. As always, Dolly confided in me as if I were a confidant, not a young girl.

It seemed Heinie had gotten so involved with Polo that he was off all the time with the boys. But, she admitted, there was more trouble than that! Heinie was a philanderer. He was fooling around with other women. It seemed fairly common among the Latino men to engage in extramarital sex. Dolly was actually in a quandary over what to do. Being a converted Catholic, she was bound not to enter into divorce.

Amazingly philosophical for a girl of sixteen, I advised, "Aunt Dolly, if you are unhappy with this marriage, surely you can get some type of dispensation from the Church. One of Mother's friends, who is Catholic, was able to get the Archbishop to arrange for an annulment. She can never marry again, but she said she had no intention of doing the dirty deed again. I'm sure if you talked to your priest, he would tell you how to get out of this marriage."

Dolly turned to me and batted her eyelashes saying, "Darling, you are so mature for your age. I will certainly look into that."

We disembarked from the car which she handed over to Julio and we proceeded into the Edgecliff Lane home.

She gave me the grand tour.

It was a palatial mansion that overlooked the crashing sea. She told me that below there was a 'dreamy' little cabaña. When she swam, she could change out of her wet clothing, shower and get in a dry robe and not track sand into the main house.

Dolly then led me to the kitchen where she instructed the help how to present the lavish luncheon to be set immediately out on the terrace that viewed the pummeling surf below.

The fog had lifted and the temperatures had climbed to the low seventies. It was a perfect, glorious Santa Barbara day.

Enrique arrived with several men for the previously planned lunch.

Penny arrived, her hair windblown and she was flush-cheeked from the convertible ride. As expected, one of the gorgeous Latinos had indeed hitched a ride with her. She looked smug as well as enthralled.

The arriving guests chatter was lively so the conversation of Dolly's problems were lost in the festive atmosphere of the luncheon.

A sumptuous buffet was served out on the patio of seafood salad and other delectable gourmet treats.

I followed the conversations of many of the handsome young gentlemen, but could not help noticing how Enrique and Dolly ignored one another. Though Dolly seemed the bright and bubbly hostess, I knew better. Beneath the smiling exterior, Dolly was an emotional wreck.

I thought it so sad that four years ago, my godmother seemed so happy. A few short years had changed a great deal.

We spent the entire rest of the afternoon touring the property, going down to the little cabaña, and then walking with Dolly down the beach.

She seemed thrilled to get away and just visit with Penny and me, 'catching up on our lost time'. She chatted amicably about our European trip and other events that seemed paramount in her mind.

With the long walk over, I insisted that we head for home. We had promised our parents to be home well before dark and it took two hours at least to safely drive from Santa Barbara to Los Angeles. That would put us home around seven o'clock.

Penny was getting enormous attention from all the gorgeous Latin men and was peeved that I pressed that we depart. I insisted, so we left for home at four-thirty.

Dolly later told me that with our departure, she left the men to carouse, drink, and smoke smelly cigars.

She made a tentative phone call to the Archbishop of the Good Shepherd Church in Beverly Hills. It seemed that he could perform an annulment if that was what Dolly desired, but it would be so much better if permission was obtained directly from the Pope, himself.

Dolly, never adverse to travel, phoned about availability of flights to Rome in the next few weeks.

CHAPTER THIRTY-FOUR

Author's Notes:

Much of this part contains thoughts that Dolly relayed to me after the Polo luncheon. I am relating her thoughts to the reader as she disclosed them to me.

BRIEF INTERLUDE

Dolly got cold feet regarding dumping Heinie. She really liked Enrique. He was quite the lover. The Latinos were so hot blooded. The thought of giving him up completely was simply out of her plan.

Perhaps if she lectured him a bit more about his infidelities, he would come back more into line. She would speak to him and see if they could work things out.

One thing she determined to rectify was reconciliation with me. For the past four years she had been so wrapped up with Enrique and all his detractions, she had forgotten how much she enjoyed my company. It was time she got re-acquainted with her beautiful child who had been a sadly missing part of her life. Perhaps if she and I saw more of one another, Enrique's shortcomings would not seem so glaring to her all the time.

The night after the Polo luncheon, she and Enrique discussed his 'other ladies'. At first he vehemently denied that he was seeing other women and blamed it all on his friends and their poker parties and card games. 'Boys night out, was a Mexican custom', he professed.

Dolly would buy nothing of it. She had already engaged a private detective who had followed him to one of the supposed, 'Boys night out'.

She produced a letter that stated that Ronald Julian, Private Investigator, P.C. had followed Enrique on numerous occasions to a Señoras house on Picacho Lane. The time of arrival coincided with the supposed poker party at a friend's home clear across the town.

Dolly had Enrique, dead to rights.

He promised to be a better husband.

She would forgive him if he would stop seeing the other 'Señora'.

Dolly also put her foot down and said she would not tolerate no longer seeing her beloved godchild. Enrique had made her sacrifice her godchild for him and she would not abide this anymore.

So for a while, things resumed a semblance of a normal routine.

I was back in Dolly's life. That was to my delight and Dolly's as well. We began to see one another again a great deal and the bond was re-established stronger than ever before.

CHAPTER THIRTY-FIVE

Author's Notes:

I had come to the conclusion that Heinie was not long for Dolly's world, when I heard exactly how Dolly had ensnared him in the first place.

According to Maria, the entrapment scenario was set to snare Heinie by Dolly many years previously.

Dolly, who feigned liking sailing on his yacht by gulping handfuls of Dramamine, had trapped Heinie over several other competing Señoritas.

Dolly had finally gone off with Heinie on his ship alone. Dolly set her cap for him and ultimately prevailed.

However, after they were wed, Heinie went to Guadalajara to get his yacht. He sailed his ship up to the Santa Barbara Harbor to triumphantly present his lavish silver collection to his bride.

Dolly boasted of the silver being her grand prize, but the boat needed to go.

Heinie had gradually been induced to sell the yacht, as Dolly referred to it the 'dreaded barge'. She hated sailing vehemently.

It was just another one of Dolly's 'little white lies', but once again, they worked well for her for a while.

Things went downhill as soon as Heinie no longer had his adored yacht to sail about in the bay.

THE MEXICAN FIESTA

Over the next two years there were ups and downs for Dolly with her marriage, but at least I was there to help her with the good and the bad.

Dolly staged parties all the time at the beautiful mansion on Edgecliff Lane. One particular event I would remember all my life because it would prove pivotal in my future. However, I never knew it until years after the occasion.

I recall all the events that led up to the night of the gala.

Dolly's private secretary, Elinor Logan, had been there all day working on correspondences for 'La Grande Señora'. It was the first and only time I met my mother's personal secretary.

I later learned much of the secretary's thoughts, because Maria always clued me in on things of this nature. It was paramount how distressed the secretary was at the time. I never would know how much this brief encounter set the tone for what the secretary would do to me later in my life.

Elinor had spent the entire day with Dolly doing secretarial chores. She knew Dolly was staging a gala of major proportions, as she'd addressed the invitations to all the notables, and received the replies when the guests responded; they were thrilled to attend.

Dolly staged epic parties. They were written up in the *Los Angeles Times,* as well as the Santa Barbara rag. No one refused one of her invitations. The only legitimate excuse to miss one of her bashes was a letter of your being deceased, from the coroner.

The house was decorated with artifacts from Mexico, huge paper flowers, piñata's, gala streamers were everywhere. In the center of the patio, a huge glass fountain spewed Margaritas for all to partake.

Elinor secretly hoped that since she had driven all the way from town to help Dolly catch up on her correspondences, that her employer would ask her to stay the night. After all, she viewed herself as family, having been in the Green employ for a multitude of years. She expected Dolly to include her in this exciting event. Fully expecting her employer's inclusion at the gala, Elinor had even packed a very festive Mexican style dress.

As it got later in the afternoon, anyone with a shred of compassion, would have asked a loyal staffer to join the party, stay the night and head for home the next day. Dolly certainly had plenty of unfilled, guest rooms.

Dolly, offered nothing.

Elinor hung around commenting on how fabulous the home looked, all decorated for the Mexican Fiesta. She hinted how she dreaded the thought of driving all the way home to L.A.

While her secretary stalled, Dolly instructed the servants where to position the iced bowls of Beluga caviar, the smoked salmon and the gloriously executed canapés for the appetizers. She was consulting with 'Cook' regarding the separate set up of the lavish Mexican buffet, when I walked into the room.

At that point Elinor was about to ask Dolly if she minded if she stay for the festivities.

I entered and asked, "Aunt Dolly, do I look all right in the new dress you bought me, yesterday?"

Elinor had heard the other servants talk about me, but had never laid eyes on me before that night. She recounted to Maria the next morning, how amazed she'd been by how much she thought I looked like Dolly Green. This was natural because I'd called Dolly my Aunt.

Elinor was unaware that I was a 'godchild', not a niece. She'd passed off the family resemblance as coincidence, until she learned there was no relationship at all.

However, again she dismissed this as well.

I was dressed in a beautiful, water-silk, empire-style formal of white and turquoise flowers. They looked as if painted by Seurat. My hair was piled high on my head in a chignon.

Elinor later related to Maria that she had thought the Hunt child a 'complete, stuck-up, little bitch'. I had refused to even look her in the eyes which Elinor thought was crushingly rude. Logan had felt fury rise over the attention Dolly paid me. Dolly was flat out ignoring the secretary who was obviously in the room.

Dolly did not even introduce me to Elinor.

Dolly turned her back on the secretary and focused entirely on me saying, "My God, Di, darling, don't you look positively divine! But sweetie, the guests will be arriving any moment and I need to get dressed. Be sure Julio chilled the Cristal just right. And, darling, tell Maria to get my Tiffany diamond necklace and matching ear clips, for you to wear, tonight."

According to Maria, as soon as I rushed off, Elinor was finally able to interrupt. She asked Mrs. Green if there was anything further before she drove all the way back to L..A.?

Dolly said, very businesslike, "No, thank you, Elinor. Respond to the correspondences as we discussed, and have a safe drive home."

That was that. 'Have a safe drive home'.

The world had seemed to stop when that 'little Hunt bitch' walked in the door. It was if Elinor vanished. Poof, gone, the moment I had appeared.

According to Maria, the following morning, the secretary phoned Santa Barbara way too early. She knew full well that Dolly would not be about, and thus wanted to get Maria on the phone. Elinor asked the maid who the dark-haired niece was that had been there last night.

Maria explained that she was Mrs. Green's 'godchild' and then launched into the horrible brew haw-haw that occurred at the gala.

"The Señor had gotten way out of line," Maria happily gossiped. It seemed that during the course of the evening Señor Schondube had gotten horribly

171

drunk. Dolly, who drank only champagne, remained fairly well under control."

Maria then relayed to Elinor, "The Mrs. was dancing with one of the gorgeous, Mexican Polo players, when she observed Heinie pushing me out the patio doors. Everyone could tell how drunk Heinie was, because he was weaving so badly. He could barely stand.

Dolly broke from her partner, excusing herself, saying she had to check on her godchild. Grabbing Julio by the arm, she rushed to the garden to find that Heinie and I had completely disappeared. When they finally found us, Heinie was tearing at my gown and mauling 'little Diane' like a bear. I was struggling and screaming and was fighting with all my might but ninety pounds against two hundred of brute strength, that was used to bringing a horse under control, was not a fair match at all.

Julio pulled out his gun but Dolly stopped the butler from firing, saying, "Julio, no! Don't murder the bastard. It's too God-damn good for the filthy, son-of-a-bitch!"

Dolly then grabbed a stake from the garden path that served to hold an errant camellia plant from falling down. She launched into the fray, driving the weapon into one of Heinie's marauding hands. He was stunned. Howling with rage and horrible pain, he charged like a wounded bull to the home!

By then, most of the revelers were standing about waiting to see the resolution of the missing hosts. They were determined to stay for the battle of the century and were rewarded with quite the show.

Heinie, sobered by the brutal attack to his hand, rushed into the house, howling in pain. It was not five seconds later that he fled in his Jaguar screaming that Dolly was a maniacal bitch. "Unna Punta, Loco!" he'd yelled as he peeled off in his ebony Jaguar up Edgecliff Lane.

Dolly appeared seconds later with me. I was ushered into her room and Maria then helped me undress and got me into bed. I'd been so shaken by these events, I'd promptly fallen asleep.

With me taken care of, Dolly continued the party as if nothing had caused alarm. The guests certainly saw little reason to halt the proceedings if their hostess was willing to continue, so the gala went long into the night.

"Maria happily continued, "the party went on swimmingly without Heinie." When the party was over and all the guests departed, Maria had been instructed by Dolly to "toss the filthy Mexican's belongings, onto the lawn.

Enrique was lowered in status, that night, from the 'divine Spaniard', to the 'filthy Mexican', all in the period of a stupidly misplaced indiscretion on his part."

Maria concluded, "Early that next morning, a crony of his from the Polo team, came by to pick up his belongings."

Those were the exciting events of the Mexican Gala as relayed to Elinor Logan on the phone.

Maria and Elinor were fairly good friends at that time and Maria confided, "No one do nothing like that to 'my Mrs.' little Diane. She no stand for that."

Elinor offered to Maria, "The girl probably baited Heinie. She more than likely deserved every bit of what she got!"

Maria defended, "That not what happened! Diane would never do nothing like that. Mr. Heinie is an animal, that is all!"

Dolly threw him out of the house that night and he was never heard from again, except when the divorce proceedings were filed. Then it was from his lawyer. Dolly washed her hands of him that night.

But being young, I passed over it quickly and it was soon forgotten.

Secretly, I was glad Enrique Schondube was gone. I never really liked him and after all, he was responsible for taking my mother away for so long.

Now, Dolly would always be there for me and we would see one another all the time.

CHAPTER THIRTY-SIX

Author's Notes:

By 1964, Dolly had resumed residence in Bel Air. Santa Barbara was fine for a vacation home, but her social life was based in Los Angeles and she needed to be where the action was for her.

Dolly changed her name back to Green. She told me one time 'that everyone recognized the name Green, but no one had any idea who Dolly Schondube was'! So she changed it back to Green and did so with nary a backward glance.

Dolly and I resumed our routine of the relationship and continued to see one another a great deal.

It was as if no time had ever passed.

I continued to court Dolly and became more and more within the Green family.

It was then that I began to seriously hang out with Ms. Saundra Grey both in Bel Air and Santa Barbara.

Sandi was Burtie's daughter and so far from the manning crowd. She drove a little Nash Rambler convertible and we would all tool around Bel Air and Santa Barbara with the top down, winging our way through the streets.

When I sued the Green estate, Sandi disavowed any knowledge of me and Penny. We joy rode the entire length and breadth of Santa Barbara and Bel Air in Sandi's little grey Nash Rambler. Later, Sandi, on many occasions stated that she has no clue who we were to this day.

Sandi Grey Nowicki would, in the will contest, completely disavow any knowledge of me. But Michael Gross vehemently confides, 'the ones that have the most to hide, usually are the ones who run screaming bloody murder when I make the inquiry call'.

Sandi did just that to Michael Gross when he called her regarding me in his quest for knowledge during his compilation of Unreal Estate.

When Michael approached her, he told me that she hung up the phone. My, he certainly must love that kind of rejection.

However, in an interview with him on a show called 'Obsessed' hosted by a woman by the name of Samantha Ettus, I quote excerpts from that interview. Michael states, "I write Enterprise Journalism. Unless people get upset with what I write, I am not doing my job. The only people who freak out when I call are the people who have something to hide. Everyone has secrets. I write about people who are public figures that have an influence on public life. If they 'sic' a lawyer on you as they did me with the 'Met', they have secrets they want to hide."

My, oh my, oh my!

So Sandi, here's one for you who does not recall our top down days...

I really do exist! Perhaps your memory is just not that keen.

THE IDYLLIC SANTA BARBARA DAYS

July 1965

It was the summer that I was eighteen and was soon collage bound. I had been wait-listed at Colorado College and was not certain when I would be traveling to Colorado.

Marie Hunt and Dolly got together and decided that before our annual trip to Yosemite, I should spend two quality weeks with Dolly that July in Santa Barbara.

That was fine with me. I was dating a boy from Harvard Military Academy and getting a bit tired of that relationship. I was ready and willing to get away from that whole scene. The Santa Barbara home was just far enough away to discourage him from coming up.

Positioned on Edgecliff Lane, the property was jauntily perched on ocean's edge and the crashing waves always lulled me to sleep at night. I loved the Santa Barbara home. I think it instilled in me my consummate love of the ocean. Even now, when we decide to take a trip, it is almost always to somewhere near the shore.

The home was palatial. Not as large as the Bel Air mansion, but still an awesome beauty all unto its own. The floors were marble throughout, as I assume it was an issue of upkeep and dealing with the sand. The home was right on access to the beach and had a small cabaña down on the ocean itself. As always, the home was decorated in white, gold and red. The house was a sprawling affair with the kitchens to the south end of the home, as well as the servants-quarters.

Maria and Julio and 'Cook' were the only staff that stayed there while others remained in Bel Air.

The windows looked out over the Pacific and we would sit there in the evenings with our cocktails. We would chat and watch the sun sink into the water as it painted the cobalt sky with red fingers and tinged the horse-tail clouds that drifted over the crashing ocean below.

To say those two weeks were idyllic was an understatement!

I have looked back on that time with Dolly as one of the most treasured times of my young adult life.

Dolly was raised in the height of opulence and thought nothing of having a little tin of Beluga with her champagne every night. We both ate it as if it was popcorn. I never thought about the money. It surrounded me in both my lives and I simply took it for granted.

Dolly Green was part of the 'fabled elite world' in which I was raised and Dolly felt she was entitled to live this way and so she did.

I never reflected then on what it might have been liketo be raised by her. I had my parents, my sister, and Dolly. So I thought the arrangement just suited me fine.

There would be an occasional time that the staff was off. Thursdays, were the designated day. I guess there was some credo about Thursdays and Sundays in the vernacular of hired help.

So Dolly and I were on our own.

Dolly marveled at the fact that I actually not only knew how to cook, but liked the process as well. It flat amazed her. She had no clue how to boil water let along assemble a gourmet meal.

Her answer to eating on 'staff's day off' was to go to the Biltmore Hotel or one of the other 'kitschy' eateries that peppered Santa Barbara in those earlier days.

But when I was there we were like two kids in the kitchen. I would fix all manner of dish while she sat on a stool and sipped her Korbel Brut Champagne. We chatted about everything under the sun.

My adult relationship with Dolly was somewhat of an enigma to everyone.

My mother, Marie, commented about it the most. She simply could not understand how Dolly and I could spend so much time together and not get bored.

How could you get bored with a woman who had so many amazing stories to tell about the early Beverly Hills days? The movie stars tales, the wild parties, everything simply fascinated me about her life.

Dolly was an avid reader and passed that passion down to me. In fact, I still have quite a few of the fabulous books she gave to me from her own library. Dolly was widely read.

She freely admitted her hatred of school as related earlier in this book. But reading was a passion for her, and she spent enormous quantities of money on books.

She was not a particularly good writer. I learned that when she let me read her little journal. But the things that were recorded there were still very vivid anyway.

Our Santa Barbara days were spent sailing all up and down the coast. Dolly hired an instructor to take me out on a beautiful forty-foot boat. She really hated sailing as it made her very sea-sick. It was the reason she had made Heinie sell his boat in the first place and nothing about that had changed. But for me, she toughed it out as it so appealed to me.

We lunched almost daily at the Santa Barbara Biltmore. Then we would avidly peruse the pier where there were little souvenir stands and even a fortune teller who read my palm. She said I would have much conflict in my life!

Wow! Wish I had listened to her! But how could I have changed the course of my pre-destined fate?

CHAPTER THIRTY-SEVEN

Author's Notes:

Twenty-twenty hindsight has always been something I have mastered over the years. Looking back on these events makes me wonder what I could possibly have done to avoid the happenings that eventually occurred? The more I reflect, the more that I realize nothing could have been done! Life dishes you lessons. But no matter what or who you are, you can't help but wonder about the 'what ifs'?

Maria and I talked long into one night regarding the possibility of my confronting Dolly regarding my knowledge of her being my mother. We discussed the ramifications of Dolly knowing I had never forgotten the bond and decided that I simply needed to face up to the facts that I knew, even if Dolly was upset.

Maria expressed great relief over my decision and pressed that I continue to write everything in my ever building journal, saying, "Chica, someday you may wish to relive all these things and it is best that they are written down. Even someone with the memory you have, should have notes to recall all these events. But you are eighteen now, if you ever are to face your mommy about her giving you away, now, here in Santa Barbara, is the time."

How fortuitous she was in her forecast. I would confront my birth mother and we really would finally clear the air!

My conversation with Maria late into the night, confirmed what I had always believed. Dolly had executed the adoption only because she felt it truly was the best for me. Her life style simply was not conducive to being a mother, despite what she had initially thought. However, her greatest disappointment had always been that Neil McCarthy had never succumbed to marrying her. She never would get over that. He was after all my father, and she resented that he never admitted parentage to her and questioned that he had been my father at all.

Maria admitted that Dolly had over the years, been a tiny bit indiscreet. However, given my looks, she was certain that Neil McCarthy was my father. I did, however, favor the Greens with my eyes, nose and ears. I definitely had the Green 'schnozzle' as some of my Jewish girlfriends referred to as 'the nose'.

Maria still seemed sorry that she had not had the opportunity to raise me. She had tried to stop Dolly giving me away but Dolly was bent on the hand off. After all, once the contact was re-established, I was with them a fair amount. So with Maria's encouragement, I did the adult thing and talked it out with Dolly. It was I think, a great weight of both our minds.

After the discussion, we went about the remaining two weeks enjoying the closeness of our relationship as we never would experience such a proximity again.

We spent each glorious day together and I learned far more about how my intricate godmother 'ticked'.

What later became blindingly apparent when I studied Psychology, was that Dolly displayed classic symptoms of someone with a Narcissistic personality. This paramount understanding was quite the revelation for me.

The key reveal was that Dolly's entire life revolved around pleasing just herself. It had been the guideline of her life.

That summer of such intense contact we enjoyed, had finally made me realized exactly what she was truly all about. It made it far easier for me to understand why she'd handed me off, but also why she could not completely say good-by.

It all boiled down to the supreme selfishness of a woman called Dolly Green!

THE BIG CONFESSION

I had spent a rather restless night after another celebrity event at Dolly's Santa Barbara home. It was always such an amazing happenstance when Dolly had her parties to see who would attend. The list was beyond A+ and no one failed to attend.

The Milners, the Hernando Courtrights, the Linkletters, the Edgar Bergens, Alfredo DeLavega, the Regans, James Stewarts, the Mervin LeRoys, and the Bloomingdales all flocked to her estate that night before.

As always, the event was lavish and this time, catered by a company that brought in all the food and set it up in the kitchen. This was much to the Green's staff disgruntlement. Dolly's 'Cook' was furious at the invasion, but later did admit "that the 'hired intruders' had indeed done a lovely job".

Dolly was dressed to the nines in a stunning Dior that was red as the poppies at her front door.

This party was far more lavish than the little Mexican Gala. Plus it was a black tie affair and was regaled in the Santa Barbara newspaper the following day, as the 'Party of the Century', because of Dolly's star studded guest list.

The morning after the event, I got up early, as I just could not stay in my room. I went for a walk on the beach, down from the little cabaña.

It was seven-thirty when I got back and I was surprised to find Maria sitting quietly in my room. She said that Dolly had been up for some time and was asking for me.

We had a busy day planned. Lunch at the Santa Barbara Biltmore was forecast on the agenda, as well as, a walk on the pier. There was going to be a huge carnival that day.

Though it was unusual for Dolly to be up at the crack of dawn, I did not anticipate what on earth the summons could possibly mean.

I, however, had finally prepared myself for the ultimate confrontation as Maria and I had discussed. So, primed for the exchange, I hurried to her room.

Dolly was propped up in her bed in her usual crimson dressing gown and was sipping coffee, reading the L.A. Times and had her breakfast tray set aside.

"Sit down," she instructed me. "You and I need to have a little chat."

I sat on the side of her bed and got comfortable. She poured me some coffee. Obviously, she had planned this tête-à-tête.

"Darling," she began. She was famous for the eye-bat and the 'darling' was de reguer. She continued, "There is something I want to discuss with you. Now that you are eighteen, I think you are old enough for this conversation to take place."

Before she could even progress I stated, "I am your daughter. I will never forget those early years."

She sat there for a moment, just looking at me. Then she sighed and said, "Of course you could not forget. I guess we all just severely underestimated you."

I did not know what to do. Laugh or cry. *'Of course you did not forget. I guess we underestimated you'*. If she had hit me over the head with a rock, I would not have been anymore thunderstruck than I was with those words.

However, being the consummate smarty, I quipped, "Pretty good actress, don't you think?"

Dolly laughed, "You know that is one thing that Ralph and I can't agree on. I say you should go into films and he adamantly says 'no way'. I think you would out do most of the actresses in Hollywood if you tried."

I heartily agreed but said, "It is not on my horizon. Daddy would never allow me to be an actress, and I will honor that conviction. In addition, I don't believe I would ever have the drive."

Dolly agreed, "He could be very wise with that belief. It is a very demanding world. I never had the feeling I could commit to film either. Perhaps like Mother, like daughter is a truism after all."

I wanted to go back to what I perceived as the real reason for the fireside chat. "Dolly, why the elaborate charade? I mean why not just let me go? I was finally settled with the Hunts, why on earth come back into my life when I was six years old?"

Dolly batted her eyes again. "I couldn't keep you as my child, but I simply could not let you go. You do know that your father, Ralph, never knew of our true relationship. Just Marie and I knew I was your birth mother."

"I know that. Daddy is pretty outspoken about Penny's mother giving her away. That is probably why Mother insisted on the elaborate ruse. But that is not really what I am asking. Why did you need to give me away in the first place? You could have kept me and had me raised by a governess."

"I could very well have done just that. But Di, darling, I thought you needed a father figure in your life and I could not get Neil to be that man. I have loved Neil McCarthy all my life, but he would never acknowledge you as his daughter. I decided for your own good, that you needed to be properly placed in a family that would raise you, cherish you, and where a father would be present in your life. I felt that my lifestyle would never be what you would need."

I could not really think of a rebuttal. There was nothing I could say that made more sense. I knew in my heart that Dolly was selfish and thought a great deal more of herself than of anyone else. But at that moment in time, all the back years flashed past and I recalled all the wonderful moments I had with Ralph Hunt. I could not fathom what my life would have been without him. To say nothing of living without Penny, or Marie Hunt.

I decided that the bottom line was that Dolly had given me a chance at a real, down to earth family. What more could I say? I lived in two worlds. A normal one with the

Hunts and my 'fairy tale' life with Dolly Green. What child could boast of that? None that I knew.

So I said, "Dolly, I will always treasure the times we have been together and look back at them as a princess in a fairy tale. It has always been a privilege to be your daughter and 'goddaughter'. I just hope it will always be this way."

Dolly then said, "Di, darling. I will always see that you are well cared for. I will financially provide for you forever. I have set up a trust for you to inherit a vast amount of the Green fortune and you will never want for a thing. My hope is that you marry well and find the man of your dreams. But despite that, I will always provide for you by leaving you, everything."

Never in a million years did I disbelieve what she told me on that day! She was my birth mother, she admitted that fact and told me implicitly that I would be left everything by her.

Later on, I would learn how deceptive she had been regarding even that promise. But on that day, I felt very secure about my future because of both my family affiliations. I would never be in trouble financially because both families were very well heeled. Little did I know the trouble that was brewing in the castle Green. Nor could I ever imagine that most of her promises to me on that day were simply more of her 'little white lies'.

Those two weeks of Santa Barbara bliss were the last days that I spent any quantity time with Dolly. I was never certain whether the admission to being my mother and giving me away created a bit of a mental issue for her. But it seemed that after that, she got so wrapped up in the horses, that being available for me was not in the cards.

I really thought little about the whole situation. I was in the throes of my college years and dealing with that trauma.

Dolly was a constant in my life and it never once occurred to me that things could ever go wrong. Little did I know what was transpiring behind my back.

I was off to Colorado College and only home for the precious summers. I very often flew directly to Fresno to go to Yosemite.

So my contact with Dolly after that eighteenth summer, was limited mostly to conversations on the phone.

Until the year I returned from college and was then planning with both my doting mothers to become a beautiful bride. Then again, Dolly became a paramount influence in my unfolding life.

CHAPTER THIRTY-EIGHT

Author's Note:

I only met the secretary, Elinor Logan, once in my life and never knew how this woman had set her cap against me then.

Little did I know how that secretary hated me. Because of the instance that took place before that one Santa Barbara Mexican Gala and the unintentional, chance meeting with me, the tide of my life would forever be altered.

In some people, there is a certain pattern of psychological behavior where the person can conceptualize an erroneous idea, and in fact, over a period of time the vision becomes tangible in their mind.

It is of no consequence that there is no concrete evidence of truth in the perception. Unequivocally, it becomes set in stone in the believer's psyche.

This was the mindset that evolved around Elinor Logan.

Because she had worked so long for the Green family, she believed that she should be privy to everything the Greens had ever done.

Further, she honestly came to believe that because of her intimate dealings with her recent, primary employer, that over the years she had become Dolly's closest confidant.

Had in fact, the secretary been even remotely close to Dolly, she would have known the background of the Greens.

Had she ever been anything but a servant, she would have known of her employer's past.

If the secretary ever had been treated more than an assistant, she would have been privy to the relationship between Dolly and me.

But she never was anything but an 'aide-de-camp' to the 'Divine Dolly'. For that matter, she was never anything further to any of the Green family; she was simply, 'Elinor, dear,' secretary, nothing more.

Never would she be part of the paradoxical family that sequestered their enterprises from few but those of the inner sanctum.

Elinor never had a key to the gate.

Dolly and I shared those priceless moments in the sun. We basked in our relationship for all the years we were able to love each another in our unique and extraordinary lives.

During our time together, Dolly and I shared her secrets, triumphs, fears, loves and hates.

Maria Rivera and I were Dolly's confidants! Between us, there was nothing we did not know about the mysterious woman called, Dolly Green.

Not knowing the hatred the secretary had towards me, I simply proceeded with my life.

It would only be later that all the evil, hatred and despair would come to light when Maria finally clued me to the bitter truth.

ADRIFT AT COLLEGE, LITTLE GIRL LOST

I had a rare opportunity when graduating from Westlake to attend my freshman year at UCLA. This enabled me to study a special battery of art courses.

Another unique class was sponsored by the Cordon Blue School of Cooking, from France. Cooking had become a passion of mine, so I spent the year learning the culinary arts.

I took enough additional classes at UCLA that I could transfer to Colorado College, my dad's Alma Mater.

Ultimately, it was this campus I wished to graduate from, having fallen in love with the college on a visit there when I was just thirteen.

Arrival at Colorado College was frantic with all new freshmen scrambling to their dorms, getting organized, and finding their new roommates.

As a 'transfer student', I had status far above lowly freshman. The transfers were older, usually more savvy, than the wet behind the ear, new, freshmen girls, because they had already been in a college atmosphere. Generally, they were the target for the suave, debonair, upper classmen. This year there were ten transfers into C.C. from coast to coast. The most talked about however, was the UCLA import, Diane Hunt.

In those days at C.C. every freshmen and transfer students' profiles had been perused by all eligible guys in the school. This, courtesy of a guy named Jonsie, who worked in admissions and had access to the new arrival's files.

News around C.C. had traveled like wildfire across campus that a girl from Beverly Hills had transferred in for her sophomore year. So my pending arrival on campus had the small college in an expectancy buzz.

Several boys sat on the Slocum Hall lawn, surveying the arrival of the new incoming girls. All were speculating on what the "Beverly" chick would look like. All bets were stopped short by the arrival of a gleaming black and white Chrysler with California plates. I wheeled the big Chrysler around the dorm circle like I was pulling up to the starting gate at La Mans. I screeched up to the dorms entry and parked the car. Daddy went around and opened the door for me.

Sophomores were allowed cars if their projected grade points were high. My freshman year had been high B's and low A's which easily qualified me to have a car. Dad and I had driven across country in a fancy, gleaming, new set of wheels.

We pulled from the luggage compartment, several Yves St. Lauren bags, then slammed the trunk with a definitive thud and headed for the dorm.

There was no question in the minds of the observers, that the Hunts were more than your normal C.C. upper crust. This was the much talked about, chick from Beverly Hills. The society belle they had all heard so much about, had arrived.

Her father was a charter member of the Elite, President's Club at Colorado College, who annually donated 'beaucoup bucks' to the fund each year. This definitely was a family to get to know.

The transfer information said Mr. Hunt worked for Twentieth Century Fox. No one knew what his rank was, but Ralph was movie-star handsome, so it was possible he was a screen actor.

Dad was dressed in grey slacks, shod with spats, sporting a blue blazer and Panama hat. He looked every bit an actor who just stepped off the set of a Gatsby film.

Daddy scanned the boys, lounging on the lawn, with a fair measure of disapproval. He hated sloth and most of the young men seemed to be sitting around perfecting the pastime, to state of the art form.

He was distracted from the men by noticing that his limousine had already arrived in the school parking lot. It was scheduled to take him to the airport at one o'clock. Right on time. Ralph liked punctuality.

I briefly scanned the boys, but displayed no emotion over the lazing crew. Pointedly, I ignoring them, asking Dad to not tip the contents of one of the heavier bags.

The boys immediately dubbed me 'a snob'. "Wouldn't even give us a look!" they muttered among themselves. "Who did she think she was? Ms. high brow, Beverly Hills? Why did she come here anyway if she was going to blow off the local cream, of the 'Studley' stock?"

No matter their wounded pride, the audience continued to observed in awe, as Dad and I disappeared into Slocum Hall.

Snob or no, the observers deemed me as 'world class'.

Purposefully, I made no eye contact for fear my shyness would engulf me and I'd be frozen to the spot.

Yet, I'd vowed to myself that coming to Colorado, I would lose the horrible self-image of myself. I'd not been able to abandon it in Los Angeles or Paris, so Colorado was my last great hope.

Unbeknownst or unaccepted by me, I looked pretty hot. I was wearing a pure, white, halter top and snowy short-shorts. They were contrasted flagrantly by my darkly tanned skin. My glossy, ebony hair, hung like a silk fan to the middle of my back. Chunk diamonds were in my ears. A heart of pearls hung at my throat. I was a diminutive ninety pounds.

On the lawn below, the attractive group of boys sat speculating about the foxy, dark-haired chick who had snubbed them so thoroughly just moments ago. Talking amongst themselves, they started betting on the size of her monthly allowance. Then they speculated as to what classes she would take.

Bill Wharf, Steve Grey, Power Booth, Ace Bush and Steve Stockmar continued their scrutiny of the procession of other new girls who were arriving at the same time as me.

Within a few minutes of the girl from Beverly Hills arrival, Steve Stockmar rose to leave.

Steve Grey tossed out a chiding, "Seen enough?" He stood to join his roommate, Stockmar.

Steve shook his head. "I guess I'll reserve judgment till I hear her talk at dinner, but I've just seen my lady for life."

Grey dissolved into gales of laughter. "Who?" he asked, "the coy little chick that just arrived in the pink sweater and matching short skirt?"

Steve was unruffled by the teasing, "Nope, the foxy chick from Beverly Hills is mine. Grey, mark my words!"

With that they walked away and got into Grey's GTO. They drove away with a roar of exhaust from the 'souped-up' American car.

The afternoon was occupied with my unpacking trunks in my room all the while, lecturing myself about being a stupid, taciturn, wimp. I cajoled myself that I no longer could be the withering, violet type. Everyone told me that. It was finally time to come out of my shell!

I was getting settled in my room when three girls knocked on my door. I asked them to come in. They had heard that I was from Hollywood and they wanted to know if I knew any stars. I was a little flabbergasted by that as I really did not know who to name. Seemed these ladies all wanted to see if I could get autographed pictures of the 'stars'.

Between Westlake, parties at Dolly's and my friends, there were very few 'stars' I had not met. It cracked me up that anyone would want to have autographed pictures of 'Hollywood stars', but I would provide them anyway.

Before going down to dinner, I looked at myself in the mirror and thought with some despair, why couldn't I look more like Penny? Why did I have to look so exotic and dark? I was way too tan, way too thin and worse, way too short.

I dressed in what I considered 'art student chique'. Denim jeans, paint spotted shirt and sandals on my feet. I tied back my jet hair at the nape of my neck which served to make my look more severe than usual. This only enhancing my huge black eyes. The last touches were to pinch color into my high-boned cheeks and put white lipstick on my lips. Very, very hippy. Definitely the flower child look that was invading the corridors of C.C.

Disgusted, as usual with my own self image, I turned away from the offensive mirrored picture and bolted out the door. At nineteen, I was still crushingly shy. No amount of pep-talks from my friends or doting sister had ever gotten me over my horrible attacks of insecurity. Or even worse, the remembrance that once I had been compared to a 'Troll' loomed oppressively in the dim recesses of my mind.

So upon entering the dining room that first night at dinner time, I felt an assault of insecurities about to engulf me. This was one of major proportions because I knew no one and the crowed room seemed filled with hostile faces. I started to turn around to bail out and go back to my dorm room, when someone touched my arm.

I recognized him as one of the boys who had been sitting on the lawn. Though I had not seemed to see them, I had perfected the art of sideways glance scrutiny, way beyond the normal ability most people possessed.

He stuck out his hand in greeting, "Hi, I'm Steve Stockmar. Would you like to have dinner at my table? You look kind of bewildered right now."

"Thanks," I timidly muttered. Taking his offered hand in greeting, I did not meet his searching eyes. As we waited in line for dinner, I scrutinizes him.

Afraid of instant speech paralysis if I looked him head on, I unobtrusively observed that he was neatly dressed in faded jeans, a denim shirt that had seen better days and his feet were shod with worn leather cowboy boots.

He looked rugged, sexy, rough. He scared the hell out of me. He was so good looking, his black hair, lanky well-muscled frame and tanned, chiseled features, put me on my guard.

We went through the line helping ourselves to the offerings. All the while Steve bantered, getting absolutely, minimal response.

We sat down with a group of other boys that Steve introduced as 'The Arthur House Crew'. They were "GDI's!" he announced.

"Oh, cool." I softly replied, having not a clue what that meant.

"God Damned Independents," he enlightened.

"Super." I chirped.

Steve tried once again, "What's your major, Diane?"

"Art." I was conducting a brilliant monologue.

Steve was perplexed and thought to himself, wow, this girl is all looks and not a single brain cell is available for an interview. He had about concluded that I had gotten into C.C. not with board scores, but my father must have bribed the school to take me into the fold.

Another transfer, Corky Martin, rushed up to the 'Arthur House' table with her laden tray. She had already met some of the motley crew so joined them without hesitation.

"Diane Hunt?"she inquired.

"How on earth did you know?" Then I smiled and I guess according to Steve, it was at that moment that I melted his heart. His attention was snared. I had a melodic voice and when I smiled, I looked even more fabulous than ever. Steve also suddenly recalled that Miss Hunt was a graduate of a girls' school. Was there a chance that she was nervous around guys? Perhaps, horribly shy?

Corky enlightened, "I saw the picture of you and your dad on your dresser in our room." She extended her hand, "I'm Corky Martin, your new roommate."

Corky clearly knew her way around boys because her banter was light and friendly. Attention focused on her the rest of dinner, relieving me from further social stress.

Steve, used to most of the guy's moves, speculated to himself that one of the jocks, Thor Thorson, would target Corky. She was his style; flashy, blond, good-looking and probably had no morals at all. So Steve's evaluation was, that the new 'Beverly chick' was his.

Steve figured that with Thor going for Corky, petite Diane would be an easy mark for him. In his brief overview, she was way more his style. Stockmar himself was slight, athletic hard from years of breaking and riding horses. He was just six foot tall and walked straight and assured. His long fingered hands constantly raked back surly coal black hair from his high browed forehead. He had intense hazel eyes, lashed with dark fringes of black. He moved with the agile grace of a stalking jungle cat. On his own, a stand apart, strikingly, handsome young man. Surely more Hunt's type than the big hulking Swed.

So it was with all Steve's own attributes that he felt he would be the choice for dainty Diane who was barely five-foot-five. She couldn't weigh more than ninety pounds and to pair her with most of the jocks at the table, would be a joke.

Especially Thor, who was a virtual giant. He was six five, over two hundred pounds of hard muscle from skiing year round. He bashed Colorado powder in the winter and in summer, frequented the Andes of Peru. Thor was one of the regulars at this dinner table and was by far the most conceited of the group. His tall, blond, Nordic good looks, always turned the ladies heads. He was a natural to choose the bubbly blond, Corky, as his latest conquest.

Steve spent little time that evening recalling that he was already seeing a foxy girl by the name of Darci. Upon seeing Diane for the first time, he determined that his current relationship was coming to a screeching halt. Diane was to become his next conquest.

Darci was conveniently out of town for the next few weeks training with the school's ski team.

I quietly excused myself from the table, muttering something about continuing to unpack. I left everyone with attention focused on Corky.

However, Steve followed my departure with his eyes. He did not look away until I disappeared, up the stairs, and out of his sight.

Dinner over, Steve and Steve Grey, headed to the library.

Grey's parting shot was, "Good choice, Steve old man, the 'Beverly Hills chick' turns out to be as fiery as a jump in Grand Lake in December. Excellent call, my friend! My bet is on Darci any day of the week."

Steve was undaunted, but his plan of attack altered. He checked out my classes and dropped several he'd registered for, in order to pursue the 'Beverly fox'. He enrolled in several art classes as it seemed that was where I was mainly focusing that year.

CHAPTER THIRTY-NINE

GETTING INTO THE SWING OF THINGS

As we attended the studio art classes together, a tentative friendship was established.

Steve learned that I was sharp witted and smart, but as he'd previously analyzed, crushingly shy.

Observing me interact with other students, Steve learned that until I was completely comfortable with another person, I would not meet their gaze. At first he thought I was rude, even disinterested in the other person. Rumor actually spread that I was a Beverly Hills snob! I ignored people and was flat out, impolite. But Steve knew better, I was a complete introvert until I felt on friendly ground.

After some weeks of monitoring this behavior, Steve confronted the issue as being a problem as he saw it. One day at the breakfast table in Rastall Hall, he announced to me that I was creating an image of being a social snob. The usual crew was at the table that morning when Steve imperiously challenged me with this bold affront.

The group looked on as Stockmar leapt into the icy pond of friendship termination, by saying, "Diane, can you ever be introduced to anyone, cold turkey, and actually look them in the eyes? No, I bet you can't. You know, it's a real character flaw of yours not being able to meet someone's stare."

The blatant statement was met with silent shock from the gathered crew. No one, not Courtney Marten, Steve Grey, Bill Wharf or Susan Walsh expected Steve Stockmar to walk away from the table in one piece that day.

I rewarded Steve with a full eye to eye, lock! It was in all truth the first time Steve had even seen me look at him, other than from beneath my fringed lashes. In that second of leveling my stare, Steve realized I had the most beautiful eyes he'd ever seen in his life. Huge and round, they were brown, but flecked with black and gold. They reflected like mica, glittering with suppressed mirth.

"Actually, Steve," I admitted, "No, I can't. I have been so horribly insecure all my life that to meet someone's stare head on, stops me in function's tracks. But there, I've met yours, perhaps this is a start."

Everyone dissolved into hilarity except Steve who continued to hold my eyes locked with his.

Steve admitted later to me that it was at that precise moment that he fell deeply in love with me! He realized that I was a very introspective lady until you got to know me. Then when I opened up, I was far more than anything he'd ever guessed. Once relaxed, I could keep pace with any rhetoric anyone dished out and could aggressively hold my own. Plus, as seen that morning, I could swallow constructive criticism and not even break my stride.

But it had taken time for me to relax and get settled, let alone, to make friends.

And, though it could have gone the other way, after that small breakfast confrontation, Steve turned out to be my number one pal.

Unfortunately, for the budding relationship, Steve's girlfriend burst back on the scene. Seated at a table in Rastall Hall, Steve and I were studying anthropology while enjoying a cup of coffee. Darci, reappeared into Steve's life. She rushed in and flung herself onto Steve's lanky frame like a Cheetah, pouncing its' prey.

Darci was a statuesque, reddish-blond. She was striking, athletic, and made no bones about her physical contact with Steve Stockmar. She thought the young man belonged to her. It was certainly clear to me that Darci and Steve were romantically attached as she hung over him like stuck with Elmer's glue.

Steve pushed her away and introduced me!

Darci sized my petite, dark haired form and said, "Oh, I didn't see you. I heard you transferred in from So Cal and that your daddy paid your way here. My, I didn't realize the college was getting so loose with admissions. I guess they'll take anyone these days."

The uncalled for nasty remark stung me and mortified Steve.

It was true that dad had made contributions to the President's fund, but that had been ongoing for years. I had gotten into C.C. like anyone else, I just had been wait-listed for the lack of space.

However, seemingly not bothered, I rose, pecked Steve's cheek with a kiss and excused myself.

Over my shoulder I hurled as I left, "You should know, Darci, after all, they admitted riff-raff like you. That must have been when the C.C. standards started going all to hell!"

Darci took an instant hatred of me. She made it very clear to Steve that she did not approve of her guy's new little girl pal, Diane Hunt.

On top of everything, Darci truly grossed me out. I had never been into public display of affection. My parents relationship, though over forty years strong, never had been one of obvious physical display. I had been raised to respect that passion had its place and that was in the privacy of one's bed chamber, not the campus rec hall.

I knew what motivated girls like Darci. Having spent my career in a girl's school, I knew her type, all too well.

Where I was shy, Darci made up for her insecurities by being insulting and overacting. I had seen it over and over at Westlake School for Girls.

Darci's possessive nature did nothing but goad me to pressing my friendship with Steve. I went out of my way to be with Steve because I knew that it agitated Darci so much.

From the moment Darci came back from the ski training trip, she stayed attached to Steve as much as her classes allowed.

Steve still liked Darci. The fact that he had mentally replaced her with me did not prevent him from wanting to continue his association with her. He liked her as the friend she already was at that time.

Steve was feeling caught between a rock and a hard place by the two girl's dislike of one another. He thought perhaps if they got to know one another better, they could still become friends.

CHAPTER FORTY

QUESTIONING THE WISDOM OF MEN

Several months flew by and we were just maintaining status quo.

Steve was caught between me and Darci and decided he might change things around with an exciting little alpine adventure.

Steve suggested that a group of us go ski at Arapahoe Basin one day. He decided that perhaps a little excursion together would allow a friendship to nurture.

He invited Thor to go along because then the Swede could keep pace with Darci and Steve would be able to ski with me.

He suspected that coming from California, I had not had a great deal of practice on the ski slopes, which of course was very true.

This suggestion was met with limited enthusiasm on my part as I was marginal, bunny hill status at best.

Of course, marathon woman, Darci couldn't wait to go.

Eventually, we took the excursion. The four of us piled into Steve's BMW and headed up to the hills.

I did my best to keep up with the advanced skiers, but Darci was intolerant. She made fun of me as I was unschooled on mountains as advanced as the A-Basin slopes. The most advanced run I had ever attempted was Big Bear in the hills above L.A.

In a final coup of cattiness on Darci's part, she told me to stay in the warming hut at the base and have a hot cider while she and the 'boys,' did what they came to do, ski, not babysit.

Both Thor and Steve were furious with Darci, who had insisted from the outset, that they ski slopes far beyond even the average advanced skier. She was obviously setting me up for failure, even though I had been nothing but a sterling sport.

The guys told Darci to go ski alone. They wanted to rest themselves. Darci huffed off and skied till the lifts closed down.

As much as the guys tried to console me, I set my mind against Darci. Therefore, the ride home was tolerated with gelid silence on my part.

On the way back to the Springs, Darci bubbled about her huge jumps from the cliffs and how much the stupid guys had sacrificed hanging out with me.

She was silenced within a mile of A-Basin by Steve who said, "Darci, who even cares about your big air. There is plenty of time for everyone to ski in these mountains and I think it would have been real nice on your part to accommodate our California visitor with a pleasant experience. Diane would have enjoyed more gentle slopes, rather than you turning her off to skiing entirely."

So it was a very quiet ride down the hill back to C.C.

Steve was tired of Darci and her immature ways. He had fallen hopelessly, head over heels in love with me.

A couple nights after the ski fiasco, he'd invited me to have dinner with him. He intended to make me an incredibly fabulous meal, then hustle me off into his bed and make mad passionate love. Then he would propose. Everyone would say we were too young, we needed to finish college, but Steve had it all planned. We could live in Colorado Springs together, finish college, and get married right after we graduated.

He loved me and he wanted to marry me, or at the very least live with me right away.

Finally, after all the girls he'd entertained and terminated, due to lacking depth, he'd found a woman of substance and brains.

The evening was scheduled, he'd fixed a culinary triumph. Seared lamb chops with fresh asparagus and hollandaise, his special Caesar learned when he was a

Sous Chef at the A Bar A Ranch. He planned to top it off with Champaign, chocolate and strawberries for dessert. Then, propose. The perfect touch.

As he prepared the sumptuous meal, he was going over all the things we had in common. We were two peas in a pod. Everything he loved, I did as well. Foremost, we adored cooking. Then as if the hours spent comparing recipes were not enough along the similar path, he discovered my avid love of animals, especially horses.

I had been afraid to mention how much I adored horses for fear Steve would think I was a too much of a 'Tomboy'. Then I learned he was just as interested in them as I was which seemed amazing to me.

We also were fascinated by the same cars, avidly listened to Ian and Sylvia, Peter Paul and Mary and the only artist we conflicted on, was Bob Dylan. Steve thought he was awful and I called him an artiste.

We had such striking similarities that we often finished sentences started by the other, so tuned we were to the same wave length.

Steve was convinced that our being together had been fated by the stars. So that night he deemed it perfect to make love to me. We had been dating for weeks. Steve felt tonight was just the right length of time for us knowing one another.

I arrived for dinner and spent the whole evening talking about Thor, who had invited me out the next night. I was excited about being asked out by Thor. I thought of Steve as just my good friend.

Steve realized in a blinding flash, that was exactly what he had allowed himself to become. He'd never once pushed me into an awkward position and let me move at my own pace.

Darci had been a deterrent because she was perpetually hanging around.

That night, unhappily Steve realized, I had completely slipped away as a romantic possibility. He was just good old Steve Stockmar, Diane Hunt's new best friend.

I began dating Thor and in a few weeks we were an item. He gave me his Senior Class ring.

Unbeknownst to either Steve or me, Thor had gotten wind that Stockmar had set his personal cap for the 'Beverly chick'. That made his need for me as a conquest, a must. Steve had always been a bit of a rival since he'd snagged Darci out from Thor's clutches. The Swede's revenge was to be quite sweet.

Romantically, I fell hopelessly in love with Thor, who seemed the catch of the school. He whisked me to parties and showed me off as his trophy. Generally, he treated me like dirt.

Habitually he would arrive hours late for a date, or not show at all, never offering a valid excuse. But I put up with it because he was the envy of all the girls at C.C. Having never had much of a serious relationship before, I mistakenly took Thor's affections, to be love.

CHAPTER FORTY-ONE

A ROCKY PLACE IN MY HEART

Life at Colorado College progressed with a fair amount of routine. Events were predictable in that there was a constant flux of new and old romances that came and went with the seasons.

Quietly, Steve bided his time and remained in my classes, continuing to be my constant, attentive friend. Hoping against all hope that the Swede would tire of me as he had of all his other conquests.

Amazingly, this did not seem to pass. It seemed Thor had made a decision that the Beverly Hills girl was a keeper and he intended to hold onto this prize. But because the Swede and I studied different majors, we saw little of one another daily.

It was my 'good pal' Steve and I who went everywhere together. We had lunch together, attended classes together, walked across the quad, talking endlessly. We studied in the library in the afternoons and often went into Colorado Springs and shopped for clothes and just hung out.

We sat in Rastal drinking coffee with other co-eds such as Steve's friends Bill Wharf and Steve Grey, for hours and talked about everything from Haight Ashbury to the Viet Nam war.

Steve and I were best of friends!

I liked everything about Steve but never considered a romantic relationship because of his bond with Darci. He was my constant buddy, my best friend. I liked him far better than most of my pouty girlfriends who were always complaining about this or that. Steve was always so 'up'. The fact he was always there for me when I needed him was so important to me.

On time, no excuses, never an interruption cropped up that prevented Steve from being there for me...but only as a good friend.

One day, we were sitting in the quad, reviewing for an anthropology test when I realized my best friend's attention was not on his books. I looked up and caught him with his attention, absolutely riveted on me.

"What's up with you, Stockmar?"I asked, my voice laced with sarcasm.

Steve answered without hesitation, "Do you have any idea how beautiful you really are or do you just take your looks for granted?"

This rewarded him with me blushing the color of a blood-red, setting sun. Flustered, I sputtered and was utterly speechless, unable to offer a reply. I just sat there negatively shaking my head.

Taking hold of both my shoulders, Steve squared me off with his strong hands and stared at me. It took me some moments to meet his glare."Jesus Christ," he observed, utterly amazed, "you are the most beautiful woman I know on the face of this planet and you have no clue, do you? You are drop, dead, gorgeous, but so insecure you can't come to grips with the truth? Oh, holy shit."

"Steve, drop this crap!"I commanded and wrenched away. I rose and started to rush across the Quad as if bitten by a wasp.

He quickly followed and grabbed me by the hand, halting my flight by spinning me to face him. Then he realized I was crying.

Steve was stunned. "What the hell is this all about? What on earth did I say to upset you so much?"

"Nothing! Just leave me alone!"I shrilled and headed off at a dead run to the dorm.

Dumbfounded, Steve stood motionless on the grass, watching my retreating form. For the life of him he could not fathom what he said that afternoon to bring on this type of reaction. If I took that well to compliments, perhaps next time, he should cut to the chase and just slap me across the face.

In my dorm room, I stood and looked at myself in the mirror. Tears had trickled black lines down my high boned cheeks. My mascara was smudged and I looked a wreck.

Hatefully I spat, "Corky is beautiful! Darci is 'drop-dead-gorgeous', but I am not attractive at all!" I railed at the image of myself. "Maybe, just possibly I'm too hyper-critical of myself. I'll go I'm okay, but I'm still deep inside, that ugly 'troll'! A freckle-faced little 'Shrimp', I'm simply nondescript!"

Corky walked in as I was criticizing myself and asked, "What the hell is up with you talking to yourself in the damn mirror?"

I turned to my roommate and challenged, "Am I beautiful?"

This caused Corky to double over with laughter on the bed. "Christ on a crutch," she roared. "Did your parents keep mirrors from you all your life? Do you need glasses now? Are you legal-fuckingly-blind?" she howled. "Fucking A, Diane Hunt. Unbeknownst to you, stupid," she howled with mirth again. "You were just voted the most beautiful chick on campus by the underground pole. So that should answer that, cookie. But you'll be horribly distressed to learn that your 'Blond God' got aced out by your pal, Stu. Stockmar won the coveted, "Hunk" award, not Thor. I guess 'Blond Gods' are out and the 'dark silent, type' is in."

Corky flung this information over a retreating shoulder, "By the way, ugly duckling, as much time as you and Stu spend together, campus rumor is, Thor is out, and good old Stu is in. Any truth to that gossip?"Corky did not bother to remain. She was on her way to the shower and having dropped her bombshell, unceremoniously left the room.

I sat in silence. I'd heard about the fraternity-sorority underground, straw poll that took ballots on the campus 'cuties' and 'hunks'. But never in a million years did I expected to be on the ticket, let alone win the coveted vote.

It made me horribly uncomfortable. "What a bunch of garbage!"I informed the walls. "Who puts any credence in what those fools say?" I sagely advised my bed. "Anyway," I concluded to the receptive audience of my stuffed animals, "it's that type of drivel I hoped to avoid by remaining a 'God Damned Independent', not some stupid, sorority chick!"

Then the parting shot...'Thor's out and Steve is in'. What the hell was that all about? Could you not spend time on this campus with a male friend without rumors flying?

Christ, I hated life. I was glad the semester was almost over so I could go home and not play these trivial games. I longed to just ride my horse and be plain old Diane.

My horse didn't care if I was ugly. My horse didn't give a shit if I wore make-up or came to the ranch looking like dirt. My mare cared less if I was thick with the 'Blond God' or the 'dark silent type'. And who was spreading that rumor, anyway? Oh, who cared? I shrugged it off.

Fixing my face I reapplied some mascara and dabbed blush on my cheeks. Satisfied that I was okay, I went down to the snack bar and treated myself to a banana split.

Steve caught up with me and sat down at the table.

"You okay?" he questioned.

As usual I refused to meet his questioning eyes.

"Fine!" I lied. "I just am having a bad day. It's nothing for you to get all hot and bothered about anyway."

Steve was nonplussed. He could not figure me out. I was beautiful, had more money than God when it came right down to it and I had everything going for me. But I simply chose to act as if nothing was on my side.

Steve sat watching me as I toyed with the ice cream in the dish. He loved me, but no matter what line he came up with, he could not convince me. If he brought it up, he was sure he would be shot down. So being the consummate optimist, he continued to bide his time in hopes that Thor would give this girl up and Steve, could then move in for the kill.

But it seemed the Swede had no intention of letting his prize go.

CHAPTER FORTY-TWO

Author's Notes:

This continuing view back to the C.C. days comes from several accounts. My perspective, Steve's recollections and input from a friend by the name of Steve Grey. He was eventually in our wedding and was instrumental in helping point my affections in the right direction. He revealed his perceptions about my relationship with Steve after the Homecoming Dance.

ZINGED BETWEEN THE EYES

Parents' weekend brought my mom and dad from California. They met and were enthralled by Thor. The dazzling Swede asked my father for his daughter's hand in marriage and eagerly Ralph agreed. Mom and Dad were elated by the match and looked forward to the day I became Thor's bride.

As a senior, Thor graduated and was enrolled in graduate school in Minnesota. He was leaving me with a promise of marriage and a promise ring which he gave to me before the Homecoming Dance.

At that same soirée, I experienced the oddest thing. Thor and I were dancing very close when I looked across the floor and saw Steve and Darci also dancing. But what Darci was doing to Steve was merely a step above obscene. They might as well have been making love on the dance floor for all the gyrations she was performing on Steve.

I felt a wave of heat. It stunned me! I thought that I recognized it as jealousy, but how could I feel jealous of Darci when Steve was just my friend? As the other couple continued to dance, I became horribly annoyed at the girl. She was so slutty, why did Steve allow her to treat him that way?

They were dancing so close it made me feel embarrassed for Steve. Or was I feeling envy that Darcie was in his arms. His long artistic fingers were clutching her bare shoulders, his tan cheek was pressed against her mouth that continuously kissed him. He glided her toward the door in an embrace that left me feeling confused with the emotions that washed me at that moment.

I surmised they were leaving to go home to a night of lust as they disappeared from the room. I had little time to ponder further, because Steve ended the suggestive scene by steering Darcie from the room.

The scene that everyone on the dance-floor missed, was conducted outside in the hall. Steve told Darci, under no uncertain terms, "I'm done with this crap. If you want to do that to a guy in bed find someone else. I'm not your man. I'm not interested in you anymore."

Before she could lodge her intended slap of his face, Steve turned heel and headed back onto the floor where he asked Thor if he could cut in for a dance with me.

Being a gentleman was one of the Swede's better features, he yielded to Steve, knowing there was no contest. I was his girl for life now, he saw no reason not to allow the poor chump at least one dance.

I was stunned that Steve had returned. He held me far tighter than propriety allowed.

The band performing was a little recognized group called 'The Doors'. Steve had hired them having heard them play some time ago. They were just getting hot on the charts. It probably would be their last college gig. They were playing a song called 'Light My Fire'.

But Steve and I were not dancing to the beat. We were moving single time as if to a tune of our own.

He spoke first, "Are you anxious to see summer come and get home?"

"I need to get away from college and be me for a while."

Steve drew away and looked at me in the eyes, "What's that supposed to mean?"

I darted away my gaze. I hated it when Steve stared me down. I always saw a different person in those eyes, a bearing of someone's soul. That night I saw something so amazing in his look that I refused to admit it even to myself. So, not to dwell on my insight, I avoided it by light banter.

"It's just that I need to think some things through. I have some career decisions I need to make. I can't see the forest for the trees here. Too many distractions."

He had pulled me close again to dance and I found myself fighting for breath. I had never been held by Steve before that night. Steve was my best friend. We had briefly hugged, we had pecked one another's cheek, even brushed lips in friendly parting, but tonight, I was dancing with him and I had never felt heat like I was feeling now. I had never felt this way with Thor. My best friend was turning me on so totally, that I was hardly able to breathe.

The dance ended and Thor rushed to claim me. He was not at all pleased with the way we had been clinging to one another. He also did not like how flushed I looked. Actually, he thought I looked unwell. He surmised I had a bit too much to drink, so left me to get our coats.

Steve gave me a parting hug and said he'd see me before we left campus, then rushed off.

While I was watching Steve leave, Steve Grey, Stockmar's roommate, wandered by. He was weaving from too much to drink and he grabbed me by my shoulders. He manipulated my chin with his hand so I had to look him square in his eyes.

"You're a tease, you know," he slurred, "a god damn, Beverly Hills, tease."

I wriggled from his grasp. "What do you mean by that?" I snapped.

"Pooooor ol' Scheeve," he continued to mumble. "Christ, you two are the biggest fools to ever avoid the inevitable. Whhhy the hell the two of you don't just admit you need to make peace, I jusssttt don't know!" At this, Steve wove his way out the door. I had no clue what he meant and Thor was there with our coats.

The trip home was quiet and when Thor asked, "My place this time?"

I opted to be let off at the dorm, pleading I felt a bit sick.

Thor readily agreed. I seemed intoxicated and he hated it when girls got ill.

I went to bed and tried to fall asleep. I was far from intoxicated. The opposite was true. I was sobered by the weight of my feelings toward Steve Stockmar.

I lay in a pool of sweat. I had never felt the jolting desires I had felt in Steve's arms during that brief dance. It haunted me. That night, his eyes amazed me. Not facing it that moment, but lying there I realizing his look was that of someone longing so much for me. There was a mist of pain veiling his deep hazel eyes.

Steve Stockmar loved me and what was far worse, I knew in that blinding instant, that I loved him back!

The dilemma I faced then was my own feelings. Is this what true love feels like? Weak kneed, melting, heat shooting from groin to chest? Well if that was the case, I had never experienced such emotions with Thor. Christ, if it felt like that to just be held in Steve's arms, what on earth would it be like to make love?

Make love?

I bolted up in my bed. Staring into the darkness, tears trickled down my cheeks. I realized then that Thor and I had never really made love. We had sex, we 'did it, we 'did the nasty'. Where in his vernacular did the word love, fall? He never once had said with words or his eyes, that he loved me. Jesus Christ! Not in all the time we had been together, did he ever say, "I love you"!

I was sad, for myself. Confused by my recent revelations, I tossed and turned the rest of the entire night.

CHAPTER FORTY-THREE

NEWS FLASH, THIS IS LOVE

Thor graduated and was off for summer break the week before I was finished at C.C. He headed home with his promise to keep in constant touch.

The day I was to depart for Los Angeles, Steve offered to shuttle me to the Colorado Springs Airport. He had seemed relatively distant for some weeks. I just chalked it up to finals and all the wind down garbage we were both going through to wrap up loose ends before the close of the semester.

Steve picked me up on time and we headed to the terminal in relative silence. He helped me with my bags by handing them to a Skycap and then offered to see me to the gate.

We walked along in an uncomfortable silence, neither of us knowing what to say. I was trying not to cry because the thought of being without him all summer with such unresolved feelings was eating away at me.

Meanwhile, Steve did not want to talk for fear of betraying his intense emotions of thwarted adoration toward me. Over the last weeks, his love had grown to a point of such obsession that he'd consciously avoided me.

We arrived at the designated boarding area. Steve said good-by and started to turn to walk away.

I caught him by his coat sleeve. "That's it, for the whole summer? Steve Stockmar, I thought we meant more to one another than just a cursory good-by on your part. I want a hug."I drew him to me.

A rushing passenger pushed by Steve shoving him fully against me. Grasping to help steady me from falling, he pulled me to his body too aggressively for just an adjustment of balance. It was at that moment that I realized he was not feeling the slightest bit platonic about our relationship. I was stunned by the fact that he was sexually aroused. I jerked away from him as if from a poison dart.

I looked him in the eyes and saw again, in the brief seconds before he left, a mixture of confusion, hurt, love and sadness. I had never seen anyone exhibit such mixed emotions. Tears welling in his hazel eyes, I realized Steve was about to cry.

Before I could say a word more he kissed my cheek and begged off, "I have to go. Have a bitchen summer. I'll see you in the fall."With that, he rushed down the concourse and disappeared into the crowd.

His contact had left me so panicked that I needed to sit for some minutes to regain my composure before I boarded the plane. The entire flight was agony!

I realized by then, Steve loved me to the core. What was even worse, I knew I loved him and had no chance to test the uncharted waters. I would have to deal with my emotions all summer long because I could make no contact with Steve. He had told me that he would be out of reach in Wyoming, so not even try to keep in contact. Boy, was I ever flummoxed.

Now what on earth was I to do about Thor?

CHAPTER FORTY-FOUR

HAUNTING SUMMER DREAMS

That summer break, as usual, we transported my horse to Yosemite National Park. We stayed for the summer. I determined that there I would sort my emotions out over this disturbing turn of events. I kept very much to myself about the matter because I had always made monumental decisions on my own. For some reason, I could not sort this one through. Frankly, I was confused, but could not comprehend my bewilderment.

I had scored the legendary Westlake coup. "Go to college for two things. First and foremost your MBA. Secondly your MRS. to an exceedingly wealthy and handsome man."

Thor certainly qualified for that as his father was one of the leading architects in Waterloo, Iowa and Thor said he intended to follow in his father's footsteps. So obviously I would be set.

But night after night, I dreamed of Steve, not Thor.

Several times as I cantered through the trees on my daily rides, Missy, almost dumped me off because I was paying little attention to riding and the horse took advantage, bucking or bolting to get my attention. I had to concentrate hard on the control of the horse, yet my mind continuously wandered back, to Steve not Thor.

The afternoon at the airport still had me mentally undone. Girls always joked about how sixteen year old guys got hard over anything. Show them a Playboy and they were rocks. But guys that were twenty, like Steve, were beyond the walking erection thing. He had been so aroused by me in the airport, he could not control himself.

I knew that could only mean he was in walking lust with me and all I had ever done was treat him as a stupid friend. How could I have been so blind?

But what about his girlfriend? I could not get Darci off my mind. This did not stop me from constantly fantasizing about Steve and me engaging in wild, erotic sex.

It began to worry me more and more every day. I kept flashing back to the night of the dance and the overpowering desires I had felt for Steve. I needed to come to terms with this before I returned to school.

That summer, happiness eluded me. No matter what I did to exhaust myself, I could not seem to rest at night for trying to solve my dilemma about Steve Stockmar.

CHAPTER FORTY-FIVE

YIPPEE KI-YAY

Steve had wiled the summer away busting broncos all over Wyoming. He decided not to take a job that had much people contact because he simply did not feel like communicating at all. He was being consumed with his love for me and could come to no rational conclusion of how to get me to leave the 'Blond God'.

Not only were Thor and I engaged, but it seemed I had been hypnotized by him.

At one point, Steve almost took me aside to tell me the truth about how much *he* loved me instead.

He chickened out because he knew how completely snowed I was by Thor and Steve felt that in comparison, he held no contest against the looming hulk of a Swede.

Thor was bigger than life. He hailed from a highly upper rank Waterloo Iowa family. Thor's father was the leading Architect in that town and was worth a bazillion bucks. The Swede drove a flashy little 150 drop head coupe of a Jaguar and just in general was a more perfect package that would appeal to the Beverly chick, Diane Hunt.

Thor, for all intent and purpose, was no question, bigger than life.

But did he really love Diane? Had he planned to do everything in his power to treat her as she deserved. Had he looked forward in to the bright future and seen all the wonderful things that they would do together as a couple, or was Thor just hung up on the dazzle and pizzazz of the Beverly Hills girl?

She was stunning, she was intelligent, she had a sense of humor that knocked Steve with hysteria, to the floor. Diane Hunt deserved so much more!

Him!

The more he reviewed it in his mind, he could tell the Swede and Diane had little in common. He knew it was nothing but a sexual attraction.

Whereas he and Diane had everything in common. There had to be a way that he could dissolve her infatuation over Thor.

As Steve broke horse after horse, going from ranch to ranch, he formulated a plan of attack. He decided to confront me in the fall. He'd tell me that he adored me and would never inflict hurt. He'd always be there for me and love me for the rest of my life. Best friend's often made the best lovers so why not give our intimate relationship a try? Corny, but who cared? He had to get through to me or he did not know what he was going to do with himself.

He realized I was his life goal and he was not about to let some hunky 'Swede' take his girl just because Thor seemed bigger than life.

Determined to succeed, he headed back to college to prepare his carefully baited trap. He would get the girl he loved no matter what he had to do.

CHAPTER FORTY-SIX

SHOWTIME

The summer finally passed yet my dilemma about Steve and Thor was still as tumultuous as in the spring.

The whole family returned to Los Angeles and I was preparing to return to college. Engaged to one man, in love with another. I literally was a wreck.

One day when together with Dolly, I discussed this matter with her.

She counseled me, "Pick the one with the most family money, then you can divorce him. You will then be 'well taken care of' if things don't eventually pan out."

Wow! That was some motherly advice!

Finally, I decided to broach the irritating matter with my mother, Marie. As much as I had tried to resolve the issues myself, I could not. I needed more than Dolly's jaded adult advice. My bond with Marie had become incredibly strong because I believed my adoptive mother was a woman of true values. Unlike my real mother whose life was glamorous, she cut through men like a scythe through the rye. Mrs. Hunt was a true lady, being always faithful to Daddy. They had already been married over forty years.

I posed my dilemma to Mother who briefly met Steve at Parents' Weekend when she had also met her future son-in-law, Thor.

Mother looked at me and said, "Now you have been away from your grand Swede's attention for three months. Go back and see what your heart tells you. If when you see Steve, you can say this can never be anything but a friendship, then it's finished. Marry Thor and never look back. But if your heart tells you that Steve can be your lover as well as your friend, go after him, instead. You say he is besotted by some other girl,

220

maybe appearances are not exactly what they seem. I have always believed that if you marry your very best friend, the love will endure, forever. Wedding for sex often never lasts. I married your dad over another man who was passionately in love with me. Ralph was my best pal and loved me as well. I've never regretted my decision. Your dad is still my best pal as well as my dearest love. He will be for the rest of our lives!

It was that amazing insight from my mother that set me on my path of logic.

The day before I returned to school, I wrapped Thor's ring in a package and sent it off to him, registered mail. I wrote him a parting letter. "I have evaluated our relationship and realize it has been a passion thing not true love. That was what I was looking for in marriage."

Signed, sealed and delivered, I sent him back his ring.

I then consoled myself. I decided that even if I had misinterpreted everything with Steve, I needed to break it off with Thor. I was pretty sure that he did not love me, it seemed it had had just always been about sex.

If Steve loved me as I suspected, then so be it. We should go on with our lives as lovers. If he didn't love me, we would simply continue our relationship as good friends.

Hopefully, I could convince him that it should be love. I was determined to make my best friend, my lover, to hell with Darci!

CHAPTER FORTY-SEVEN

TRUE REALIZATIONS

I boarded the plane to return to school on the first day of September.

That same day, Steve arrived back in Colorado Springs and registered for classes. He then went back to his apartment and made preparations for his seduction.

He'd phoned and talked to Mother who encouraged him to 'give her daughter an opportunity to make a choice'. She said that' I was confused about the relationship. My plane was due in Denver by nine o'clock'.

Steve decided to meet me at the dorm and whisk me off to dinner and then tell me he wanted to marry me. I needed to cancel all plans with the damn 'Swedish' beast! It just had to work this time.

With pounding heart, Steve Stockmar sat on the little dorm porch swing waiting for me to appear. He was forced to wait a long time.

I flew into Denver quite late that night. Delayed for hours because of equipment problems at LAX, my flight was greatly postponed. I missed the commuter flight from there to Colorado Springs, so I was forced to rent a car.

I drove the pitch black hour and a half, trip to Colorado Springs. The entire time I was thinking of Steve and how I was going to win him to my camp. I had all those hours to fantasize. I had fabricated so many plans I was befuddled over which seemed the most rational. I arrived at my dorm at eleven o'clock, well past my expected arrival.

I was physically and emotionally exhausted from my trip and the mental issues I'd hashed over during the entire flight wore me down. Plus the whole damn summer had wrung me to an emotional wreck. All I wanted to do was collapse in bed.

In some senses I was relieved that finally, tomorrow I would be able to confront the issues with Steve and get everything off my mind.

Tonight, however, all I wanted to do was go to bed and dream of Steve and hopefully resolve, in my sleep, a solution to my dilemma.

I decided to leave all but my overnight bag in the car. I could deal with my luggage the next day. Wearily, I walked up the steps of my dorm.

And, someone was sitting in the shadows on the porch swing. I was a little frightened to see anyone there so late at night.

"Hi Diane," the soft, husky, masculine voice rumbled, assuring he was friend, not foe.

For a moment I froze. It certainly was a conjured vision of my tormented thoughts. I must have fallen asleep and was again dreaming of my ongoing dilemma with Steve. I could not believe he was actually waiting for me on the porch.

He walked down the steps and grabbed the bag from my hand.

"Hey," he bantered lightly, "even though it's super late, I've got dinner fixings. Let's go to my place. I've got some things I want to run by you." He figured if he kept up a light rhetoric, I would not refuse. "There are some things that you and I really need to discuss. I hope you aren't too tired, is this all right?"

I was thankful he was doing all the talking. He'd kissed me lightly on the lips just seconds before and it was all I could do to continue to keep breathing.

I was so flamed with emotion all I could do was chirp. "Fine, just fine. I have a few things to get straight with you, too."

He talked the entire way to his home about busting horses, bailing hay and a bunch of stuff that I could have cared less about. All I could think about was holding him, kissing him, and that I loved him. Why was he talking about horses and hay? But I was afraid to initiate conversation at that point because I honestly did not know how to begin.

I wondered if anyone had ever died from the anticipation of the act of love. Maybe he didn't really want to make love to me. Maybe that day in the airport last spring, he was just having a lust flash. Oh Christ, I was so scared of his rejection, I hurt. I needed to tell him how much I cared about him, even if he did not give a shit about me, other than being my best friend.

We arrived at his house and Steve opened the door and with a flourish he ushered me into the spacious, bachelor pad. He went to the bar in the kitchen and made himself busy by opening a bottle of Chardonnay.

Steve was worried because I seemed so oddly quiet. He wondered if I felt all right. In all the time he'd been close to me, I had never been this reserved. Maybe I was exhausted from the trip. He thought I looked pale beneath my beautiful tan. He'd noticed how pinched I looked in the light of the car when he settled me for the drive to his home. I looked thinner than he remembered, which only served to accent my high-boned cheeks and large brown eyes. Perhaps this was not the night to try this seduction thing.

Steve handed me a glass of wine asking, "So, how was your summer?" he began his circumvent attack.

I took the glass and said, "Oh, absolutely groovy." I artfully lied as I took a sip of wine. Averting my gaze to a beautiful painting he had hanging over the mantel, I purposefully avoided eye contact for fear of losing my grip. "I rode a lot, sat in the sun a bunch and had a really great time in Yosemite." I fibbed some more. "One of my best summers ever! I can't remember when I've enjoyed myself more. A ton of the old gang was there for the first time in years," I rambled. "It was good to see my friend, Ed Fahlen, from Phoenix and the Nishkans from San

Francisco. It's been years since the whole gang was there."

"Great!" he said disappointedly. He'd hoped for an account of a lousy summer, as he had endured himself.

But my prattling banter was concerning him. Something was weird with me. I seemed taught and strung tight. There definitely was something coming down. Suddenly, Steve felt a cold wash of fear. He sensed that I was going to kiss him off. I had said in front of my dorm, "I have a few things to get straight with you, too." He could hear it all now as I was probably screwing up my courage to say, "Oh, by the way, it's good-by. Thor and I are getting married so we no longer can be friends. Our seeing one another so much, is cramping my style. It won't look good to the others knowing I'm engaged and still hanging tight with you all the time."

Panic gripped his heart! This seduction was not only going to be a monumental failure, but he was never going to be able to be near me again. Not as my lover, let alone, be allowed to remain as my dearest friend. His sexually aggressive actions during the past few meetings, must have made me gun shy. Why else would I be acting so weird unless I was going to tell him to kiss off?

Somehow he had to stop this collision course of failure. He could not stand the consequences. Without me, life for him could not go on.

With no warning, he grasped my chin and cupped it in the palm of his hand. He wanted me to stop avoiding looking into his eyes.

"Diane, please, look at me."

Pointedly, I averted my gaze to a near-by chair. Unfortunately, my usual lack of confidence was not being bolstered at all.

Completely out of character, snarling like a wolf, Steve commanded, "God-damn it to hell! Diane Hunt, will you just look at me, please!"He all but roared the words at me.

This seemingly innocent command was life altering.

Stunned, unaccustomed to this type of gruffness in his voice, defiantly I glared at him. The second my eyes finally met his, we were bound.

Like a bolt of lightning that arcs from sky to ground during a summer storm, that moment, the voltage fused us for life! The magnetism was so violent it physically shook us both.

"Steve..." I began.

"Diane..." he whispered.

Simultaneous our vow..."I love you!"

Wordlessly, wine glasses were set aside. As if possessed, we fell on one another and kissed for what seemed to be a lifetime before Steve lifted me into his arms and carried me to his bedroom. We collapsed onto his bed.

What transpired was, we made love, not just had sex. There was a frenetic urgency at the first encounter because both of us had longed for this union. After the initial tumultuous passion, we spent the rest of the night learning one another's bodies.

We took the time to lengthy explore. No hurry, no hesitation. We both knew from the first dance to the last moment of exquisite pleasure, we would be joined this way till the end of the earth.

Alternately, we talked and made love, resolving all that had passed. We laughed over our miserable summers and how we were our own worst enemies. I cared about Steve but because of Darci, I thought perhaps he had just wanted me as a friend.

And of course it had been obvious to Steve that I loved Thor, so out of his chivalrous nature, he made no moves.

We both were astounded over how misconstrued both relationships had been.

We rued the time spent apart, when a simple conversation could have clarified our confusion. Neither of us wanted to broach the subject for fear of being shot down.

Finally, we laughed over how simple it would have been if we had talked things out from the first moment we realized we had an emotional attraction. But both of us knew this period of testing was better because it had probably strengthened us both.

Steve and I took up cohabitation at his house.

****

Shortly after that day, Steve and I were just bumming around doing couples stuff, when a red Ferrari screeched to a stop and Thor climbed out of the car.

For one, I had never seen the little red rocket before. His previous wheels were a little 150 Jag, drop head coupe that belched billows of oily smoke and went through quarts of oil a day. So it took a few seconds for me to realize who was coming to our door.

Thor was about six foot three, a ripped 200 plus and looked a little as if a thunder cloud was hovering above his head. To say he was an unhappy camper was an understatement, at the least.

I unceremoniously told Steve to go out the back door. There was no earthly reason for him to be in the path of this furious approaching man. It was my problem to talk to Thor and I would face it head on.

Steve chivalrously protested and insisted that he stay.

Thor began to pound on the door and alternately rang the bell.

I demanded that Steve leave and after some moments of his fury over not staying to defend me, I shoved him out the back door and locked it so he could not come back in.

I went to the front and opened the door.

I greeted Thor whose first words were, "I don't accept the ring back. I want to marry you and I am here to find out who has taken my place!"

"I don't think it is your business. I explained in my letter, that it is my belief that our relationship would not survive marriage. Those are my final words."

"Who is it? Dabney Murcheson? I knew he had his eye on you. Who? You need to tell me so at least I can understand. What is it? He has way more money than I do but that can change. I intend to make a killing in business as soon as I graduate from Grad School."

"It's not Dabney! It's Steve!"

"Grey? I knew that son-of-a-bitch would potentially move in on you. Forget living in Minnesota, a California girl like you will freeze to death out there!"

"Stockmar!"

This stunned Thor to momentary speechlessness. "Stockmar? That wimp of a guy?"

"He is not a wimp," I defended, "he is shy and sensitive and merely a bit slight. You on the other hand, are a giant and have the sensitivity of a stump. I refuse to marry you, so please go away!"

"I could buy you anything you want. I really was set on marrying you, Diane."

"Too bad!" I pushed him out the opening and slammed the door really hard to make my point.

Thor shouted a parting shot, "Well at least you aren't marrying someone worthwhile. I would have really been pissed if it had been Mercheson or Grey, but Stockmar? That is the joke of the century! Good bye, Miss Hunt. Had I known you were this big a fool I would have never driven all the way from Waterloo to discover that fact for myself."

That was the last we saw of Thor.

Steve and I announced to his parents that we intended to get married in June of 1970.

The Stockmars were thrilled, as were both my Mom and Dad.

CHAPTER FORTY-EIGHT

Author's Notes:

We set our wedding date for June 6, 1970 and the months before the event flew by.

Steve graduated from Colorado College in June of 1969.

I returned to Beverly Hills to make all the arrangements for the wedding that would transpire the following year.

Steve moved home to seek employment in Denver, which was to be our chosen home.

It was during the year before we were wed, that he joined the Banking team of the First National Bank. He was hired to train on the teller-line. This began his initial step up the corporate ladder to the top of the financial hierarchy.

Steve was getting his affairs in order for the rest of our married lives.

THE MOTHERS' OF THE BRIDE

I was busy getting things down to the last minute detail of our wedding in Beverly Hills.

While Mother and I spent months fine tuning every detail of the beautiful wedding plans, Dolly oversaw the whole orchestration, as well.

Looking back on our wedding day, it was in fact a fairy tale come true.

Everything came off as beautifully as planned and the costuming was, to quote Dolly, 'divine'.

I had chosen to buy a dress from the design house named William Cahill. It was, at the time, the Beverly Hills choice of couturier for dresses of the upper echelon brides. All the gowns were completely original and his reputation was known far and wide.

Both Dolly and Mother went with me for that choice and the two women bickered like hens over a chick. I remember Dolly wanting my gown to be all of lace and frills and Mother insisted that I was just not the lace and frills kind of girl. Between them, there was a great deal of tension and no one seemed willing to budge. The poor saleswoman was beside herself. I think she was about in tears.

At one point she tried to reason with Dolly, and because of the startling resemblance of Dolly and me, she called Dolly, Mrs. Hunt. Dolly hastily corrected her with an uncomfortable laugh, saying, "I'm her 'godmother', dear girl!"

The salesgirl then excused herself. She was the color of a beet and I concluded she was about to suffer a stroke. I was stuck in the middle, adamantly agreeing with Mother, but not wanting to offend Dolly when William Cahill himself stepped into the fray. I am quite certain it was not a new experience for him, as he walked in with a sample dress that simply blew everyone away.

It was elegant, silk peau de soie, trimmed about the bodice, neck and sleeves with guipure lace. It had a Juliet pin-tucked panel front, lace collar and long pin-tucked sleeves. It was empire in style. The gown was long with a sweeping train, a complete classic that Cahill produced for the two mothers and me to view.

It received unanimous acceptance by all three of us. Of course it needed to be made to fit me, as at that point, I was wearing a size two.

I chose the bridesmaids' dresses at the same time and did something that in that day was a bit unconventional. I chose to have my girls all in white dotted Swiss.

When we were in Europe, Mother had purchased a veil of exquisite Belgium lace. I knew it had been for Penny, but her grand wedding never happened; she eloped instead. So the veil was to be my beautiful prize.

Much of the preparations were orchestrated by only Dolly and me. They were primarily by me because of

Mother's recently challenged health. I chose the menu for both the rehearsal dinner and the reception, discussing it carefully with both my parents.

When asking Daddy what kind of a budget did he expect his reply was, "I'm just along for the ride. Do exactly what you want. All we got with your sister was a lousy elopement. Go to town, 'Shrimp' on this party. It is your mother's only shot with you girls."

So I did.

I hired Ray Huff to do the photography. At the time, he was the darling of the Hollywood celebrity photographers.

Hernando Courtright, who owned the Beverly Wilshire Hotel, was a dear friend of Dolly Green's. He offered services of his grand establishment and personally helped the Hunts and the 'godmother', plan the rehearsal dinner, and the lavish evening reception that would follow the wedding ceremony. Without Dolly's connections and input, I could never have hoped to have such an unbelievable affair. Dolly arranged for the lavish reception be catered beyond first class at Hernando's Hotel. Dolly went with Marie and me to choose the appetizers, the elaborate menu of the sit-down dinner, as well as, the many French wines and Champagnes that were to be endlessly, poured, that night. Ralph Hunt never knew how much of my wedding was footed by the 'divine' Dolly Green. Marie never told him either, as it was part of the bargain struck so any years before.

The Los Angeles Times announced the upcoming nuptials with reverence due to an 'Angel Town' child. The society editor of the L.A. Times, Jody Jacobs, went on about the wedding as if it were the most important ceremony ever performed. I was extolled as being the most beautiful girl, from a very distinguished Beverly Hills family, marrying a tremendously prestigious man from Denver. Our wedding was extolled as the wedding of the year.

CHAPTER FORTY-NINE

Author's Note:

Pre-wedding was absolutely amazing. I was so proud of the entire group of my peers for pulling together and getting there from as far as Colorado and Washington D.C.

The plan was a series of parties starting with Dolly's on Thursday night. Several Denver People were able to attend including the Ted Stockmars, the Valentine Logans, the William Kelloggs, the Arthur Cowperthwaiets, and the Cowperthwaites' daughter, Jill and son, Tee.

Dolly's home was overwhelmingly opulent compared to Denver residences, but all were very blasé about being entertained there. I have a photo of Ted, Suzanne and Mother standing at the far end of Dolly's living room in the Bellagio mansion. There is a beautiful Sevres vase to Suzanne's left and a massive display of Cymbidiums behind Ted. All are formally attired and Mom is gorgeous in a white Elizabeth Arden creation of lace and seed pearls that she and I picked out for the occasion.

The planning of the wedding was beyond that of the orchestration for a princess bride. That is how Dolly treated me throughout the year we took, to plan the elaborate affair.

The wedding gifts we received were piling up and I was having a hard time keeping up with the thank you notes. I wanted to get them done but finally it got so overpowering that I realized it would not be until we were back in Denver that I would be able to respond. So I just kept careful notes of who sent what.

Dolly sent six place settings of our sterling flatware and a check for one thousand dollars. The check was included with a beautiful wedding card that was lovingly signed,

'Much love to you and Steve, Diane darling. Devotedly, Aunt Dolly'.

Lily sent four place settings of our flatware.

Burtie sent an amazing antique sterling tray with a provenance that said it was Louis Quatorze, from her Antique Store. She had a little hobby shop that she dabbled with in Beverly Hills.

The rest of the gifts were lovely and they simply kept flocking to our door.

Interestingly, it must have been the year to give silver trays. My God! To this day I never run out of silver trays!

GODMOTHER OF THE BRIDE

In the spirit of my upcoming nuptials, Dolly insisted she host an extravagant party for the Denver wedding guests.

The gala was to be held a few days before the wedding. The entire bridal entourage and attending out-of-town guests were invited to her home for cocktails and dinner.

The godmother was thrilled to host the Denver dignitaries.

The exciting night of Dolly's lavish party, most of the bridesmaids and six groomsmen attended. So did the Hunts, the Senior Stockmars and several couples who flew in early for the festivities.

A dressy dark suit and cocktail frock evening, all the gentlemen looked distinguished in their formal attire and the ladies were glamorous in various confections of silks and laces.

As the guests of honor, Steve and I were ushered in the door by a man trumpeting our arrival with a saxophone.

There was a band, lavish food, and a sit down dinner for all the honored guests. Champagne flowed freely all night long.

Late in the evening, Dolly took Steve aside, leading him into the unoccupied, upstairs library. She needed to tell him a few things that were of upmost importance to her.

Dolly instructed him to always treat 'her darling Diane' with respect, as if I were a Queen. Dolly said she had overseen her godchild all her life. She insisted that Steve now was the one who must pick up the gauntlet and carry on. She told him that one day all her things would come to them both, but not to count on getting anything from her too soon, as she intended to live for many more years.

Steve, knowing in fact the real depth of the relationship, was anxious to convince my real mother that her precious daughter would be cared for throughout her life with him.

Steve assured her that he would always safeguard me. He'd fought too hard for my hand to ever allow me harm.

Dolly took him by the shoulders and cautioned that she could only do so much, especially since they were going to live so far away. She wanted Steve to know that if they ever needed help of any kind, all they had to do was call. She could and would arrange anything! Then, she told Steve that money always had its proper place. She was certain he would learn that, in good time. She saw them accomplishing wonderful things for themselves, but the bottom line was that if they needed something done properly and top flight, always pay the highest price. And never hesitate to come to her. She would always be there for them no matter what.

Steve assured Dolly that he knew he would never be financially in her league, but he hoped to provide me with everything I could ever want. He felt we were kindred souls, so much alike, driven by so many of the same goals. He assured her that when we got into a place where we were highly visible, and needed protection, he swore he would provide the best for me. He intended to run a bank before he turned forty, that was his goal.

Dolly embraced him warmly, saying, "You're a wonderful, young man, Steve Stockmar. I pray you both obtain your every goal."

They rejoined the party and continued to enjoy the fairy tale night.

The godmother was assured then that Steve Stockmar was a man of his word and would indeed care for her little Diane. She felt trust in this man. Even though he seemed so slight of build. He was a gentle boy with dark soulful eyes and a tall stature, but still immature and young. Dolly recognized that someday, Steve would be an incredibly striking man, but now he seemed like a young kid trying to play grown-up.

But so did her Diane. All ninety-pounds of the little waif. They were both only twenty-two. They seemed so vulnerable. Dolly only hoped this marriage would be a good one for her child.

The next morning when Dolly rushed into the pantry to make sure her silver was being wrapped in Pacific cloth, she saw the servants dutifully putting everything properly away.

Elinor Logan was helping tidy the disarray and inquired about last night's party. "How do you like the prospective groom?" nosily she asked her employer.

Dolly handed Maria a wad of protective cloth from the closet saying, "Wrap this up well, it may be a while before I entertain again, if I go to Italy, as planned."

She then turned her attention to Elinor, "Oh, Elinor, he really is a sweet young man. He seems very intelligent, but of course, no match for my Diane. I only hope she isn't in for a fall. He seems like quite a visionary, I just hope he can carry out his dreams. If he can, I'd say my little girl has hitched her wagon to quite a star. He said last night," she turned to help Maria tightly pack the candelabras in the brown cloth, "that he intended to run a bank before he became forty years old. That's Steve Stockmar's goal."

Elinor snorted with disbelief. She had looked at some of the Polaroid's that morning of the party. Maria identified Steve Stockmar to her. Elinor thought he looked far more capable to instruct a class in romantic poetry or lie in a meadow composing prose, than become a leader of a tough, banking team.

Elinor offered, "Time shall show I suppose. He's an attractive fellow, but I wonder what the years will bring?"

Dolly went off on an entirely different tangent, about how dreamy the Stockmar father was, and Elinor knew her motives there. She would hear little more about the qualities of Steve, when an older man was in competition for Dolly's attention.

CHAPTER FIFTY

Author's Notes:

I had spent the better part of 1969 planning for my wedding. Mother was not capable of the grueling meetings because of her frail constitution, so much of the planning was orchestrated by Dolly and me.

Dolly was the one who accompanied me to the Beverly Wilshire Hotel to make the arrangements for the elaborate rehearsal dinner. Though of course the Stockmars were responsible for the financials for that dinner, it was far easier for me to make all the plans as I was in California. Furthermore, we were having the reception there so I simply volunteered to do the arrangements of both events.

Dolly insisted that at the reception we serve only Champagne and that there could be an open bar for people that did not want to imbibe in the bubbly wine. Canapés and all manner of hor d'oeuvres were to be served. It was, after all, a late afternoon wedding. People were content in those days with heavy hor d'oeuvres and lots of libations.

A sit down dinner was to be served for the family and wedding party later, once the bride and groom had departed.

PRE D-DAY

June 5, 1970

The rehearsal dinner was to be held at the Beverly Wilshire Hotel where all the arrangements had been overseen by Hernando Courtright's skilled head of staff. Hernando oversaw much of the preparations at Dolly's insistence. She and Hernando were lifelong pals. The Courtwright children were her godchildren as well.

The rehearsal at All Saints Episcopal Church was routine. By then all the young groomsmen who had been asked to take part, were there, as were all my bridesmaids.

My sister Penny was my matron of honor, my bridesmaids were Susan Walsh, Katey Harris, Marsha Logan Geiger, and Annie Stockmar.

Steve's best man was his brother, Brian. The groomsmen were Steve Grey, Bobby Hawley, Reggie Fitz and Jay Geiger. Quite a handsome group all around.

My niece and nephew, Kelly and Scottie Martin, Were the ring bearer and flower girl.

The Rehearsal dinner, at the Beverly Wilshire Hotel was attended by many. Dolly was present as were Bami and Arthur Coperthwaite, their daughter, Jill and son Tee. My cousins, Linda and Johnny Martin, Penny's husband, Ted Benglen. Courtney Martin, my roommate, Steve's grandmother Mabel Harl, his Aunt Kitty O'Neale, all the bridesmaids and groomsmen were in attendance as well.

We were seated at long tables and the dinner was quite wonderful. The Beverly Wilshire Hotel was much respected for its dining experience and it excelled that night. I am quite certain that Dolly had a hand in that with Hernando overseeing everything.

One more day...the wedding would be upon us. Time was flying by too quickly for me to believe.

CHAPTER FIFTY-ONE

Author's Notes:

Maria Rivera related these happenings to me several weeks after the wedding when I called to check in. Dolly was away for the day. Maria related this sequence to me and it made me feel really quite sad.

Maria relayed that she was helping Dolly get ready for our wedding and this was how the afternoon proceeded.

WEDDING DAY BLUES

Dolly sat before her looking glass and adjusted the silk tie of her Bill Blass dress. She looked critically at her reflection in the mirror and was not particularly thrilled at what she saw. Her neck was wrinkled with crêpe and her eyes seemed to sag. She really needed more nips and tucks. She'd told Maria that she had plans to have plastic surgery in Naples next month, but until then, she would have to make do. Age was creeping up on her. She did not like the mantle it was cloaking her in the slightest bit.

She told Maria, "I long to be young again like my darling, Diane. What a beauty the child has turned out to be after all. Everyone thought Penny was going to be the staggering beauty, but my Diane had turned from an ugly duckling, into an enchanted swan. Steve is to be her prince. He is such a handsome, young man."

Carefully, Dolly applied the final touches of her make-up. Black eye pencil accented her eyes. They needed work, too.

"God, Maria how I hate growing older!" She was sixty-four now and felt the years had been none too kind.

Of course her excessive tanning in the early days had done nothing to help the aging of her face. For years she had baked herself to leather on the beach of Santa Barbara and all the foreign shores she roamed. She always had been a sun worshiper. So now she would have to pay the price. Lately, she had been having little cancer spots removed from her face. The doctor said they were not serious but to absolutely stay out of the sun.

Dolly rose from her dressing table and surveyed herself in the full length mirror in her room. She felt she looked quite elegant in her red and white silk by Mr. Blass. It was scrolled with embroidered, red silk at the cowl and on the sleeves. Her diamond and drop pearl Van Cleef and Arpels earrings were a dramatic jewelry touch. That and her enormous marquis diamond on her left hand, were all she wore in the way of jewels. Dolly looked very elegant as the unofficial Mother of the Bride.

"I feel a twinge of envy, Maria. Only a very few will know who Diane's mother really is at the wedding today."

Dolly went to gaze out a window that looked over 'the forever view of Los Angeles'. How her town had changed over the years. She recalled how she used to be able to look out and see all the way to the misty cloaked ocean of Venice Pier. She remembered when there was no airport in her town.

"Maria, I remember how in the olden days it was not unusual to look out the sash and see ladies and gentlemen riding fine horses down my unpaved street on their way back to the stables up at the end of the road."

Maria had joined her at the window looking down with her mistress. Dolly had sighed, "Times were more simple then than now."

Two Rolls Royces passed below at the intersection of Bellagio and Stone Canyon, roaring to their respective destinations. Everyone was in such a tear these days.

Dolly then checked her diamond-encrusted, Van Clef and Arpels watch. It told her it was only two-fifteen. The

Hunt wedding was at four, so she had plenty of time to reminisce.

Gliding down the winding marble staircase, Dolly and Maria went into the sun-room that overlooked the vast expanses of sculpted landscape that surrounded her property. Sunlight flooded the gorgeous room. Cymbidiums were positioned all around the glass doors that were flung open to admit the warmth of the early June day.

Dolly stood admiring the beautiful pictures of her daughter that crowded the top surfaces of each table in the room. She went from high-boy to chest, gazing at the snap-shots. Finally, she stood before an impressive portrait that hung on the sun-room wall. She had commissioned Peter Hurd to do the likeness of herself and her beautiful daughter, Diane. He had captured the darkly enchanting loveliness of them both.

Dolly stood there for some moments admiring the fabulous portrait. They looked so alike. She was always amazed that no one else seemed to notice! But it didn't matter, she knew the truth.

To Maria, the 'Grand Dame' said, "Is she not an exquisite girl?"

Maria replied, "No more enchanting that her mother, Mrs. Green."

"I only hope that my Diane's life experiencing a dual family has made her a fuller person. I feel reasonably comfortable with Diane's experiences. As always, the shadow of remorse raises its ugly head, taunting me that I failed as a mother." Dolly stood there trying to come to grips with her roller coaster emotions. In her own eyes, she always had been a travesty when it came to motherhood. She had repeatedly told Maria that fact. She was continuously remorseful over shirking her obligation to pursue her own life. This, above her commitment to raising her own beautiful child. Perhaps she was even envious of her own daughter's happiness in light of all the failures in her own life?

241

On this important day, she certainly knew she was jealous of the Hunt's involvement with her child. All these selfish feelings left her continuously plagued with maternal guilt. All those years ago it seemed so important to be foot-loose and fancy-free. Yet, she could never completely let Beau go. Dolly had to hold on to the child, insisting beyond contest, that she become the baby's, 'godmother'. She probably would have been far better off had she never seen the child again. She had to have her cake and eat it too.

This June day, Dolly's selfishness was paramount in her own eyes! If she had been more kind, less turned inward, she would be at the church today, recognized as Mother of the Bride, not simply the 'godmother'.

Easily, she could have raised Diane. But at the time, it seemed so out of the question. She was driven to get rid of her 'bothersome' child.

Dolly shook her head with remorse saying to Maria, "Had I only known then what I know now. If only I could turn back the hands of time and have my baby back. If only when the Hunts came that final time, sealing my decision's fate, I should have told them to go away. That I had changed my mind. They could not have my baby, 'Beau-Beau'. Not then, not ever! I was the little one's mother and I had decided to raise my own child. Not give her away like some unwanted, dolly. My selfishness and nonchalant attitude about the responsibility of the beautiful infant overshadowed my need to be accountable. My own pursuit of my life, unshackled by a child, pushed me to the decision to eliminate Beau from my everyday life. Now it is far too late to alter things, Maria. Twenty years, too late!"

Dolly had then deeply sighed, "Maria, the only thing I can do is carry on with my life the way it is, one day at a time. I am hoping against hope my guilt will not consume me completely over the passage of years. Diane will be moving to Colorado. Away from me forever. I will rarely see my daughter again."

There was nothing she could do to prevent this. And in all honesty, the Stockmars seemed like wonderful folks. Dolly believed that they would treat Diane well. She knew how horribly she would miss Diane.

But it was she who chose to give her child away. All those twenty years ago she made the choice. And today, she wondered if she had done the right thing? What if she had kept 'Beau-Beau'?

She stood there looking up at the portrait as if the oil image could answer her plea. No, Dolly rationalized, as always in the long run, her choice all those years ago was probably by far the best.

Then why did she always feel so ridden with guilt? Would she ever be able to sleep peaceful nights not wondering if giving up her child had not been the most selfish move of her life? The older she got, the more it preyed on her mind. If she had kept Diane, things would have been very different. For one, she never would have met Steve Stockmar. She would have met some potential studio executive or prospective lawyer and probably lead a far more up-beat life here in Los Angeles.

Certainly, if Diane had stayed with her, she would not be packing off to the wilds of Colorado with this Denver boy. Dolly never would have allowed her child to go so far afield to college.

Assuredly, if Diane had remained with her, she'd have found some nice LA man like all her Westlake classmates. They were all getting married and staying right here in their home town. Then Dolly would not be losing her child.

She blamed the Hunts for allowing Diane to venture so far away. If they had insisted she stay at UCLA, her Diane would probably be marrying a local boy.

Dolly prayed her daughter had carefully thought this marriage through. Steve seemed to be such a nice young man, but Dolly doubted he would be the force that could inspire Diane all her life.

Actually, Dolly feared it was more of a passion thing that motivated their union. All her marriages had been based on lust. When the flames cooled, so did the interest in one another. Then the whole thing crumbled like water against a sandy shore. She hoped it would be different for Diane, but like mother like daughter, that was the way the old saying went.

But was Diane like her, or had the girl subscribed to many of her adoptive mother's philosophies? After all, Ralph and Marie Hunt had been married almost fifty years.

Perhaps Diane was more like Marie than Dolly in her loyalties and goals. Only time would tell.

Dolly turned from the portrait and looked out over the view of the town. What would make Diane choose Colorado over this beautiful place? Dolly rationalized, she would never really know what motivated Diane to choose to move. She only hoped she would keep in touch and that her marriage would turn out better than all her mother's failures.

Impatiently, she checked her diamond-encrusted watch. It was three-fifteen.

She continued, "Maria, though All Saints is only fifteen minutes from our house, I absolutely do not want to be late!"

Her chauffeur, was waiting for her in the front hall.

"Whooee!" he whistled. "Don't you look exquisite, Mrs. Green?"

Dolly giggled and said, "Thank you. If you wouldn't mind, my dear charmer, get the car. I can't be late for Diane's big day."

He hurried off to fetch her Cadillac.

While Dolly and Maria waited, they did a brief tour of the downstairs. Dolly stopped at each gilt framed picture of her beloved Diane. Every coffee table, low-boy, high-boy and visible surface had a photo of her child encased in gold or silver. It was a walk down memory lane of all the fabulous events they had experienced together. They spanned from when Diane was six and seated on Dolly's massive, black Hunter horse, to pictures of them in Guadalajara, Santa Barbara and by the pool at Dolly's Bel Air home. One photograph was of Diane in the lovely blue and green formal the night of her Mexican Fiesta. It caught her attention. She picked it up and held it for some time. Dolly gazed lovingly at her daughter and was suddenly startled when Elinor interrupted her.

"Mrs. Green, you had better hurry or you miss Diane's big day. James honked, didn't you hear him?"

Dolly handed the photo to Elinor and said, "Isn't she the most stunning girl in the whole world? Oh, Elinor, I can't wait to see my darling Diane, as a bride." Not waiting for the secretaries' reply, she was off in a rush.

The ride to the church was brief. Dolly was ushered into the church and seated directly behind the family pew where her two sisters were awaiting her. She was thrilled to have such a good spot. Before she knew it, the processional was starting.

All rose to see the bride.

Tears sprung to Dolly's eyes when she saw her beloved, Diane. A vision of beauty in white. Her daughter was to her thinking that day, the most striking girl ever to be born. She adored her, had watched over her and in all effects, had guided her toward this wonderful day.

As she listened to Steve and Diane repeat the marriage vows, Dolly whispered a prayer that they would be forever in love the way they were on this day. That all their lives they would remain this close. That they would have a wonderful life together, and Dolly intended to continue to do everything that she could possibly do, to make their wishes all come true.

CHAPTER FIFTY-TWO

Author's Notes:

To my way of thinking, this was the day I had waited for all my life!

I was deeply in love and had made what I believed to be the right choice.

How could I know what lay ahead of me. Not only had my upbringing been tumultuous, but all my life would be something along the lines of a script for a Hollywood soap.

We have always had high drama in our lives and this was just one step along the way.

WEDDING D-DAY

June 6th, 1970

I had arranged to have a beauty day with Dorothy at Arden's. It was pretty amazing. Poor Dorothy had to do Mother, Penny and me all in the same morning! The rest of the girls did their own make-up and hair.

I remember arriving at the church and the photographer was there. I was dressed in a little mini-dress and I had never expected Mr. Huff to be that early and he caught me going up the stairs to the rectory to get dressed.

What a busy day.

Everyone was dressed and ready and the time was drawing to the hour of four.

Penny was fussing with my veil, adjusting it so it hung just right. "You look really beautiful, Beau. I always thought you were a lovely child but this is amazing. How gorgeous you are today! Steve is going to faint."

"Man, I hope not!" I quipped. "I'd hate to give CPR at the altar instead of exchanging rings and a kiss."

Penny and the rest of the girls giggled at that.

Susan Walsh added, "Hunt, you really are the consummate card."

We were told by the woman who oversaw the rectory that it was time to go to the front of the church.

We all rushed outside to get ready and hurried to the courtyard. The wind had come up and was blowing all our dresses around. We were all worried that our hair would get messed by the breezes. Fortunately, they stopped when we got in front of the Church.

The chapel was filled to capacity. I was truly amazed and actually thought then that we should have engaged the main church. But it was a little late for that.

The photographer was snapping pictures right and left. He caught a wonderful one of my dad peeking into the church with me happily smiling. It is one of my favorite pictures from that day.

The organ music began to trumpet the traditional Wagner's Bridal Chorus of here comes the bride. It was show time for us then.

The ceremony went without a hitch. I look back at the pictures today and it was exceptionally beautiful.

If any girl could have envisioned something more lovely than my wedding, it could only have been topped in my mind by someone like Lady Di's.

The reception was through in a flash it seemed. Champagne flowed like water, canapés were passed and everyone seemed to have a glorious time.

We posed for Mr. Huff. He managed to get Dolly, Burtie and me together in a wonderful photograph.

I thought the reception would never end. It was really exciting, but I was so busy talking to all the guests, that I never even had a glass of Champagne.

Penny insisted I go and change. Then Steve and I were off for the evening in a hail of rice. We drove away in our new Camaro that was a wedding gift from Mother and Dad.

We spent the night at the Westlake Village Hotel.

The following morning we were meeting Ted and Suzanne at Mom and Dad's to pack the van for the trip to Colorado.

Our honeymoon was to drive to Vail and spend some time at the Stockmar home there. It was an idyllic trip. We took our time and stopped at Bryce Canyon Arches, where we were in no hurry. It was a very fun and leisurely journey for a couple very much in love.

June 11th we celebrated my twenty-third birthday in Vail. It had snowed six inches overnight and Steve and I, the consummate young married adults, went out and had a snowball fight and built a snowman.

It was not exactly what anyone would call an exotic honeymoon, but we were anxious to get to Denver and set up our own little home.

****

The day following the wedding, the Los Angeles Times proclaimed these facts in its society column again written by Jodi Jacobs:

Miss Diane Melanie Hunt, daughter of Mr. and Mrs. Ralph Van Nice Hunt of Beverly Hills California, became the bride of Stephen Harl Stockmar of Denver on Saturday afternoon in All Saints Episcopal Church in Beverly Hills. He is the son of Mr. and Mrs. Ted Paul Stockmar from Denver.

The double-ring ceremony was performed by Dr. Kermit Castellanos. The church was decorated with white chrysanthemums, peonies, baby-breath and gladioli. A reception in the San Sourci Room of the Beverly Wilshire Hotel followed the ceremony.

The bride was given in marriage by her father, Ralph Van Nice Hunt. She wore a William Cahill Original gown of silk peau de soie and guipure lace with a Juliet pin-tucked panel front, lace collar, long pin-tucked sleeves and train. Her specially designed illusion veil of heirloom lace was fastened to a small cap. She carried a colonial bouquet of white baby roses, daisies and stephanotis and baby's-breath.

Mrs. Theodore G. Benglen of Canoga Park, California was the matron of honor, Miss Anne Stockmar, sister of the groom, Mrs. John Geiger of Denver, Miss Susan Walsh of Vail and Miss Katherine Harris of Washington D.C. were attendants.

They wore William Cahill gowns of white dotted Swiss with empire bodices, high necklines and long sleeves. They carried colonial bouquets of vari-colored flowers.

John Brian Stockmar was the best man for his brother. Robert Hawley Jr. and John Geiger of Denver, Steven Grey of Mound, Minn. And Reginald Fitz of Albuquerque, N.M. were ushers.

The bride's mother wore an Elizabeth Arden turquoise and white print dress and coat ensemble, white kid shoes and bag and a white bow in her hair.

The groom's mother wore a short tucked gown of cameo pink chiffon with a high round neckline, long bishop sleeves and a full hip-pleated skirt.

The bride was graduated from the Westlake School for Girls. She attended the University of California and graduated from Colorado College. She was presented at the Coronet Ball in 1965.

The groom is a graduate of George Washington High School and Colorado College.

The bride is the granddaughter of the late Mr. and Mrs. H.G. Pfost of Clinton, Mo. and the late Mr. and Mrs. George A. Hunt of Denver.

The groom is the grandson of Mrs. Maple T. Harl and the late Mr. Harl of Denver and Mr. and Mrs. Ted Paul Stockmar Sr. of Denver.

After a wedding trip to Vail, the couple well be at home in Denver.

Guests at the wedding included the groom's grandmother, Mrs. Maple T. Harl, the bridegroom's aunt, Mrs. Felix O'Neill, Mr. and Mrs. Arthur T. Cowperthwaite and their daughter, Jill and son Tee. The William Kellogs of Lajolla, Courtney Martin of Kalamazoo MI. and the Valentine Logans of Denver were reveler's as well.

Other guests that joined the party were Mrs. Dorothy Green and her sisters, Mrs. William Bettengen and Mrs. William Raines.

CHAPTER FIFTY-THREE

Author's Notes:

From here till the nineties when Dolly died, I am going to give the reader vignettes of our lives. I won't bore you with the minutia, just the higher points that culminated to where we eventually landed and are to this day.

We had a lot of bumps, humps, lumps and hurts. But in all, in retrospect, we learned a lot with every jostle and jab!

We had a lot of highs as well, but the old adage that you remember the challenging issues more than the everyday joys, often rules the day.

DENVER DAZE

Shortly after our marriage, Dolly announced that she planned to visit Denver and wanted me to get her set up in the Presidential Suite at the Brown Palace Hotel.

Excited by this prospect, my mother-in-law, Suzanne, bustled about setting elaborate plans in place for a huge party honoring the 'Grand Dame'.

All the blue-bloods of Denver society would be invited, even a few Cherry Hills couples would be invited to be in the mix at the Stockmars' gala at the Cherry Street home.

Dolly was duly picked up at the airport having been flown there in a friend's private jet.

After greeting one another, we drove Dolly to the Brown where we got her settled in her luxurious suite.

I was a bit concerned what Dolly might think of our small home, but there was nothing we could do. We were a young married couple and the little house was very special to us. When she eventually saw our home, she was polite but I am sure was secretly appalled. Our first home was approximately the size of her bedroom suite.

One evening all the Stockmars arrived at the Brown Palace Hotel's, Ships Tavern for dinner. Dolly picked up the bill after fighting over the chit with Ted. It was 'her trip and her treat' and she would hear of nothing otherwise. So that was to be the deal of the entire stay.

The party at the Stockmar's was lavish by Denver standards. There was a cast of thousands there. Suzanne had it catered and it was a very sumptuous affair. She'd had florists bring beautiful arrangements that were placed throughout the home.

It was a magical night where people enjoyed visiting with Dolly immensely. She was truly a fascinating individual and at parties, really could put on the 'Grand Dame' show.

During Dolly's stay, we drove her around the Denver Country Club and Cherry Hills to show her the beautiful homes and for her to get a feel for the lay of the land.

Dolly said, "Diane, there is nothing here as grand as Beverly Hills or Bel Air. These homes are stately, but hardly mansions. I hope you have chosen well by moving here. When Steve is finally in the upper financial leagues, where on earth do you plan to live?"

I was at a bit of a loss after that comment, as I thought many of the lovely areas that surrounded Denver had stately homes. I would happily live in any one of them.

I answered, "We will manage, Dolly and we don't really aspire to live in a 'mansion'. We'd love to have a nice, manageable home as I will more than likely always be the hired help."

Dolly had a lively sense of humor and retorted, "Well, I hope that will be the case about the housing, but not about the help."

The trip was a whirlwind and Dolly seemed satisfied that her 'little chick' was well taken care of. But it was shortly after she got home, she pressed on me her need to send me monthly checks.

Dolly insisted, "You seem fine, but I would feel a great deal better if I could help a bit!"

Steve and I actually argued about that gesture. Initially, he refused to take her 'hand-out'. So I secretly accepted the gifts and we ate far better because of Dolly's help.

It was not a lot, one hundred a month. But in those days so long ago, one hundred was a huge amount of money. I look back to then and think of my weekly food budget which was around twenty dollars and we ate quite well. Now twenty dollars at the market will buy little but some butter, bread and eggs!

As for us, with an income of four-hundred-seventy-five dollars a month, the hundred was positively a Godsend.

In October of 1970, Mother and Dad were also to come to Denver. But on the eve of the trip, Mother was stricken by a massive heart occlusion and barely survived the trip to the hospital. She did live, but was very ill and I traveled out to California every third weekend of the month to be with her. Daddy would buy my ticket and send it to me. No way could we have suffered the expense.

We were able to buy a lovely small home on High Street in 1972. Mom and Dad helped us with a down payment and Steve sold stocks and bonds to come up with the balance of the six-thousand dollar down payment.

I asked Dolly if she could help with a loan, but she actually seemed surprised that I would ask her.

She said, "Di, you should be asking Ralph and Marie. They are your parents after all and I am just your godmother. If they don't give it to you, then I will help. However, you would need to pay it back!"

I had asked to 'borrow' the funds in the first place and was actually offended by her alluding to the fact that we would not repay the debt. So I *never ever* asked her for any funds again.

Fortunately, Mom and Dad came through, so we got the house. So our early married life marched along.

I was working for a dentist and traveling back and forth to California to be with my ailing mom.

She and Daddy celebrated their fiftieth wedding anniversary in September of 1972 and then two weeks later she died as the result of an operation.

We went to her funeral and Dolly and Burtie attended. It was a tragically sad affair. Daddy was devastated over her death. I was as well and hoped that I would be able to have a visit with Dolly. I needed to be consoled concerning my mother's loss, but that was not to be. I was not able to have a separate visit with Dolly at that time. She was too busy to fit me into her schedule, so we promised to meet again sometime soon when I was next in L.A.

It was not until I got home and back to normalcy, that I realized how much I was going to miss my mother, Marie. She had been such a constant guiding force in my life. She had been a rock upon which I placed so many of my life decisions and with her gone, I felt adrift at sea.

CHAPTER FIFTY-FOUR

Author's Notes:

Looking back on those early days, Denver life was pretty simple for a little gal from such a dazzling town as Beverly Hills. Denver was a relatively small, quiet and unsophisticated city, so far from the maddening crowd of L.A.

I remember being amazed that very often I could not get artichokes in the market. They were a particular favorite of Steve and mine. You could get them any time of year in L.A. but not in Denver.

Of course we had little money but it seemed we did just fine.

We were in love and everything was rosy. Now it was time to start family life.

BABYHOOD BLISS

Steve had been promoted to a senior position in the bank, so it was determined with his increased salary, it was time to think of having kids.

We were planning to have a baby so I quit working for Dr. Don Larson as soon as I learned that I was pregnant.

We had known Steve would be coming along in the banking field and the timing was good.

Dolly was in touch with me a great deal during that time and she was elated to hear that I was pregnant. We spoke far more frequently then as she was monitoring how things were progressing.

I was playing tennis everyday and just lounging around the pool waiting for the birth of our child.

Timothy Hunt Stockmar was born August 23rd, 1973 after a long, hot, Denver summer.

Getting used to parenthood was as all new parents know...trying at times. Tim was challenging to put it mildly! But we tried to go along with the day to day flow.

Tim was a very active child and it was interesting for me to be a mother, as I really never had adored children at all.

Tim was a very busy child and I did his early rearing very much on my own. Steve was traveling for the bank a great deal in those days.

I was inducted into the Junior League and went through the training routine. Friendships that were built through that particular affiliation, we both enjoyed as couples.

Life went on from there with busy motherhood and just the days of our Denver lives.

In 1975, Dad was planning a move from Thousand Oaks to San Marino. He had fallen in love with a woman who had been a previous acquaintance of my parents.

He was planning to move in with Mary B. Taylor at her San Marino home. So he had sold the home in Thousand Oaks and was liquidating his furnishings.

I went out to help him stage a garage sale. I took a break from the item pricing routine and arranged to have lunch with Dolly in the middle of the week.

Tim and I arrived early for the lunch. As per usual, Dolly was late getting home from a morning appointment.

Maria and I were able to catch up on things while we waited for Dolly to arrive and I put Tim down for a nap.

Dolly shortly arrived and cooed over Timmy who immediately was charmed by her. He played on the floor with her enormous Saint Bernard, Leica.

We had a huge white Shepherd at the time named Bismarck, so Tim was entirely used to large dogs mauling him.

We had lunch together at Dolly's home on Bellagio Road and she was much her old self. She was chatty and interested in my life in Denver, particularly thrilled that

I had joined the Junior League. The luncheon was a nice interlude in a week of work with Daddy's sale.

I was back in Denver before I knew what happened and back in the swing of things there.

Steve was rising in the bank and business kept him very busy. He was promoted to be a Vice President in the Real Estate department of the First National Bank of Denver.

In the late seventies, he went on to be a senior Vice-President at First Bank, and was climbing all the time.

About the same time, we became involved with the Rocky Mountain Jaguar Club when we acquired a vintage Jag Saloon. We began restoring both Healey's and old Jag's. The club was a source of a couples' friendship and connection. We were members for many years. Many fun events, races, drives and parties were staged by that club. Steve was the President of The Rocky Mountain Jaguar Club for seven consecutive years and I was the Treasurer.

I became involved in a newly founded chapter of Achievement Awards for College Scientists, and later in the seventies, was appointed the President of that organization.

I served on a plethora of additional committees from chairing the Children's Hospital November Noel, to the Debutant Ball Committee.

Little Tim was growing like a weed. Much of my time was occupied with his care and shuttling him to events. It was a very busy time in our lives.

I continued to have good contact with Dolly, as we chatted at least bi-monthly. She frequently called me to keep in touch.

In 1978, Burton Green's Belridge Oil Company was sold to Shell Oil for 3.8 billion dollars and the ten shareholders got millions.

Steve noticed the article in the *Wall Street Journal*, Thursday October 18th 1979.

The article proclaimed:
'Family Fortune: Belridge Oil Heirs React to 3.65 Billion
in Shyness':
An excerpt from the press release:
'Shell Oil Company announced today that it has
bought a Bakersfield based oil company, Belridge,
owned by the late Burton Green.

Green, who died in 1958, was one of the founders of
Beverly Hills'.

The primary shareholders were reluctant to talk to the
press.

Today the Whittiers, Bucks and Greens don't rank
among the super-rich, but they are certainly wealthy. The
Whittier and Green families, in particular, have
considerable holding in other oil properties outside of
Belridge. Thus say the family member who will talk, the
Belridge millions won't change their lives that much.
One member of the Green family who won't be
identified put it this way: "When you have all you want,
some more doesn't mean that much!"

The three daughters of the founder, Burton Green were
reluctant to be interviewed.

"Publicity doesn't make it nice for us," explained one
of the sisters, Liliore G. Rains.

Another Green family member says that the sisters
who own 63,284 shares worth $231.9 million are
particularly fearful of kidnappers."

****

Dolly called me and was ecstatic over the fact that with
this money, she intended to 'seriously get into horses, as
I have longed to do all my life'. This allowed Dolly to
really get into the full swing of race-track life.

Dolly was very open and conversational about her
newly inherited money. That year she upped my
Christmas check to three thousand dollars. She had

previously been sending the one hundred a month and then twelve hundred dollars at Christmas.

****

After a legendary party at the Bistro, Jody Jacobs, the Society Editor for the Los Angeles Times had splashed the Social Page of the morning paper with the details of the bash:

This article that was published in the *LA Times*, dated July 23, 1980 by columnist Richard Hoffer read:

DOLLY GREEN, MYSTERY WOMAN!
Racing's Hot New Owner

'Dolly Green whisked into Lexington, Ky., the other day in a chartered jet. Before whisking back to Los Angeles Tuesday, she had bought five thoroughbred horses in Keeneland's July Selected Yearling Sale. She had paid $2.0 Million, including $1.4 million for a bay colt of proven parentage.

Although not a record, it was topped Tuesday by a Greek shipping magnate who paid a world record $1.7 million for a similar bay colt-Green's bid was nevertheless newsworthy.

Except for a paid subscription to the Racing Form, delivered daily to her Bel Air home, Monday's bid was said to mark her fist fiscal involvement in a very expensive, very chancy sport.

Green's bid took all of horse racing by surprise, both for the amount bid and for her obscurity in racing circles. Nobody could recall seeing her around the Kenneland stables before. Nobody, for that matter, remembered seeing her around Southern California tracks. No turf people had even heard of her, unusual in a sport where the money is nearly as inbred as the horses.

Described as a "mystery woman" in early wire service reports, Green did little to lift the veil before leaving at the start of the second and final day of the sale. She was back on her jet before all but a few reporters at the sale had an opportunity to talk to her. And there wasn't that much talk at that. She originally gave her address in its entirety, as California. She elaborated for one reporter, "Los Angeles," she told the reporter, "But please don't print that."

So there wasn't much at all known about horse racing's latest high roller except that for a novice she sure spent a lot of money.

"Put it another way," a horse racing buff said, "for anybody, she spent a lot of money."

As it turns out, Green can well afford it and, if her sudden stable doesn't pan out right away, she can do it again next year if she wants. A newcomer to horseracing-"This is my first venture into thoroughbreds." She told one reporter-she is no newcomer to money. She is the daughter of Burton Green, the man who is popularly believed to have "built" Beverly Hills. And she is an heiress to Belridge Oil Co., recently sold to Shell Oil Co. for $3.65 billion. It was reported that Green, a major stockholder along with her two sisters, received $231 million from the sale. "And she was rich before that," an observer of the Los Angeles social scene said.

Green's entry into the world of horse racing may have been sudden, but those who know her and are willing to talk say it is not ill-conceived. According to Brownell Combs, whose father, Leslie Combs II, owns Spindrift Farms and who owned the five yearlings Green bought, Green has been, "coming around as a spectator for thirty years. She goes to the races and has just generally kept up with it. She's an old friend of my father's and apparently has been planning something like this for a long time. She's gotten the best advice, arranged for the best trainer and I think has bought the best horses. That's the only way to succeed in this business."

'Green has prepared in ways additional to subscribing to the Racing Form. She enlisted the help of Jimmy Kilroe, director of racing at Santa Anita and Hollywood Park and one of the most respected and knowledgeable men in the horse racing to begin with. Kilroe did not make the trip because of illness. But his wife, Martha Kilroe, Green's good friend, did. So much for the right advice. Green also contracted for the services of Laz Barrera, horse racing's leading trainer the last four years. And finally, Green went for the best horses money could buy.

Her $1.4 million bid went for a horse by Northern Dancer, the 1964 Kentucky Derby winner, out of Gold Digger. Buying horses for the purpose of racing is considered one of the world's great long shots, but buying horses by Northern Dancer, is as close to a sure thing as you can get. Northern Dancer has produced 64 stake winners. The colt Green bought is a half brother to Gold Standard, who earned $160,000 racing, and to Mr. Prospector, who earned $112,000.

She also paid $275,000 for a filly by Raise A Native, $250,000 for a colt by the Ax II out of My Guest, and $135,000 for a Majestic Prince colt out of Easter Robin. "She's been thinking about this a long time," said the junior Combs, who handles the day to day operation for Spendthrift Farms.

'Although Green had no previous experience in horse racing except that gained from visiting Combs at his Lexington horse farm, she reportedly has been around horses for a while. She was involved in steeplechase jumping and Hunting horses at one time and recently served on a social committee at Santa Anita for the National Horse Show.

She is "Just a great Gal," one acquaintance was quoted saying, "Suddenly competitive in horseracing, but she is still a mystery woman for most and always will be."

****

A Subsequent Article in *The Los Angeles Times*:
Times Staff Writer Richard Hoffer on July 24, 1980:

SHE JUST LOVES HORSES, MYSTERY WOMAN SAYS:

'Dolly Green, the so-called mystery woman who came from nowhere (or at least Bel Air) to plunk down $2.2 million for five yearlings at the celebrated Keeneland sale, is evidently more than just another oil heiress with money to burn.

She is also an excitable horse lover whose reaction to her new heady status in the world of horse racing, is: "I feel like I'm going to faint."

'Green, who paid 1.4 million for a bay colt in the Monday bidding at Lexington, Ky., returned to Los Angeles in a chartered jet but not to judge by the breathless quality in her voice to earth. "Oh, it was the most exciting thing." She said referring to the auction. "I couldn't believe after all these years, I was actually bidding on a horse. I'd never been there(to a sale)before. My goodness, all I'd ever done before was go to the races-that's as close as I ever got. And I watched them from the director's room at that. And then to bid that kind of money for a horse. My I did have some trepidations."'

'She is the daughter of Burton Green, developer of Beverly Hills, and recently profited from the 3.65 billion sale of Belridge Oil Co. in which she was a large stockholder.'

Plenty of help: 'She was aided in her venture by counsel from Jimmy Kilroe, director of racing at several California tracks. And she made sure to buy her horses from one of the sport's leading breeders (and close friend of Leslie Combs II.)'

"With these people helping me, it made it a good time to get into horse racing," she said."I'd always thought about it but just never did. I had a feeling this year, I said, 'I'm just going to do it.' I decided to be very brave and go ahead."

"Oh, I know all the pitfalls-horses break down and what not. For all the fun you can have, it can be hell, too. Somebody told me long ago not to ever get married to a race horse. But I just felt I was ready."

Love at First Sight:

'It helped too, that she fell in love with the bay colt at first sight. "Let me tell you about this big brown colt," she said breathlessly. "Just everybody wanted him and I knew he would go very high-the prices are just astronomical. But he's by Northern Dancer, the Derby winner(1964) and out of Gold Digger, a pretty good horse, too. So I was prepared to go high."

'The British Bloodstock Agency of Ireland offered $1.3 million for the bay colt. "I never would have bought him if I didn't like his looks," Green said. "I don't know about all the proper angles of the feet and legs, but I just loved the looks of that horse. I petted him and kissed and hugged him after I had bought him. And his eyes-they say if their eyes aren't kind, if they don't look human, don't take him because he'll resist you-they were beautiful. It's still a gamble, I know all about that, but I just love that colt."'

Dolly seemed suddenly to become a darling of the press as she had been so formerly reclusive. As had the entire family Green.

****

This article was from the Los Angeles Times dated January 30, 1981 and was reported by Jody Jacobs:

THE SUBJECT WAS HORSES AT THOROUGHBRED PARTY

'Dolly Green isn't new to racing. The daughter of Burton Green, (one of Beverly Hills founding fathers

263

and former owner of Belridge Oil Corporation), she's always been interested in horses. But it wasn't until July when she spent $2.2 million for five thoroughbreds that the interest became serious. "And now that she is in racing," said a good friend and advisor, Mrs. Frank Kelroe, "she wants to meet the horse world." The horse world; or at least a great portion of it was in Los Angeles a few days ago for the Thoroughbred Racing Association meeting.

So Dolly Green invited quite a few of them to a black-tie seated dinner dance at the Bistro.

A large horseshoe filled with red carnations greeted her guests as they reached the top of the stairs at the popular restaurant. In the party room, Flower Fashions had taken Dolly's racing colors-red and gold-and run with them: masses of red carnation and roses anchoring racing silks to the walls, tall epergnes overflowing with the flowers on lace over red covered tables.

The hostess stood in the doorway with her guest of honor, Leslie Combs II, who owns Spendthrift Farms in Lexington, Ky., and from whom Dolly acquired her thoroughbreds. She wore a red silk broad-shouldered jacket and long skirt embroidered in gold thread designed by Karl Langerfeld of Chloe.

"I'm wearing Chloe perfume, "Dolly added with a happy chirp to her voce as she extended a hand to welcome Gloria and Jimmy Stewart, Alfredo de la Vega, and Mervyn and Kitty LeRoy.

Some of the Regan 'inner circle' who'd been in Washington for the Inauguration were clustering about talking about past events.

"Good thing we're here tonight," commented Gloria Stewart, part of that circle, "otherwise we'd be at home suffering from withdrawal."

Betsey(in a pale peach strapless Dior with satin coat) and Alfred Bloomingdale, Campbell Bradt, Virginia

Milner, Erlenne Perkins and Marion and Earle Jorgensen all agreed it was so.

Cuban-born Laz Barerra, for the past four years the leading trainer in the United States, was just back from Venezuela and saying the race track in Caracas is "the best in the Americas." He also had some nice things to say for the hostess who had chosen him to train her horses, among them Arco and Premier Minister, both of whom have already won big races. "She's a great woman," he told Dorothy Lauglin (down from Santa Barbara) and Dorothy's-in-law Wheelock Whitney. "And I want her to enjoy racing."

Liz Whitney Tippet, Marjie Everett, Clement and Lynn Hirsch, Mrs. George Pope of San Francisco, Whitney Tower, Howard and Libby Keck, Robert and Betty Strub and Jimmy Kilroe were all on one subject, most of the evening-horses, naturally. Sonny Werblin, who was once and agent(Ronald Regan was one of his clients) but switched later to horses, commented that it was 'all the same kind of business...selling tickets!" And no one denied it.

A race track trumpeting of sound brought everyone in to dinner and from then on it was dance, dance, dance to Joe Moshay's music. Some of those on and off the floor were Gladys Knapp with Gaylord Hauser, Palmer and Charles Ducommun(who was recalling that as a young Navel officer he'd attended President Harry Truman's swearing in) the Ricardo Montalbans, Hernando Courtright (Fiorenza was not feeling well) Ted Besinger nursing a bruised leg, Daniel Donohue, Frances Bergen wearing violet sequins, Irene Dunn, Lorena Nidorf in Bill Blass' velvet and silk dress, Bill Frye(off to England in a few days to start working on his new film), Jim Wharton, Richard Gully, Lou and Bill Dougherty, Mary and Brad Jones, Curt and Priscilla Tamkin, Mrs. Sidney Brody, the Howard Keck Jr's., Joan and Pat Cotton and Bob Foreward.

At the last moment a few guests phoned in sick and a few guests brought a few friends. It kept the hostess busy rearranging her place cards, but it didn't dampen her spirits in any way.'

****

All the sudden press coverage should have been a tip-off to me that she was becoming slightly mentally challenged. Because before, Dolly absolutely refused to be interviewed. Then suddenly she seemed to become a real media darling.

Several articles appeared about her in various presses.

I remember one *Los Angeles Times* article, where she was pictured in her home with her beautiful Saint Bernard, Leica. A friend who lived in L.A., knowing my connection to Dolly, sent me the clipping. It was sometime in the early eighties. Had I focused on the fact that she gave such an in depth interview, I would have been alarmed. Greens never did things such as that.

Red flags were being flung into the air and I was too immersed in my own daytime soap drama of our own lives that I completely missed the danger signs.

Dolly had been so paranoid of someone kidnapping me as a child, that she and Ralph constantly argued over that. We had male protection until I was well into my teens.

But the Green that was most concerned about the kidnapping was Dolly. She had told me why in one of our numerous fireside chats. There was an attempt on her early in her life, Dolly saw the kidnapper gunned down before her very eyes.

Once I was off to college and Dolly was sure that I was not under that frightening threat, did she allow the constant shadowing of me to finally cease.

CHAPTER FIFTY-FIVE

Author's Notes:

The eighties brought about many changes in our lives, some wonderful, some memorable and many best forgotten.

Dad became severely ill with cancer in August of 1981 and died in early September. I was able to fly out to be with him immediately after the illness was diagnosed.

He was in the hospital and I was there with him over the Labor Day weekend. The following weekend he was dead.

It was a horrible time for me. His illness was sudden, as an undetected brain tumor had been affecting his speech a bit. Then, like a wildfire back-draft, went out of control and Daddy was gone.

So for me, it was an unbelievably tragic and sad time.

I talked to Dolly when we were in L.A. for Daddy's services, but she was not available to attend the graveside service at Forest Lawn.

GOODNIGHT SWEET PRINCE

Mary B. arranged Daddy's funeral. It was a horribly tragic time for me as I just was not prepared to lose Daddy. He had seemed such a young eighty-one. A prince of a man, my dearest father. I could just not believe Daddy was gone!

Tim was only eight at the time and it was a traumatic time for him as well, losing his doting grandfather.

In order to try to alleviate the trauma, we decided that Tim and Steve should go to Disneyland while I went to have lunch with Dolly.

Steve had become the President of Marvin Davis's Metro Bank in 1980. It was the same year that Davis bought Twentieth Century Fox.

I told Dolly about the fact that Steve had become the President of Davis's bank and she was displeased that he was working for Marvin. After Davis bought Twentieth Century Fox, he changed everything at the studio. He even fired one of Dolly's long time friends. Dolly was really pissed. Marvin fired many of her pals and Dolly told me what a jerk she thought Davis was. She made a comment that "it would be a cold day in hell before Marvin and Barbara Davis were on *her* party guest list."

During my luncheon visit, Dolly was accompanied by her Saint Bernard Leica, who lay faithfully at her side.

Maria bustled in and out.

Maria was always thrilled to see the two of us together and made no bones about how pleased she was to see me. She hugged me enthusiastically at the door every time I arrived.

Dolly and I visited, I showed her pictures of Timmy who was still small at eight. We had a lovely lunch of Crab Louis and 'Cook' had fixed a yummy dessert of poached pears.

During the lunch, again Dolly took off on Marvin Davis. She went on and on how people in the movie industry hated the man! This was even to the point of laughing heartily over the fact that her pal, George Lucas was going to portray Davis as a slug like creature in an upcoming *Star Wars* movie called *Return of the Jedi*. Again she railed about how Lucas was going to get his licks in on Davis. His whole Twentieth Century Board of Directors would all be portrayed as horrible slug-like creatures in the movie to pay Davis back for his heartless takeover the studio.

I thought it was bazaar!

However, when I eventually saw *Return of the Jedi* in 1983, it took me no time at all to realize that Jabba the

Hutt and his band of boys, were exactly as alleged. Marvin Davis and his merry band of men were portrayed in the movie as the aforementioned slugs. I recalled Dolly's words then and laughed over the sly Lucas payback. Betting to myself, that Marvin would probably never figure it out!

But that idyllic luncheon interlude, with my godmother, would prove to be the last time I would see Dolly in good health.

****

When we got home from California, I received a note from Dolly that read:

Di dear,

What a shock your father's death was. It was a blessing though that he did not linger. I am sending a donation to the American Cancer Society. I know it is always a terrible thing to lose one's Dad.

It was so good to see you, even though a sad occasion. I send you deepest sympathy and much love always.

Fondly,

Your Aunt Dolly

CHAPTER FIFTY-SIX

Author's Notes:

Being the token 'Wonder Goy' of Marvin's bank had its drawbacks for me. I needed to constantly shop for clothing to attend the myriad of 'events' to which 'Mrs. President Goy' needed to attend.

I have never been one to LOVE shopping, so for me it was an utter bore. Not to mention what an enormous financial drain!

I the meantime, I had begun my literary career and was writing a book called Merlin's Ring.

Steve bought me a really good word processor after dad died. So all the social whirl was interfering with my time when I wanted to write.

But to the best of my ability, I bucked up and played my part as 'society queen'.

MARVIN DAVIS' 'WONDER GOY' AND HIS FAITHFUL SIDEKICK, DIANE

Our lives went on with Steve at the helm of the Davis bank. Therefore, it was imperative that I play the President's wife.

Our financial status with my dad's inheritance and Steve's increase in salary, enabled me to support the horrible wardrobe dilemma that presented itself. I shouldn't ever appear at an event in the same outfit. So I was a great client of Auer's, an exclusive shop in Cherry Creek.

It was during this time that Barbara Davis conceptualized the Carousel Ball. The committee, though made up of many prominent Jewish women, also had a few token 'goys'. I fell right into that category.

There were several events that built up to the Balls happening. The very first meeting was at the Davis home on Sunset Drive in Cherry Hills. I remember going with my mother-in-law, Suzanne, who was the press liaison. She was also a very close friend with Pat Smedley who was the Society Editor of the *Denver Post* at the time.

Naturally we were all three dressed to the nines to go to the 'Queen Bee', Barbara Davis's court. As we arrived and parked, the drive was clotted with cars and security men talking into wrist radios, rushing about. They seemed to grudgingly let us by, but were rude as hell. There was a cast of thousands there.

I could count the other token 'goy's' as I began to refer to ourselves.

Barbara had chosen Chartan Martin as the Chairman of the Ball. She must have felt it was imperative for her to have a important socialite 'goy' at the helm. Barbara's daughter, Nancy Davis was Co-Chairman.

Chartan had asked several of her friends to be on the committee, as she did wanted things done correctly. The Jewish American Princess's (JAPS) were notorious for not getting things done quite right. Their forte was far more along the lines of outdoing one another with the obscene 'Bas' and 'Bar Mitzvahs', that seemed all the eighties rage. Steve and I were also expected to attend those.

The luncheon was lavish and due to the massive numbers was obviously served buffet style.

We all had little nametags to identify ourselves. I told Pat and Suzy I loved meetings where the numbers were so many that it was more like a Denver Bronco game that a normal committee meeting. 'Babbs just loved to entertain!

I recall meeting Barbara for the first time as I walked through the lunch line, and she amazed me by saying, "Oh, you are the wife of Marvin's new President, the 'Wonder Goy' at Metro bank."

You know, I just did not quite know what to say. So, I replied, "Yes Mrs. Davis, I am Steve Stockmar's wife."

"Well," she smiled and said, "I will be seeing a lot more of you then, my dear." She then flashed a signature Barbara Davis smile.

We made our way into a sitting room off the living area that was decorated all in snow-white chairs. Two enormous couches and four over-stuffed white chairs completed the décor.

I was eating my lunch, seated on either side by Suzanne and Pat, when chanced to look down at the edges of the opposing couch. I could not believe my eyes. I then began to look around at the rest of the pieces of furniture. All were the same. Every corner of ever sofa and chair was bright yellow. Steve had told me that the Davis' had several enormous German Sheppard watchdogs and there was the evidence of the canines 'tagging' right before my eyes.

I whispered to Suzanne to look. At the time she had a dog named Charlie, a white Highland terrier who had never been properly potty trained. Charlie was notorious for lifting his leg on the couches in the Stockmar home.

So I leaned over to Suzanne and said, "Look the Davis couches had been 'Charlied' too!" Then I began to laugh.

It was infectious!

Suzanne leaned over to Pat who also looked and burst into laughter.

Pat whispered to Chartan, who then whispered to Sandy Clanahan who whispered to Muriel Newell, who in turn passed it on to Betty Lynn Jackson.

The whole room dissolved into a riot of gales of laughter.

I heard later that Sunny Bronstein asked her good pal Cindy Farber what on earth the silly 'Goys' in the sunroom found 'so damn funny'?

No one but us silly 'Goys' knew and we weren't about to tell the 'JAPS'.

****

During the time Steve was employed by Marvin, I developed an amazing disrespect for the young Denver society women of the Jewish faith.

Mostly they had obscene amounts of money, as their husbands were primarily attorneys. They all spent indecent amounts of dough that they felt was their right to spend. They never worked a day in their lives, many had never had any form of vocation ever.

Obviously a fundraiser of the magnitude of the Carousels Ball took a fairly large and organized committee. There were the lavish luncheons that were enjoyable, but then there was gobs of work as well.

I remember one particular meeting at which we were to address and stamp the invitations. Unfortunately for me, I got there late and there were only a few seats available. An obvious vacant one was next to a stunning blond whose hair was always a mystery to me. It was so huge that I wondered if she did not have a nest of birds living in there. But all the proper 'Japs' predominantly sported very large hair.

This particular woman was wife to one of Marvin's lead attorneys, who also performed a lot of counsel with Steve.

I sat down next to 'Blondzilla' with the enormous hair.

Materials were passed around to stamp the envelopes and I began my chore industriously. After some moments, I realized my table-mate was gazing around as if confused.

I asked, "Is there something you need?"

'Ms. B.' batted her eyes and replied, "Oh, no. I was just trying to see which side of the envelope a stamp was supposed to be placed."

I was floored but asked, "Have you never stamped a letter yourself?"

'Ms. B.' replied, "Heavens no! That is what a personal assistant is for." So that pretty much finished our lively dissertation for the day.

I did my job and went home, marveling at the intelligence of 'Ms. B.'

Oh my!

The ball went off with not a glitch and the royalty was flown from Hollywood to sit on the Dias and oversee the elaborate benefit.

Attending were John Forsyth and Linda Evans, Lucille Ball, the Arthur Linkletters and Jimmy Stewarts, to name a selected few.

It was dubbed 'the charity event of the year' by the *Denver Post* Society Editor, Pat Smedley.

Then there were the 'Bas' and 'Bar Mitzvah's'. These extravaganzas made me wonder if the women had not been raised in Hollywood and been exposed to the birthday parties as had I?

One was a *Star Wars* theme, and it was complete with all the cast of the movie this included the dreaded and feared Darth Vader! The parent's flew the cast in on Marvin's private plane.

There was one theme party set up like *Gilligan's Island,* with a tropical backdrop, complete with hula dancing women and men in Hawaiian shirts. They were clad in cutoffs and rushed around serving parasol drinks to the guests.

Another theme was the Hollywood set of the *Terminator.* It was completed by the appearance of Arnold S.

Other examples are too numerous and silly to list, but I do think you get the gist.

So between the Carousel Ball Committee and all the other committees I was bouncing between, I was the ultimate 'busy woman'.

Being Mr. President's wife, running our home and raising our child. Plus I was trying to do the unthinkable...get a book written and actually published. This was a huge amount on my plate.

The Gothic market fell cold so it was suggested that I produce a contemporary book. So I began to write in that literary style.

As busy as I was, it was little wonder that I was not concerned that I couldn't get in touch with Dolly Green. I frequently called and repeatedly was told that 'she was with her horses at the track'. I gave her barely a thought. She was busy, she was active, and she was leading a life that was a parallel existence to mine.

Well fine!

****

One Friday afternoon in July of 1985, I was sitting out on the patio sunning and Steve walked out the back door.

I asked, "What on earth are you doing home this early, dear?"

Dear replied, "I just resigned today."

Well that was a total shock!!

While Steve was home trying diligently to find a new job, I decided to go to my twenty-year Westlake reunion.

The 1985 Reunion trip which was a road trip to L.A. with Bonnie Kortz and Tish Stevenson, was when my contemporary novel, *Reservations for One in Hell*, was conceptualized.

Once home, I began to write like mad! It was the beginning of my own rest of life-long writing career.

CHAPTER FIFTY-SEVEN

Author's Notes:

I don't know for sure when things really began to go very wrong for Dolly. But I believe that it was in the early eighties. In retrospect, I had begun to suspect that Dolly's mental faculties were beginning to be challenged. Regardless, there was little I could do.

It is my belief, that in the early eighties, her personal secretary, Elinor Logan began her quest for Dolly's vast funds. The secretary had been left not one dime by the rest of the Green family. She had worked first for Burton, then Burtie and Lily too.

All deceased, not one dollar richer in the inheritance stead, Elinor must have deduced that she would fare little better with Dolly's estate plans.

According to Maria, the secretary enlisted the help of one of the staff chauffeur's to help her in the quest for a little readjustment of Dolly's estate funds.

I continued to call and communicate with Dolly, but got increasingly vague responses. So, I started writing her letters.

I believe Dolly's advanced decline began in 1985 when she suffered a very severe bout with influenza. She was heavily medicated with pain and antibiotic prescriptions at that time.

It was all downhill from there.

WHISPERS FROM THE EDGE

In October of 1985, I drove to Los Angeles with Bonnie Kortz and Tish Stevenson to attend my high school class reunion. We stayed with Mary B.

I then spoke briefly with Dolly and she told me she was far too ill to see me. She sounded very disoriented to me. She could not recall the name of her horse that had just won some huge race. She could not remember several things that seemed very odd to me.

Dolly said in closing, "Oh Di, I'm sorry I am so sick! I've had a terrible influenza. I wish I could see you, Di, but I just can't! I'm far too ill and would not want to expose you to this horrible sickness!"

I chalked the vagueness up to that illness. It was then that the little whispers of uncertainty regarding Dolly's mental soundness began to niggle at my mind. Things regarding her ability to actually focus on reality and anything in general, began to spiral down from there.

Meanwhile, our lives were in a complete chaos.

With Steve's resignation from his position of running Marvin Davis' bank, we were in quite the turmoil.

Steve was interviewing for different jobs alternating with looking for a potential company to buy. It was a very interesting time around the hacienda!

So over the following couple of years, I called the Green household infrequently, as was my usual way. I didn't think a great deal about Dolly's inability to answer the phone. Whoever answered said, "She is at the track, or out to lunch or busy." I chalked it up to her being a very active woman.

I began to write occasional letters updating Dolly on our lives. I figured that letters would probably be better for her as she could read them at her leisure, of which she seemed to have little to spare.

The Christmas check came as usual, but the one in 1985 was with an almost illegible signature on Dolly's part.

I continued to phone but got increasingly vague responses. It seemed Dolly was 'out with her horses and trainer at the track'.

I was getting a bit suspicious that things were not quite right.

CHAPTER FIFTY-EIGHT

Author's Notes:

In 1987, Steve became the COO of a company called Quinn and McGill and we traveled to California for a convention. At that same time we called the Green mansion and got an interesting response.

The following revelations are in part from documentation that I did at the time we went to visit Dolly Green. Maria insisted that we come.

Under no circumstances, had I been prepared for what we would find. However, at Steve's suggestion, I carried with me a concealed tape recorder so I could begin to document exactly what was going on in the Green household.

We both had become further alarmed over the lack of communication I had been able to establish with Dolly since 1985.

So in 1987 we went to attend a convention for his company Quinn and McGill that was being held in Coronado and discovered the shocking truth.

DISCOVERY OF THE PRISONER OF BELLAGIO ROAD

We arrived in California on Saturday and were planning to spend the night at Mary B's.

I remember sitting in her library again with a sense of déjà vu. I phoned from Mary B's library and amazingly got Maria on the phone. She sounded oddly covert.

Maria made arrangements for us to meet at exactly eleven o'clock that next day which was a Sunday. So we agreed to see her and talk then.

It was 10:49 on Sunday when we went to Bel Air and deliberately drove up to the closed iron gates and rang the bell on the side speaker box.

Finally, Maria answered, "Hallow? Who is there?"

I grasped Steve's hand in triumph over hearing a cheerful, familiar voice.

"Maria its Diane." The silence that followed was deafening.

Finally the maid replied, "Madre Dios, is this truly my little 'Beau-Beau'? You did come after all?"

"Yes, Maria, is Dolly up yet? We are here to see her as planned."

There was a formidable hesitation in Maria's voice when she finally replied with a sigh, "Beau...'my Mrs.' has been very sick over the past many months. But I think you need to see her, anyway. I know I should not do this but, I must. Madre Dios, I hope no one find me out."

I turned to look at Steve. I was confused because we had agreed upon this meeting just yesterday. As the gate swung wide we proceeded up the winding, tree shaded drive. Delightful memories flooded both our minds of glorious times past at the palatial mansion owned by Dolly Green.

I questioned, "Remember all the parties, the receptions, the infamous Mexican Galas, and the lavish New Year bashes that Dolly orchestrated?"

"Of course. I attended some with you, how could I ever forget. They always reminded me a bit of a Hollywood movie set, for all the celebrity guests. That is where I first met 'Sly' Stallone and many more of his ilk."

We both expected to see Dolly's red Cadillac sitting in the driveway with a chauffeur polishing the gleaming chrome. However, the dead-end, cul-de-sac was oddly deserted. The silence was disturbed only by buzzing bees, sipping syrup from the flowering eucalyptus trees, as we proceeded up the drive.

We swung our rental car around and parked in front of the red-lacquered door of the enormous pink stucco mansion. The home was like a glittering castle basking in the morning sun. Warmth radiated from the walls, fragrance from the blooming flowers enveloped us with a heady, tropical embrace.

All seemed well in the rarefied world of Dolly Green's immaculately, kempt estate.

We had expected Dolly to poke her head through the opened window and promise as she always had before, to hear her merrily call, "Just a second, darlings, Maria will be right down to let you in!"

But no one had joyfully greeted.

The stillness of the day was disconcerting and once Steve cut the engine, all we heard was the droning of bees.

Getting out of the car, we walked to the door.

Steve turned to me as he tapped the brass, lion's head knocker, saying, "Things seem oddly quiet around here."

I murmured, "Indeed they do. There is a complete lack of servants or any activity. This seems really quite odd."

We both heard the clicking of heeled shoes on the marble floor as someone hurried to admit us both.

Maria flung open the door. "Come in," she instructed. "Come in."

The maid hugged me so hard, she almost broke ribs.

The beautiful older Puerto Rican woman's hair was sprinkled with gray but she looked wonderfully healthy and sound. I guessed her age to be sixty-nine or seventy at the very oldest. She was a sight for sore eyes. I hugged the maid for quite some time.

Maria finally stood away and surveyed us, saying, "You have chanced upon a rare time that the household is deserted, except for myself and 'my Mrs.' All the rest of the staff is at Good Shepherd Church in Beverly Hills, saying prayers for Mrs. Green. 'My

Mrs.' had been so very ill. You need to be prepared for what you are about to see." Tears misted the faithful woman's eyes. She then mentioned, "I admit you against strict orders allowing anyone to see Mrs. Green. Her doctor warned that any disruption of her routine could severely upset her more."

Motioning us to follow her up the stairs, she'd continued to caution us of Dolly's delicate condition and to prepare us for quite a change.

"Since you have come all the way from Colorado, you should at least visit with Mrs. Green. She has been this way for quite some time now."

Steve volunteered, "Look, if Dolly is in such delicate condition, I will just wait out here while you make your visit, Diane. If there is going to be such trauma involved with our popping in, perhaps you should visit alone with your godmother."

I would have nothing to do with him remaining behind. I grasped his hand in a gripe of a vice and all but dragged him with me through the door. "I'm not going in there without you. But Maria," I asked, "let Steve and me visit with her just a little while. If she is challenged for strength because of this illness, then we will only stay a brief time."

We both went into the bedroom and seated ourselves in chairs on each side of the 'Grand-Dame'.

We then listened to the woman we had seemingly known forever, but the audience today was with a complete stranger.

Until we got into the room, neither Steve nor I had been prepared for what met our eyes.

The woman's current appearance stunned us both to speechlessness.

Dolly Green's former startlingly beauty was faded, her yellow silk nightgown was food-spotted, her raven hair was gray-rooted, stringy and disarrayed. Her usually immaculate, red-tipped nails were chipped and jagged, clearly being ignored.

The whole visage made me soundlessly weep at the pitiful sight. My godmother was a completely changed woman from what we both remembered from the very recent past.

Wheel-chair-ridden, disheveled, shriveled from loss of weight, she sat raving senselessly to herself and her unseen friends.

Apparently, over the passage of the last few years, she'd been stricken by a debilitating illness. The metal chair was her captor, blindness her veil, Alzheimer's her master as she was its' unwilling slave.

Dolly's voice finally quaked with this emotional question, "Have you come to take my baby? Have you come to take my baby, 'Beau-Beau'?" Urgently, Dolly insisted, "You can't have her. If you have come to take away my baby, 'Beau-Beau', I have changed my mind! I need to raise my own child!" Her voice was unwavering with conviction. She seemed as lucid as she had ever been in her entire life.

However, we came to later learn from Maria, that the frightened query about her child had been the first lucid verbiage uttered in many months.

Hastily, I clutched Dolly's hand and cajoled, "No. No, Dolly, we have not come for 'Beau-Beau' today. We can talk about that some other time, when you're feeling better. We are not taking your baby away from you. She is safe in her nursery playing with Maria."

Steve added his assurance, realizing he needed to placate the fear that had suddenly entered Dolly's confused mind. "Dolly, we've only come to visit. It's been quite a long time since we've had a good chat. We have not come to get baby, 'Beau-Beau'. Even, if you have changed your mind."

For some unknown reason, his answer seemed to calm her more than my previous words.

Unseeing, Dolly waved one arm in the direction of Steve's voice. He clasped her hand to still her.

So stunned by her appearance, I offered, "it is forecast to rain for a long time."

She then replied, "No, it was most assuredly not and you should listen to your elders because they are always right!"

Once this was spoken, her hand still firmly in Steve's grasp, Dolly lapsed back into the senseless babbling that we had heard upon initially entering the room.

Both Steve and I realized we had probably witnessed the only singular flash of lucidity we would hear from Dolly in the brief time we would be allowed to stay.

I sat quietly observing Dolly. The disheveled woman was a far cry from the raven-haired beauty, I'd seen on my last visit to Bellagio Road.

We stayed for quite a while wishing for some further glimmer of light in the darkness of Dolly's addled speech.

None came, again! Dolly senselessly babbled away, chatting amicably with her unseen confidants.

We were appalled by the woman's deterioration. Shocked at how completely she was lost to inner space. We had no way to have been prepared for the tragedy that we viewed.

Maria stole quietly into the room, whispering to me, "It is twelve o'clock. She must eat lunch now. She has a routine that is based on doing everything at exactly the same time each day. If this is changed, she goes very crazy. Then, we are forced to put her into restraints. Beau, I told you this would not be an easy visit. I told you how changed 'my Mrs.' had become."

Steve pried my clutching fingers away from Dolly's claw-like hand. Urging me to rise by grasping my elbow, he guided me from the darkened room.

Maria asked us to go to the solarium and wait for her, while she served Mrs. Green her meal.

CHAPTER FIFTY-NINE

Author's Notes:

From here forward the reader should note that the sequences revealed will comprise material that has been used in the formulation of the sequel to Pale Diamonds, called The Dark Side of a Fairy Tale.

Because the happenstances are so bazaar as to seem only possible in fiction, the reader may find them too amazing to believe the facts. However, the saying truth is 'stranger than fiction', applies in this entire story, tenfold.

And, sadly enough, the pertinent facts revealed throughout this book are nothing but the bitter truth.

PERTINENT FACTS WITHHELD

We went down the spiral staircase, across the marble floored entry hall. Wordlessly, we went to the solarium to await Maria. We seated ourselves on a huge red down-filled sofa. We were both silent, thinking over what we had just viewed.

I stood, then moved to the expansive picture window that overlooked the greater Bel Air and Los Angeles basin. I touched the leaves of one of the abundant Cymbidium plants that were placed in almost obscene profusion around the room. Its' beauty seemed to me such a travesty compared to the ugliness that was sequestered behind the doors in the bedchamber above.

But some things never change. The solarium was still filled with orchids, the sun streamed in, drenching the room with dazzling light. Pictures were crammed on tables, vying for the attention of anyone who cared to view the notables featured in the golden frames.

The Ronald Reagans were immortalized, as were the Jerry Fords. There was a photo of Dolly with the Howard Kecks, and a stunning portrayal of the three Green sisters. Together, resplendent among the rest of the pictures, the women had been show stopping, even into their later years.

Through the sun-room's tinted glass was a forever view across Bel Air. It had poured last night, a violent storm that washed Angel Town's smog down the gullies and ravines.

The visage was brilliant blue and gold with the sun, a Los Angeles, 'Post Card' day. But on the horizon, near the ocean hovered clouds that threatened to move in at any second and quash the luminescence of the afternoon. The later forecast was for rain and knowing the signs of encroaching weather, I silently surmised it was only a few hours before a downpour would engulf us. Rain was on the way, despite Dolly's contradiction. I did listen to my elders, but normally the ones that were sane.

Despite the brilliant warmth I felt shaken and chilled. Never had I anticipated seeing Dolly in this horrible state, so brutally affected by the dread Alzheimer's disease. Frankly, I was deeply stunned.

Steve interrupted my reflections, saying, "I can hardly believe that Dolly Green is the woman in that wheelchair. I'm shocked that things have been allowed to become so advanced without our even being notified. Someone should have at least told you she had become so ill!"

He rose and moved to stand in front of me, compassion laced his husky voice as he queried, "Honey, are you satisfied that we saw her like this or, would you have been better off not to know just how horribly deteriorated she's become over these past years?"

"I think I needed to see her this way but what a horrible shock this has been. I just never in my worst nightmares could have conjured the image of how she is now."

Steve asked, "Exactly when was the last time you actually had a conversation with Dolly?"

"You remember honey, it was when in 1986. I told you she sounded horribly vague. She had a terrible cold and could barely talk but seemed a little out there. I chalked that up to her being on cold medication. Lord knows, I'm fuzzy when I take that stuff."

"So all this has transpired since your last conversation when she was supposedly ill with a mere cold?"

"Yes. I had been concerned that she had been unavailable to me for such a long time. But between her busy schedule that I was led to believe she was leading of seeing her horses every day, hosting charity luncheons and the like, I tried to be happy she was so busy these days. Yet now we see this elaborate smokescreen about her life was nothing but an convoluted travesty! She has been sick all this time and we were not allowed to know. I am beyond infuriated over this whole thing. I mean it is as if she has had a stroke. Why in God's name have we not been informed?"

Steve patted my shoulder with a supportive gesture, then clasped my hand. He followed my gaze to view the greater expanse of L.A. saying, "Honey, I just don't know."

After some moments of reflection, Steve continued, "Dolly is so far gone. I never would have guessed what we were in for when Maria allowed us to see her, today." He became silent with his musing, then resumed, "The last time I saw her she was as vital as I have ever seen her. I would never have known the woman was Dolly in that wheelchair had I not known her all our married lives."

I choked back a dry sob, "She is completely gone to her little group of unseen friends. She did not even know who she was talking to when she begged us not to take her baby, 'Beau-Beau'."

Steve shook his head with dismay, "I wonder what triggered Dolly to become lucid enough to ask if we were here to take her child? She must have thought that we were Ralph and Marie Hunt. I would almost have to believe that even after all these years, she seemed to feel guilty over giving you up for adoption."

With anguish I sighed and admitted, "I really believe that even in her declined condition, she still feels horrible guilt over giving me away. You are right. She must have thought that we were my parents coming to get me when I was a little girl. To this day she must regret having given me up as her child. I hardly can believe it though, not after all these years."

Steve took both my shoulders between his hands and leveled his eyes with mine, "She is your own flesh and blood, Diane. No mother, I don't care who, could ever feel completely guiltless about giving their baby away. Just because the circumstances regarding your family's continuous contact was unique, does not change the bottom line. She disposed of you when you were two years old. I always thought it was heartless to foist off a baby at that formative age. So now, in Dolly's tormented mind, she is eaten alive with grief over the choice she made. Somewhere in the recesses of that addled brain, she is trying to set things straight. Dolly probably thinks that now she can deny the Hunts the right to have you, change things as if through a magic wish. 'Abra Kadabra', things are as they were when you were two years old. Well, Diane, my dearest love, it's a bit late to 'change' that mind."

"Steve, that's a horrible analogy. She placed me with my adoptive parents because she wanted me to have a shot at a somewhat, normal life. She always oversaw what went on as I grew up. I know how you feel about the situation, you never have condoned it, in that respect you were always like my adoptive dad. But under the circumstances, Dolly did what she thought was best! No matter what her motives, if she is feeling condemned now, there is nothing I can do."

"Honey, it doesn't matter. The die was cast many years ago. If she feels guilty, as I believe she should, there's nothing anyone can do! She'll have to come to terms with her own inner demons and I'm certain that every waking hour of her day, she's fighting quite a few. The bottom line is that Dolly Green is your birth mother and she refused to keep you as a child. No matter what her motivations, she gave her baby, 'Beau-Beau', away. I'm not being harsh, sweetheart, we've discussed this matter all our married lives. Your situation was very bizarre when it came down to Dolly Green. Your adoptive parents allowed your reunion by accepting her back in your life when you were six years old. From which point, Dolly orchestrated your continued relationship by becoming your 'godmother'. Even you played along. So, all of your lives proceeded from there as if there was a tiny little secret hidden from the rest of the world."

"Steve that is just harsh! She was doing it to try for normalcy in my life. My parents condoned it and I just was along for the Barnum and Bailey ride."

"No matter. I have always thought that the whole thing was bizarre! Your parents may have regarded the adoption as the answer to their prayers, but I always viewed it as the darker side of a warped fairy tale. But hey, that was just me!"

I nodded distractedly, there was little debate that the entire scenario of my life was anything but a rather unusual fable.

I interjected at that point, "Maria seems horribly nervous about our being here. If she admitted us against doctor's orders, I can understand why she is uncomfortable with our intrusion. Especially if a break in routine seems to cause Dolly to get so upset they have to put her in restraints."

This thought caused us both to fall silent and introspectively think over what we had both just seen.

CHAPTER SIXTY

Author's Notes:

I had a feeling so horrible about this entire disaster, I stood there thinking how could I turn back the hands of time and find my mother again.

How could I have been so cavalier as to assume everything was just 'peachy' when my mother lived in the 'gigolo' capitol of the world?

I remember commenting about the Doris Duke snafu, where the chauffeur stole her millions. I remember Steve commenting how it seemed so damn prevalent in Beverly Hills that money was stolen from the family when the servants gained control. Manipulating wills seemed de reguer!

When we spoke with Maria, I immediately thought I could smell a 'rat' at the Green estate.

Little could I know how right I had been. The facts were just beginning to unfold tenfold.

VIEW OF THE REVEALING PAST

At that moment, Maria walked into the room and stood in front of Steve and me, saying, "I know how much 'my Mrs.' condition has shocked you both." She heavily sighed, "But she has been this way for many months. One night she simply go nuts and start screaming at the top of her lungs, 'I want to die, I want to die'! She never been right, since that horrible night. Sadly, all the Green's have suffered this same affliction. Eventually, it claim their lives. Mrs. Green just change overnight. One day she out seeing her horses, the next she like this. The doctor say she have a little series of strokes. She will 'maybe' come back, but few of us think she will."

It always amazed me how strongly the Puerto Rican accent still lingered in Maria's speech. The servant had lived with Dolly Green since she was twelve years old, but still spoke broken English.

Continuing, the maid assured, "Diane, I know 'my Mrs.' is your mother. But anyone else who knew anything about you being Mrs. Green's child, is already dead and gone. No one knows the truth about you, *just us three.* 'my Mrs.' is too far gone to know anything, anymore. But I know you not her 'godchild', like everyone pretended for you to be."

I went to stand in front of Maria and said, "Thank you so much for letting us in today. I only hope this does not prove too upsetting for Dolly, later in the afternoon." I hugged the maid, then stood away and asked, "But Maria, why didn't anyone tell me that Dolly had declined this much? Why was this hidden from us?"

Maria averted her eyes as if afraid to tell the truth. "Her secretary, Mrs. Logan, no want anyone to know 'my Mrs.' condition. She say 'my Mrs.' get well and when she do, no one need to know the nervous breakdown that she suffer those months ago." She leveled her eyes with my glare, "Mrs. Logan, she forbid me to allow anyone at all, to see Mrs. Green. But I know you had to see her, Diane. After all, she is your real mother. It is your right to see how bad she has become and to say your last good-byes to your mommy. I hope you can remember her as she was, not what she has become."

"Thank you, Maria. I am grateful that you let us into the house. How is it that this Mrs. Logan is in such a position of authority that she can dictate what is done about Dolly Green? Even if this secretary thought I'm just another one of the godchildren, I still deserve to know her condition, not be lied to on the phone, telling me Dolly is at the race track or out to lunch. Good, Lord, how would I know any different? I pictured her leading a wonderful life in these passing years."

I heavily sighed, "Most women in their late seventies are doing more activities than I can keep up with let alone following the social schedule I was being told Dolly was pursuing. But I thought it was wonderful that she was remaining so fabulously occupied. Then, we come here today to visit and find her horribly ill, detained and in custody within her own palatial room. She is nothing less than the prisoner of Bellagio Road, held hostage by some secretary that I don't even know. This is appalling! I am furious with the duplicity of this whole sham!"

Steve grabbed me by my shoulders, advising gently, "Calm down, honey, let Maria explain what's been going on over the past few years."

Maria began to pace and shake her head. "Look, Diane, Mrs. Logan, she think you nothing but one of her many godchildren. She has quite a few. Mrs. Logan not know of your true relationship with Mrs. Green. As lifelong secretary, Mrs. Logan has assumed charge of everything. She say she act on Mrs. Green's authority. She say she no want to notify the family or godchildren so that they are no alarmed by Mrs. Green's condition. Even the Doctor seem to think she make a recovery. Mrs. Logan has run all the Green's affairs for many years. She has the right to make these decisions because she work for the family for over thirty years. In the past few years, she have to deal with everything that happen to the Greens."

I was not going to be easily placated. I continued my inquisition, "Why hide her illness? I still can't understand."

"Because Mrs. Logan say Mrs. Green was a very proud woman and she would never want anyone to know how bad she has become. Diane, even Barry and Sandi, her niece and nephew have not seen her this way. They know she no feel well, but Mrs. Logan has not even told them. Course I think they nothing but a couple a no good, money-grubbing kids, anyway. Neither one do nothing but live off their mommy's money. Neither one of them has ever had a real job, not once in their lives. I could care less when those two find out 'my Mrs.' is so ill. They gonna hang around like vultures till your mother dies. They think inheriting money is like falling off a stump."

It had always struck me as funny that Maria could never get hackneyed phrases exactly right. But today, it fell short of the humorous side, as Maria seemed to be carrying on a one-sided conversation with herself, which I suspected now happened all the time. After all, there was not a plethora of intelligent life forms present in the Green household, anymore.

Knowing Maria's habit of listening behind closed doors, abruptly I changing the subject, questioning, "Has Dolly ever said anything like what she said a while ago to anyone else? Asking about her baby, 'Beau-Beau'?"

"Not ever!"Maria assured, confirming my suspicions regarding the eavesdropping."I believe 'my Mrs.' must have thought you were Mr. and Mrs. Hunt come to get you when you were a baby. You know, she always adore you. She was selfish that way. She no could give you up entirely. She had to have her pie and swallow it too. That is why she no let you go completely. That is why she have to come back as your God-mama when you turn six years old."

I shook my head with concern over all that was being revealed. "I just can't understand why she was so agitated today? Later in life she and I had an understanding that I never held her in any way guilty for placing me in another home. Why would she be so panicked this morning over someone taking me away from her?"

"All her life she say to me, *she would 'never forgive herself for letting you go'*. I tell her she no had let you go. That she could see you anytime she want. But she never seemed satisfied with my answer. Never! All her life she fretted over giving her baby away. She say I no understand. She would tell me that only a mother could comprehend. She over and over again say she feel guilty because she send you away. She say that Glen Hart no protect you the way he should. She say he no take care of you the way a Green should be cared for. I never do understand what she mean."

I contradicted, "Dolly was my mentor, my godmother. All my life she over-saw my path. No one could have been better to me. It was as if I had two homes. One normal life with the Hunts and then a fairy tale life with my godmother, Dolly Green."

Maria shook her head in a negative fashion, reflecting, "I always tell her this is so. But I no get through to her. Not then, not ever. She sit there for the rest of her days trying to get her baby back so she can feel comfortable with her little white lies. The thing is, we know she was good to you, Diane. Remember your happy times together with your mama. She loved you, always. Her condition no can change that fact! She always spoke of you with love and admiration. And, you too, Mr. Stockmar, she respected you above any man she ever know. She tell me this right after you marry her precious daughter, Diane, what a upstanding man you were. Nothing can ever change how proud she was of you both!"

Steve nodded and patted Maria on her shoulder, "Thank you. I know she always trusted me and I am thankful I saw her when I did and at what I thought was her best."

Impatiently, Maria brushed a trickling tear from her high boned cheek, as she hugged us both farewell. She instructed, "Now, go. Enjoy the rest of your lives together. You live every day as if it could be your last! 'my Mrs.' lost sight of things that mean all the most to her. Don't you two get caught in that horrible trap."

We spent a bit more time going over things that had been conveniently not shared. Pertinent facts withheld were revealed as Maria spun the sad tale of the heartbreaking death spiral to which the 'divine' Dolly Green was succumbing. Specifics that left both of us feeling fairly stunned over the deceitful sham that had been conducted at Bellagio Road.

The manipulation that had been allowed during the fleeting months as Dolly became further deeply ill, was frankly appalling.

Finally, that Elinor Logan had obtained power of attorney and was at the helm of the deteriorating empire Green, was appalling to both of us.

Dolly was the last of the fabled siblings that could claim rightful heritage to one of the founding families of Beverly Hills. So with her pending death, the Green line was at a bitter end. Or so everyone thought because no one knew about me.

Feeling that Maria was increasingly nervous regarding our presence there, we hugged her, thanked her for her confiding in us and left her standing in the grand foyer alone.

Getting back into our car, we drove off, down the winding drive and through the enormous wrought iron gate.

As Steve paused at the bottom of the drive, the huge metal portals closed behind us with a distinctive thunk.

There was finality to that sound that neither of us would ever forget.

CHAPTER SIXTY-ONE

Author's Notes:

There have been times in my life when I realized that a page had been turned and I had been helpless to prevent the turning.

I'd been given away, then brought back into Dolly's life on a whim. I paralleled this day's pain to the feeling I'd experienced the first time she had given me away.

In this instance however, it really was forever! As a child, I could only feel horribly sad at my loss. Now, as an adult, I felt such profound despair that I could hardly voice the words.

Once again, as if for the millionth time in my life, I felt like a little girl cast aside.

Today, I wore the mantel none too well!

FAREWELL FAIR CAMELOT, YOU ARE NOW IN ENEMIES HANDS

An eerie fog descended over the Bel Air Canyons, choking the sun's rays and casting a chilly veil of moisture over the formerly, picture perfect day.

The forecast for rain was correct and all so typical of a So Cal transformation. One second it was beach weather, the next, time to bring out the rain gear.

Steve and I drove down the remainder of the drive from Dolly Green's mansion. We were somber, reflecting the dark mood of the abrupt turn in the weather.

Steve paused at the driveway's access to Bellagio Road and waited for the steady stream of Rolls Royces and Maybachs to pass before he began to nose our rental out onto the momentarily, calm street.

Checking his watch, he noted it was noon on the dot. We had spent precisely two hours with Dolly's life-long maid. Perceptually, he hesitated as if awaiting directions from me.

I was looking over my shoulder at one final glance of the beautiful pink stucco estate that I had known so intimately, all my life.

Shrouded by the rain, the pink mansion on Bellagio Road rose into the mists like some legendary castle of yore. Now it seemed foreboding, ominous, uninviting, unlike the previous welcoming visage of only a few hours earlier.

Sighing with resignation, I urged Steve to drive away by a nod of my head, impatiently I brushed away errant falling tears with the back of my right hand.

Breaking the silence I ventured, a haunting sadness trembled as I voiced, "This is the last time I shall ever see my mother's home. Things are not right in Camelot. I can feel the turn of the tide. The camp is controlled by enemies. I'll never be welcome back in the Castle Green."

Steve consoled, "Honey, things may not be as horrible as they seem. I mean we chanced here completely unexpectedly. It was not as if we were announced. Perhaps, had we given some notice, they could would have made some effort to have her a bit more spiffed up. Then we may have just come on a particularly bad day."

I gave him a scathing look as I asked, "Do you believe what you just said?"

"Not really, no. But I always give the benefit of the doubt."

"Whatever!" I looked at the small ring I wore on my hand. The tiny signet had been given to me by Dolly when I was a baby, and I wore it constantly. She had told me at one point that it was fabled to be charmed by an enchantress. I had never fully believed in the story but wore it anyway.

Holding the ring for Steve to see I said, "No enchantment on this earth will turn things around for my poor mother! Now this may be the only object of hers that I will ever rightfully possess. She is being held captive in that glorified prison and that secretary is turning the Green world upside down! I know it, I can feel it and there is not a bloody thing that you or I can do!"

Steve remained silent for a moment and then admitted, "I think you may be feeling bit maudlin, but our uncertainty as to exactly what is happening should prompt me to keep my opinions to myself."He clasped my hand in his, a comforting gesture at that movingly poignant time.

We were headed in the direction of our final destination. The exclusive Coronado Hotel was where we were required to attend a convention. So we headed down to Coronado and went through the motions of being focused on that task.

All the while, we hashed over the details of the baffling Green mystery.

CHAPTER SIXTY-TWO

Author's Notes:

The entire ride down to Coronado, Steve and I hashed over many ideas and nothing came up in a remotely positive light.

I chastised myself for being so trusting, so obtuse, and so gullible for believing all the previous lies.

But the whole truth as we saw it, was that out of sight had been opportunely and profoundly, out of mind.

Whoever was orchestrating this entire marionette show was certainly pulling all the right strings! Putting them in the fiscal driver's seat with me conveniently hidden away in a Colorado trunk.

TWENTY-TWENTY HINDSIGHT

Two hours later at Coronado, we were relieved to be in the cloistered atmosphere, where we settled into our elegant rooms.

After enjoying luxurious massages at the Spa, we returned to the privacy of our quarters where we sat for almost an hour in a lavender scented Jacuzzi.

Due to our discovery of Dolly's horrific condition, we were still, both as tight as a string on a drawn-back-bow.

That evening we attended a gourmet dinner in the sumptuous, main dining room. The convention was underway, but we were hardly willing participants.

Excusing ourselves early from the revelers, we sought the solace of our rooms. Our moods were grim, we had hardly even enjoyed the wonderful banquet food.

The visit to Dolly's had left us both deeply shaken. The outcome had been so unexpected, neither of us had been slightly prepared for what we found.

Back in the seclusion of our quarters, we hashed over and over the events of the day.

Talking things over always had a healing effect for us. To know all the angles was the best solution to a tough situation. It was a guideline of our marriage and it had always kept our bond strong!

I continued the ongoing discussion, "I told you that the last time I phoned Dolly's home, someone answered then immediately hung up the line. I got that three times and I just finally gave up once the operator said there was difficulty on their end. Now I get how badly things have gone wrong. God, how could things have gotten so out of control without our knowing it at all?"

Steve gently replied, "Honey, if I had an answer for this, we wouldn't have received the shock we did this morning. This is as disturbing to me as it is to you. It is completely subversive of Logan to take this course of action, if you only ask me."

I voiced real concern, "Exactly! Then, you know I noticed today that there was not one single photo of me in the entire massive home. Also, the Peter Hurd portrait of Dolly and me that has hung for years in the solarium, was missing. Perhaps it had been moved elsewhere, but I cannot imagine where it would have been placed. It certainly was not in her bedroom."

"Maybe it was there and we were so shocked by the visage of Dolly in her wheelchair, that it did not even register as being on the wall."

"No. You don't miss a forty by fifty portrait of me and my mother. It was huge. There is no way even in the darkened room that I would have overlooked that portrait. It was something that meant the world to us both. Dolly and I always discussed how I would get most of her personal things and it was foremost on the list. Who else would want that personal piece?"

"I can't imagine why that would have been put away. It was certainly one of Dolly's favorites. I saw it prominently displayed the last time I visited her. It was in the solarium and I caught her staring at it just as I walked into the room."

"If all my pictures have been put away, this gives me an overwhelming feeling of discomfort. If I am no longer remembered by photo, who knows what has happened to Dolly's memory about me as she recently galloped down senility's path. Perhaps, she has purposefully been encouraged to forget me. This whole thing is screaming Stockholm Syndrome to me!"

"I don't take it as a good sign," he admitted. "It is very certain that things are being very oddly conducted in the Castle Green."

Late into the night, we discussed the probable ramifications of the elaborate duplicity behind the staged secrecy of Dolly's illness.

Steve bluntly stated, "The implications are overwhelming and point undeniably toward Logan's own financial cause. It is certain she is manipulating the outcome of Dolly Green's estate. She probably has exploited her power of attorney to her advantage in the past several months, while Dolly has been in this advanced state of deterioration."

I sighed, "Oh, I am quite certain of that. From what Maria was able to say, it sounds as if most of the staff still are in place. How ridiculous is that just to care for a woman sitting in a wheelchair. She should have been placed in a nursing home by now not allowed to sit up there all alone."

Steve denied, "Oh, no. Then the truth would come out about how gravely ill Dolly has become. This way, Mrs. Logan can pull all the puppet strings from the mansion and no one is the wiser. Just like us. We were clueless to the advanced state of Dolly's mental impairment."

"I just can't believe this was allowed to happen."

"Dolly was the youngest of the Green sisters, was she not?"

"Yes, Burton's little pet. Both Lily and Burtie are gone as you heard Maria say today."

Steve consoled, "I hold firm that there is little we can do right now unless it is very covertly approached. Blatantly accusing someone who has been in the Greens employment for over thirty years would cause a team of attorneys to double over with laughter and chagrin at these types of allegations from us. Probably, any accusations that threaten Logan before Dolly dies would alert the secretary to do something far more radical than she has undertaken so far."

I agreed, "I guess there is nothing we can do until Dolly passes away. Only then, can we discover what tricks the secretary had been performing over this course of time. I just hope Maria is not chastised over our meeting with Dolly today. If Logan finds out that she allowed us access to the Green mansion, Maria may be in line for a pretty harsh comeuppance."

Steve reflected, "At this late date, if Maria is still with the household, she probably is impervious to harm."

"I hope so! I would feel horrible if she lost her job over this."

"Her employment is tenuous at best in Dolly's current state. I just wonder how long Dolly will continue to live this way. One can never tell with these things. She could go on like this for years. Look how long my grandmother was in that nursing home before she died."

Somberly I answered, "True. You really can never tell about these things."

Unfortunately, when our conversation wound down at twelve-thirty, we had resolved little in a positive manner.

Settling in bed, before drifting to sleep, I said something that would indefinitely bother us both, "I only hope that by letting us in today, Maria, will not be in trouble. She did it for me. I hope she doesn't pay too high a price."Then, I fell asleep in Steve's arms.

He, however, lay staring up at the ceiling going over and over the mystery in his mind. Nothing he'd come up with since we departed the Bel Air mansion, seemed to be the solution. He wondered if we would have been better off to never see what was going on. It was almost worse to have seen Dolly in this state. Steve felt helpless to assist me in this intrigue that had been created by a wheedling secretary to certainly gain control over Dolly's vast estate.

Thinking it over and over, he came up with the same resolution. There was not one damn thing they could do to challenge the Logan woman at this point. Having worked for the entire family for all those years gave her credibility that even the Pope would hardly challenge.

Steve was used to problem solving. Financial paradoxes were his forte. He never went to sleep without all angles of a fiscal problem dealt with or a challenging quandary unsolved. He addressed our personal life the same way. We never went to bed angry or with a debate unresolved.

Mulling over and over the facts, he again recalled what I said about Maria paying too high a price for admitting us today.

It was one thing for me to be twelve hundred miles removed, safe and sequestered in Colorado. But Maria was there, in the same house with the plotting woman. What if Logan found out we had been admitted to see Dolly Green? What would the secretary do to the life-long, maid?

Shoot her?

Rub her out?

Hire a hit man, or do the dirty deed, herself?"

Oh, Christ! He silently, scolded himself. She'd fire Maria, that's all. He absolutely needed to stop being so caught up in the thriller novels he constantly read. Things like that just did not happen in real life.

No little harmless secretary of the Greens would stoop to something as heinous as that. He was blowing everything completely out of proportion in his sleep-deprived-brain.

He could only hope that this Logan woman was completely harmless and just bent on her own fiscal gain.

CHAPTER SIXTY-THREE

Author's Notes:

Relaxing slumber had not been pals to either of us that previous night and we both awoke not well rested.

We had a huge agenda on our plate with the convention and the lack of sleep was not going to be to our benefit.

Steve later related his feeling to me and I have written them down in my own interpretation.

COME TO JESUS WITH OURSELVES

The next morning Steve dressed and went out to take a walk on the beach. The meetings were scheduled for later in the day. He would wait for me to get up and then, we would go to breakfast together. He wanted the quiet morning walk on the sand to try to sort things out that he had not been able to do the night before.

In the aftermath of the visit, the disquieting conversation with the maid still left him horribly uncomfortable with what was transpiring in the Green home.

Steve believed that no matter what happened, they had been in the Bel Air mansion on friendly terms for the last time. He had a formidable feeling about the motives of Mrs. Logan hiding the condition of the 'Grand Dame'.

With yesterday's visit, all the months of successful evasion became clear. Outside of household staff, Mrs. Logan did not want Dolly's real condition generally known to a single soul.

Last night, he voiced little about his truly heinous suspicions. Steve was emphatic in his belief to himself that Logan was manipulating things specifically against me. At this point, his only course of action was to be compassionate. We would go back to Denver, resume our busy lives and play a waiting game. Eventually we would see how the Green saga panned out.

He finished walking up and down the beach and stood outside our rooms and scuffed his toe in the fine sand. He squatted down and felt the powdery particles, allowing their grainy crystals to slowly sift through his fingers. Standing again, Steve scanned the sunrise sky, inhaling the pungent salty air. It was cool, crisp, biting, and yet not a hint of smog or pollution could be detected.

A sea-gull swooped from a nearby palm, flushed abruptly to flight in the sky. It rose upward, unfettered, seeming to touch the pink rays of the rising orb with its' undulating, transparent, wings. It disappeared on the horizon without further sound.

Simplistic events, Steve seemed to rarely take note of anymore, such as things unpretentious and breathtaking as the flight of a bird. The feel of crisp air, the sharp grittiness of the sand, all went unappreciated in his everyday important life back at home. It struck him odd that this seemed categorical, yet so important, that day of all days.

The morning before, he'd witnessed an unnerving picture. A woman he had admired all his life had been completely felled by a debilitating disease.

Dolly Green's life was at a caustic end.

It was clear she was possessed by bitterness and unhappiness over her life's chosen path. And, no amount of money in the world could undo the ravages wrought by her illness.

This was a formidable lesson for both of us to witness and from that learn.

We had a wonderful life but what we had not celebrated in a long time was our deep adoration and love. Somewhere along the way, in our deliberate pursuit of success; happiness had taken a back seat.

Steve felt the sun's warmth dance a caress on his cheek and he smelled the dew on the crystal, dawn air. Simple things he never focused on, anymore. Long ago, he and I admired those unpretentious moments. Somehow, our lives had gotten blown out of proportion.

Day in, day out, we followed a routine that did not allow us to sniff the roses. It was time we turned that around.

Yes, we were comfortable. Yes we were prominent, but something was missing in our present everyday lives. The enjoyment of down-to-earth things seemed to be rapidly eluding us.

Dolly Green had allowed that to happen and look where had it gotten her!

At that instant, Steve decided that things needed to change. At least they did in his life, which meant the family would hopefully endorse his soon to be, newly charted course.

It might take some time to accomplish but we desperately needed to reevaluate and take the steps toward change.

CHAPTER SIXTY-FOUR

Author's Notes:

I was still as flummoxed the following morning as I had been the night before.

When I awoke, at first I thought that I had experienced a nightmare, then I realized that it was true.

I had seen Dolly. She was in a wheelchair and there was nothing on this earth that I could do to change that around. It was a horrible bitter pill to swallow and I still was having trouble choking it down.

WE NEED TO RETHINK THE REST OF OUR LIVES

Peering out the window from behind a back-drawn drape, I studied Steve as he stood watching the rising sun. I felt a pang of worry wash over me. His hair was silver-black in the dawning light. He stood tall and erect and was an amazingly handsome man.

However, his posture that morning belied his normally confidant carriage. I could tell he was exhausted. I knew he'd spent a restless night worrying over what we had seen at my mother's house.

We were both still young, but after seeing Dolly, I knew we both felt horribly vulnerable. I had slept badly, as well. Nightmares haunted me all night, robbing me of a restful slumber. I allowed the drape to fall, obliterating the sight of my husband.

I needed to hurry to shower and dress. He hated to wait on what he called, 'girl stuff'. I set about completing my morning ritual.

The night before, I'd laid out a denim outfit. Hastily dressing, I dabbed on foundation and blush and pulled on jeans and a blue shirt. Hanging my habitual squash blossom around my neck, I was ready to depart.

Last I looked at the initial ring Dolly had given me. I always wore it on the pinkie of my right hand. I believed it had always brought me good fortune, not to mention amazing luck.

Dolly's fortunate destiny had finally run out. Something had happened to her protection after all her years of delicious fabrication. Her stories to avoid the truth, avoidance of actuality, the grim reaper of honesty was exacting his final, cruel punishment.

Now, all the riches in the world could not turn back the clock and allow me to communicate with my mother. I wanted to tell her how much I loved her and appreciated all the things she'd done for me over the years.

All the doctors, the best medicine and good care could not change the bitter hands of fate. Alzheimer's only took prisoners, there was never a "KINGS X", I wanted out of this random, cruel disease. It made me feel extremely mortal.

What if I inherited the dread illness that seemed to have claimed all of the Greens? The thought terrified me! But what hit me more, was that even with all Dolly's vast wealth, nothing could change what had passed. The millions could not make her well. She was past all help. She was a horribly guilt-ridden woman because of the fabrications she had contrived to please herself. The little white lies of Dolly's life were to forever be cast in stone.

I had never lived my life through duplicity. If anything, I often found myself in trouble because I shot verbally from the hip. Always calling 'a spade a spade'. Honesty was my byline, so unlike the exploitive guile's of many of my friends. I'd led my life the exact opposite of my manipulative mother. Had I purposefully chosen the opposite path?

I went to the mirror to inspect myself in the glass. Staring back at me was the image of what Dolly Green would have looked like at my age.

Seeing Dolly yesterday, made me wonder if Steve and I should not re-think the rest of our own life course. I would hate to end up wishing we should have gone about our careers differently in the pursuit of the almighty dollar. We continued to beat our heads against the wall, trying to amass more and more. "And what the Hell for?"I expostulated aloud.

All Dolly's millions seemed trite in light of what we had seen at my mother's home the day before.

Sometimes you needed a life jolt such as we had experienced, to make you see the forest for the trees.

So many of our friends had terminal cases of grandiose fiscal, tunnel vision. I wondered then if Steve and I weren't victims of that trap?

I vowed to talk to Steve about a change of life. But I would have to wait till the time was right. I knew, Quinn and McGill was Steve's new choice. It might be hard for him to make a change. Everything about this business seemed to appeal to him. But it had been leaving me a bit cold. I never had been in favor of the partnership and made no bones about that fact. I sort of hoped that at one point we could break this off, but only time would tell. I'd just need to bide my time.

I needed to get on the road. Steve was surely getting impatient over my stalling. We needed to get to the meetings that were scheduled for the day. I certainly could not solve this here.

****

Once home and re-settled, life went back into normal. I was working with Steve in the company and the time just flew by.

This missive was included with the 1987 Christmas check. After that year, I received no more Christmas checks at all:

12/14/87
From the desk of Elinor F. Logan:

Dear Diane,

I was sorry to hear that you were taken by surprise at Dolly's condition when you dropped in at the house not long ago. It had not occurred to me to notify you as we have tried to protect her from people knowing in the hopes she would improve. She did show improvement after her hospitalization 1st March.

Please let me know if you need to inquire about her as we are handling everything for her here at her office.

Best wishes for a Merry Christmas.
Elinor Logan
Secretary to Dolly Green

CHAPTER SIXTY-FIVE

Author's Notes:

We were just plugging along. Things were going fairly well with Steve's new company, Quinn and McGill and I was trying to catch up on my weekend housework, when the phone interrupted my cleaning quest.

Because of the circumstances and both our beliefs that things were going horribly wrong at the Green mansion, Steve insisted that I attach a tape recorder to the phone. So if Maria called, we could record her conversations. We informed her that we were doing so. I did this and found myself ready to record every time the phone would ring.

Of course this was well before caller ID, so it was a crap shoot every time the phone buzzed as to who would be on the lines.

Maria began to call quite frequently in 1987-1989.

Once I finally reconnected with Maria after the 1987 visit, she admitted that it was in 1985 that Dolly began to slip and mentally decline.

Apparently Dolly consulted a glaucoma specialist in San Francisco, begging him to give her an eye transplant. He refused due to her advanced age.

Dolly's decline, according to Maria, began primarily when Dolly began to lose her sight.

This conversation was recorded in early January of 1988.

WHISPERS FROM THE CASTLE GREEN

It was Saturday afternoon some weeks after we had arrived back home from our California trip, when the telephone rang interrupting me from making the beds.

"Diane?" The voice on the other end was thickly accented, Puerto Rican. I instantly recognized that it was Maria Rivera.

A feeling of panic enveloped me. "Maria, is something wrong?"

"Well, nothing is different with Mrs. Green." She sounded hesitant, "It's just that I did not have much time to talk when you were here, that other day." She paused, "I am here alone right now. Mrs. Logan is not coming back today and I am in my room. I know we chatted quite some time but I want to go over some things with you again a little further. I need for you to understand some things that I was not able to tell you about on that day because of the time."

I spoke into the phone, "I'm really glad you called. When we were there last, I was so shaken over Dolly's condition, that I'd like you to go over some other things so they are more clear in my own mind."

Maria interjected, "I need to tell you some things that are going on. Maybe I'm crazy but I think things are very wrong. And, Beau, I am very nervous about 'my Mrs.' chauffeur. He is someone who needs to be watched. I no have time to tell you about him the other day, but he's a scary man! I don't know where he came from but he had 'my Mrs.' eating out of his hand. He almost get her to marry him. Oh, my God!" she sighed, rushing on she continued, "I think he and Mrs. Logan are in cahoots. When 'my Mrs.' get so sick, they got rid of everyone but me and 'Cook'. Then they go hire a bunch of other staff. They fire people who work for 'my Mrs.' thirty years. It's spooky, Beau. I'm more than a little afraid of those two."

I offered, "I think you should be. Tell me this, can you explain again why you think Elinor is being so overly secretive of Dolly's illness."

"Well," she sighed and continued, "she say that it's because she want to protect Mrs. Green. You see, Beau, this crazy thing of 'my Mrs.' came on so sudden like. One day she was out petting her horses and feeding them sugar at Hollywood Park, then the next day, she's nuts.

She would have good days and we all begin to believe Mrs. Logan has reason to protect Mrs. Green. We all believed that one day, 'my Mrs.' just wake up and be her old self again." She sighed heavily, "But since she went into the hospital in May, refusing to eat, she never been the same. Mrs. Logan say she only protect 'my Mrs.' image. She no want the world to know how sick 'my Mrs.' is, when Mrs. Logan say she will get well any day."

"Maria, was there anything particular that seemed to cause Dolly to snap?"

"In my opinion it was a combination of things. First, 'my Mrs.' became almost blind. It was gradual, but over six months, she was really unable to see. It was happening gradually but she hid it very well. 'My Mrs.', she has always been very able to act. Once, she tell me, 'Maria, if I ever go completely blind, I no can see my horses or no can read my books, I'll kill myself! I don't want anyone to see me like I am becoming! I look horrible with age. It just isn't fair. I don't want my godchildren to see me this way. And certainly I don't want my 'darling Beau' to know what I've become'.

"And mark my words, Beau, she tried to kill herself not long after she tell me this. It was God's intervention that prevented her from falling headlong down the marble stairs the night she went nuts, for good."

314

I was saddened by this rhetoric, but urged, "Maria, go on. Tell me what happened that night."

"It was right after the sisters died. Mrs. Lily was the oldest, you know. Lily went nutty two years ago and locked herself up in her house seeing no one. Everyone here make fun of her, call her Mrs. Howard Hughes. She died and it wasn't six weeks after that the other sister, Mrs. Burtie died. But she took too much alcohol and pills. She always was in trouble with the booze."

"God, Maria, I had no idea. So this could be part of what set Dolly off?"

"I am sure of this. One night, a few months after her horse won at the track, Mrs. Green, she started screaming like the demons of Hell were after her. I jolted from my sleep and raced from bed to find 'my Mrs.' at the top of the stairs tangled in the banister with her bed clothing wrapped around her. She was screaming at the top of her lungs, 'I want to die. I want to die, too! I want to be with my sisters, my daddy and Mommy, too'!

"Beau, she tried to throw herself down the marble stairs. If it had not been for her getting all tangled in the banister, she would have fallen all the way down the stairs and probably broken her neck. That is what she tell me she wanted. It is my opinion that the death of her sisters drove 'my Mrs.' to take her life. But fate intervened because God needed her to be punished for what she did to you."

"Maria, what on earth do you mean by that?"

"Well, I think that she never should have given you away and sometimes life has justice after all. 'My Mrs.' was too lazy to bring up her own child. But, she no could completely give you up either. She had to have her pie and swallow it, too. She was that way all her life. If it did not please her, she get rid of it, or she make it so it was the way she wanted it for her own sake. She never think of anyone but herself! I believe that God won't let her leave this life until she has done some penance for all her ways, Beau."She exhaled a heavy sigh as if the weight of the world was resting on her shoulders. "'My Mrs.' tell me the day she give you away, she go to confessional. She say she been forgiven by a priest. But you have no idea how this tore at her in the later years. When she get her marriage annulled from Mr. Schondube, she go to Rome to get a dispensation from the Pope. She tell me while she was there, she asked Monsignor himself to forgive her for giving you away. I tell you Beau, no matter who forgive your mother, she no can get what she done out of her head. She lie so much all her life, she is gonna do penance until she die."

"Maria, I certainly believe what goes around comes around, eventually. But I do not believe in the divine intervention of any supreme being to punish someone who gave away her child some forty years ago."

"Now Beau, I no talking about just that. I talking about all her mortal sins! 'My Mrs.' all her life told nothing but 'little white lies'. She tell me this. 'Oh, Maria,' she say, 'I no like this, I no like that, we just tell a 'little white lie' and make it go away.' If she no like a situation, she fix it with a 'little white lie'.

"Beau, she no like her first husband, she tell her father he beat her up. Mr. Green, he make the man go away. Mr. Walker, she get tired of him, she tell him to get out because he is no good. She lied. Mr. Neil your father, he no want to marry, because he already have a wife. But it's okay to have an affair. It's okay to have little 'Beau-Beau', but we gotta get rid of her before we hurt the Green families name.

"So we get rid of Beau and tell Mr. Hunt she only care for you for a friend. That you no her baby, so she could come back as your godmother. Your Daddy never knew your mommy was Mrs. Green.

"She got Mr. Schondube with her little white lies, he think she in love with him, but she not know what love is. She dump him as fast as the rest, especially when she catch him fooling with you. Do you remember that night in Santa Barbara when the Señor treated you so rough?"

"Maria, I was never in my life as scared as I was that night. I really thought he was going to molest me."

"Yeah, well your mama took care of that fool."She laughed even though the memory was not a peasant one. "Beau, the closest thing 'my Mrs.' ever come to loving anything, was her adoration of you."

"She did always dote on me, didn't she, Maria. You know that is the one thing I have held on to. That no matter what happens, I know to the bitter end, my mother dearly loved me. She always gave me wonderful things, material and inspirational. She was my mentor from a very early age. She was responsible for my appreciation of the beautiful things in life and certainly inspired my literary career as much as she encouraged me to read. I'll never forget that. But I do know she built all her life on a house of 'little white lies'. Perhaps you are right, this is some superior being's way of showing her it was not right. I'm not horribly religious, Maria, but it's possible that someone has determined that she must live the rest of her life talking to inner demons. She was certainly clear on one thing that day we were there. She did not want anyone to take her baby away."

"Well, it's too late! All the prayers in the world will not change things for 'my Mrs.' I always feared because of her deceptive ways she would have a horrible fall. You know she built a life on spider webs of white lies. Now she is caught in the final sticky trap. She gonna sit in that web of deceit until eventually she dies."

"But I still don't really understand why Mrs. Logan is being so secretive about Dolly's condition? What can she hope to gain by keeping it from the family and friends?"

317

"Oh, she no keeping it from people she think should know of 'my Mrs.' illness. She talk to the important ones every other day. She make out like Mrs. Green is gonna get well again. But 'my Mrs.' is never gonna get better. She's too far gone to ever get back.

"I think Mrs. Logan covers this up because she don't want anyone to know how much money she is using of 'my Mrs.' in order to pretend everything is okay when it is not right, at all. Mrs. Logan is setting her own self up very well. She uses 'my Mrs.' money as if it were her own special fund. You should see what she has bought for the help for Christmas, it was positively sick, overboard, expensive stuff!"

Feeling this was not productive on her account, I wanted to steer the conversation back on track.

"Maria, why are all my photo's gone? Especially our portrait by Peter Hurd?"

"That one big argument she and I did have. She say 'my Mrs.' no can see no more so she get rid of your pictures. We fight big over that. She say 'she no can stand the sight of all those sickly sweet pictures no more'. One day she just took them all away including the painting by Señor Hurd. I love your pictures, Beau. I pull them from the garbage and hide them in my room. She no get rid of you so easy with me! I have no idea what she did with the painting. I never see it again. She just never did like you, Beau. I think maybe she and 'my Mrs.' got in some huge fight over a call she never tell 'my Mrs.' about one Christmas a long time ago. I remember she and 'my Mrs.' no talk for days."

I sighed, "I can't imagine why she dislikes me? I only saw her once in my life."

Maria informed, "I no really sure. I think she no like anyone who has any ties to Mrs. Green. I no so sure it has anything to do with you, in particular. She simply wants no one to be close now that 'my Mrs.' is so ill."

I encouraged, "Maria, what else is happening?"

"Other things, they have been going away. I can't find 'my Mrs.' big diamond ring. Mrs. Logan, say she take it to the vault, but I think she sold the thing. Mrs. Logan wears a lot of Mrs. Green's things like her furs, clothing and her jewels."

"That's just wrong. They are Dolly's things, not Logan's to flaunt about while Dolly is so ill."

"Well Mrs. Logan she no think so. She tell me that 'my Mrs.' would have wanted her to have some of her things. She is acting like 'my Mrs.' is already dead."

"This is really too much."

"I could no agree more. Mrs. Logan's buying lots of things for herself and she say it's for her new position as 'my Mrs.' spokes-person. I don't know Beau. I just worry about you and what she gonna do with your mama's things. She say she send out furniture pieces to be repaired. They don't never come back. I just don't know. That woman is up to no good."

"Maria, do you think that Mrs. Logan might have some inkling as to who I really am?"

"No. And I am not gonna be the one to tell her. I'll tell it to a lawyer before I tell that nasty cow anything about 'my Mrs.' family life. She was never privy to it when 'my Mrs.' was well, I no gonna give her privy now that Mrs. Green is so sick. That woman is working things to her advantage, I just know it, Beau.

"She had some big meeting a few months ago. All closed doors and lawyers. She got herself made so she can sign papers and things. She can even sign checks because 'my Mrs.' is too sick. But the lawyers they come out of the meeting saying how wonderful 'my Mrs.' looked. Well of course she did. Mrs. Logan had Arden come do her hair, make-up and nails. Dressed her up real fancy. For a while there, the Mrs. was just blind not crazy like she is now, so 'my Mrs.' pretend everything was okay." Maria sighed as if the retelling of all of this was almost too much for her to bear.

I moaned, "Go on, Maria, I know this must be hard on you to tell."

Maria continued, "When her father's Oil Company sell to Shell, she have more cash than ever before so she buy and buy horses. She go out to the track every day to feed sugar to all those nags. Even when she was pretty sick, she went to the races with bodyguards, supporting her on either side to help her walk. At one point, she had six goons. It was only for appearance sake. Mrs. Logan insist 'my Mrs.' keep up appearances. 'My Mrs.' kept buying more horses. Mrs. Logan tell her to do that too, so no one think anything was wrong. She have more horses than anyone need. I don't know what we ever gonna do with all those nags. Up to the day she went crazy, she had 'that chauffeur' take her to Hollywood Park where "her darlings", she call them, were stabled, to feed them sugar from her hand. I think last count she had seventy-four. With all her Daddy's enormous wealth, she still no could keep this horrible illness away. All the Greens go crazy like this. But she enjoy and spend the dough when she had it from her father's Oil Company sale."

I interrupted, "I remember when Steve showed me the article in the Wall Street Journal about the ten majority Belridge Oil Company, heirs. They interviewed a few but Dolly did not respond. But after the sale of Burton's Company, Dolly started sending me substantially larger Christmas checks. I was a bit surprised to receive a three thousand dollar check as opposed to the usual one."

"Yes," Maria agreed, "she was so pleased to do things for you. But, when she go crazy all that changed. Mrs. Logan take charge and everyone has been cut off. I know as soon as that big meeting was over, Mrs. Logan give orders from 'my Mrs.' office to stop the checks to the godchildren, after Mrs. Logan was made able to sign the checks.

"Well that was certainly a surprise. After so many years of receiving Dolly's Christmas check, the lack of it this year was a real shock."

"You know, Beau, Mrs. Logan still run the offices on Wilshire Boulevard as if Mrs. Green will be coming back at any moment. They run the house the same way. We still have a full time staff."

"This just gets stranger by the day."

"Well a lot of things have gotten odd since 'my Mrs.' become so ill."

I answered, "I should certainly say."

Maria continued, "Well, even 'Cook' remains to fix 'my Mrs.' chicken wings. They are all she now will eat. 'Cook' is still employed here to boil chicken wings when I could do that. But Mrs. Logan she say, any day Mrs. Green will become well. She has the doctor in three times a week to give her vitamin shots. But other than him and the immediate staff, no one really knows how bad Mrs. Green has become."

I interjected, "Maria, if Mrs. Logan has changed Dolly's will to hurt me, I may be forced to contest it as her daughter. Other than my sister, you are my only witness with knowledge that I am Dolly's birth child. Steve thinks that my sister, Penny, might be disqualified because she was too close to the situation. Her credibility could be heavily scrutinized as being a 'biased witness'. Not only that, I received my birth papers some years ago and they are some elaborate smoke screen saying my mother was someone else. You might have to testify that I am Dolly's child. It could be dangerous. Steve and I fear the worst. We believe that Mrs. Logan certainly has manipulated Dolly's estate plans to her own behalf and perhaps harmed me."

There was no hesitation on the maid's account, "Those birth papers were the bunk! Mr. Green got them because they needed legal stuff when they think

you were going off to that *'whaddyaucallit'*
Orphanage. Those papers cause nothing but trouble.
Your adoption to the Hunts almost blew up because of
that mess."

"We figured something like that. Somewhere along
the line I heard Mother and Dad discussing it
privately. Penny and I were always the consummate
eavesdroppers. I said to her once that when she and I
died we would have our ears bronzed and put in the
'Eavesdropper's Hall of Fame'."

This caused Maria to really laugh for the first time
all day. "I think Mrs. Logan may have made some
changes in the will. But also she make some additions.
Herself and that 'chauffeur' being the ones added to
great advantage. If she added, then she'd have to take
away. 'My Mrs.' have a lot of money, but the way Mrs.
Logan is spending it, there won't be much to go
around when 'my Mrs.' dies. Beau, if she has harmed
you, I will swear on a bible's stack that you are Dolly
Green's child. I was at her bedside when you were
born. Mr. Green got some phony papers he got from
Mr. Ford that were from some other ladies baby that
died. Those papers were for when they think to put
you in that Orphanage, Merryvale. Remember, I tell
you all that when you a little girl. When that friend of
your daddy Hunt got in the picture and got you for the
Hunts, the papers no were no longer needed. But
Beau, I remember it as if it were yesterday. You were
born in 'my Mrs.' home, in her bed attended by a
nurse and me. I was only a little girl but strong and
wise for my years. They let me assist. I swear this
Beau. You need help with getting your momma's
things, I help you fix these crooks! That's all they are.
Mrs. Logan and that 'chauffeur', they plotting against
your mother and maybe even you."

"Maria, what do you mean by plotting against me?"

"I just caught a little of this and that the other day. I no sure. I think Mrs. Logan and that 'chauffeur' are trying to push 'my Mrs.' over the brink. I think if she die soon it would be a relief to everyone. But I think they maybe are trying to help her along."

"Maria, perhaps you are in jeopardy staying there with that pack of thieves. Steve said with all the money at stake, you should be cautious yourself. Maybe even get out while the getting is good."

"Beau, people no resign from a lifetime position I hold, like taking a stroll down the plaza, I work for "my Mrs." for fifty three years."

I offered, "I wasn't suggesting resignation would be a walk in the park, but maybe you should consider the options. Maybe it's time for you to go home. Frankly, Steve and I are horribly worried about you!"

"I don't pose no threat to them. Anyway, they don't know what I know. Only you and I share our secrets. I'll be just fine. I need to stay and care for Mrs. Green till she goes to her final rest. Mrs. Logan, she find out I let you in to see 'my Mrs.', she scream a lot but she all wind, little harm."

"Good Lord, Maria, how did she find out? Now I really am worried about you."

"Beau, I'll be fine."She assured. "I am one tough lady to have been through all this and survive. Aren't nothing gonna take me behind my back."

My doorbell rang interrupting further lengthily discussion. I concluded the conversation, saying, "Maria, keep me updated. I need to know what's going on. I thank you so much for you caring and I love you, Maria, you know I always have."

"Yes," she agreed, "I always knew you did. You are a wonderful woman. You were my favorite child. What a credit to your mommy, darling Beau. I love you too. You will be hearing from me soon."

I hung up the phone and rushed to answer the door. It was a dress I'd ordered and was being delivered by UPS.

I called Steve and relayed the conversation later that afternoon.

As before, he advised, "There is little we can do but bide our time. You did record the call?"

"Yes, as we agreed."

So life continued on and on.

CHAPTER SIXTY-SIX

Author's Notes:

Several months after a number of these very negative conversations with Maria, I took it upon myself to send Elinor Logan a letter just to let her know I was miffed over the whole duplicity of the circumstances.

I don't know if it had a harmful effect or not. We had broached the castle walls and she knew it. I don't know if Maria and my continued conversations had a bearing on the outcome, I cannot help but think that the die was cast and that Maria sealed her own fate by staying.

I begged her to leave, but she was far too loyal to Dolly.

Then Maria paid the ultimate price for that loyalty.

THE GAUNTLET IS FINALLY TOSSED DOWN

MY LETTER TO ELINOR F. LOGAN : JUNE 14TH 1988

Dear Mrs. Logan,

It has been nine months since I visited Aunt Dolly and I thought I would check in with you to see how she is doing.

It was a sad visit with her as the previous time Dolly and I were together she was very vital and full of life, as well as extremely sharp.

I kept fairly regular telephone and written contact with her, with the exception of the last year and a half, during which time, Steve and I were negotiating the buyout of a company.

In the fall of 1986, I had a phone conversation with Dolly that greatly unsettled me. It seemed she was getting quite vague. It seemed she was not quite sure who I was, where I lived and did not ever remember the name of her horse trainer or the filly that had won several recent races. I began to be troubled then, but placed it aside because after all, she was getting older. Sometime certain periods of the day are more lucid than others for the elderly.

Some months later, I saw her in the winner's circle at the race track where her filly Brave Raj, received the first place award. Dolly looked good, so as we all do, I did not worry excessively about her. I only learned of her illness when I traveled to California in October of 1987 and dropped by, unannounced.

Dolly was always such an influential factor in my life and to see her in an advanced state of deterioration was, needless to say, a horrible shock.

Dolly and I were exceptionally close as I was growing up. I would say far more so than most godparents to their godchildren. I love her very much and though I can never again get that across to her with her current illness, I wish you to know she is ever on my mind. She has always been in my thoughts but with the current illness far more so.

If it is not too much trouble, I should appreciate an occasional update on her condition. Because you have been so close to her over these years, Mrs. Logan, I know you can appreciate how concerned I am as to her well-being.

My prayers are with her and those who much care for her in this bewildered state. I have had the responsibility of dealing with two of my husband's aunts who suffered with the disease and know how trying it can be.

Please, realize that I wish to know of her status because of my deepest love for her. I only wish I were close so I might be of some aid or comfort, if only to sit with her and hold her hand and quiet her fears.

I can think of no more cruel a fate for Dolly to have become blind, and suffer this debilitating disease. She loved to read, to see beauty, and to be with people who were of quick wit and mind. She was reveling in the enjoyment and love of her horses. I wonder sometimes what cruel twists of fate govern our lives.

It was gratifying that in our visit I truly believe for a moment, if only for that, she remembered who I was. She displayed some of the old Dolly spark by scolding me for contradicting her when I told her it was going to rain for a long time and she said "No, it was most assuredly not and for me to listen to my elders because they were always right!"

I look back on my brief time with her that day as a mixed cherished memory. Mixed because I was so distressed over her condition but grateful to be with her again once more.

I sincerely hope I may be with her again and though she did not fully remember who I was, she did at one point seem to realize who I was and that made the visit more than worthwhile.

When my father died in 1982, I was called to be with him in the last weeks that he lived. At first I hesitated to be there because he had a stroke and was in a similarly deteriorated condition as Aunt Dolly. I chose to be with him because I felt if there was a chance he would recognize me and realize how much I care about him, it was worth my effort to help in his difficult time. He knew me far more than I had hoped, and I have never regretted being with him at the very last.

Dolly will undoubtedly live for quite some time in this altered state, but I am gratified that when I was there, she knew who I was and was glad to be with me again.

Please update me, if it is not too much of a bother. I really wish to know because she has always been more than a godmother to me.

Thank you for your time.

Diane H. Stockmar

It was not all that long before I received this charming letter from Elinor.
July 11, 1988

Dear Diane,

Please forgive my delay in replying to your earlier letter. Time really does get away from me as these are busy times in our office as well as at Dolly's house.

As you know, we five at her office are deeply fond of our dear Dolly and are doing everything possible to keep things running smoothly on her behalf. Since the loss of her two sisters, there is no one to look after her, however, her two sisters were not really able to do so anyway, and we were doing the same for them.

I have been with the Green family since 1/1/60-and that is quite a long time! I looked after Mr. Green first-then the same for the rest of the family. That's sheer devotion, I guess.

I do wish you could have contacted me before having to endure the shock when you unexpectedly dropped in at her house. Her darling Maria who has been with her for so many years, also, immediately told me of your visit and I did mean at that time to contact you. However, Maria said you were going to call me but perhaps your time was limited. I was somewhat waiting for your call. Finally I decided to write as I thought it easier to contact you through a letter than on the phone as I know your time must be busy what with your upcoming move.

Dolly has been failing for several months. Her memory was gradually going and she had no remembrance of many of her good friends.

For quite some time she has needed to rely on me to fill her in. She was quite an actress, as you know, so she managed to carry things off out in a crowd. I believe that as her eyesight was going, her brain was going also. Her appearance on television at the Breeder's Cup in November was the last thing she did, and she managed to carry that off to the best of her ability-with two body-guards and myself assisting her. Bless her heart. At this point, she doesn't remember even having any horses. From that time on, it was down-hill.

Earlier this year we needed to hospitalize her because she was refusing to eat. We pulled her through and from then on have had her home with nurses around the clock.

The Doctors have not specifically diagnosed her condition as Alzheimer's, however, the symptoms seem similar. It is a dementia of some kind. You are correct, as you mentioned in your letter that it might possibly go on for a long time with all the good care she is receiving. She is still the charming Dolly, in spite of everything-always thanking the nurses and everyone caring for her. She speaks very clearly-which was not the case with her sister Lily, who had trouble expressing herself, or finally not being able to speak at all. Dolly hallucinates and seems to be living in her own little dream world. She is in no pain whatsoever. I meet the Doctor there three times a week and we keep careful check on her. She has had a catheter in ever since she was hospitalized, but I finally convinced the Doctor to remove it recently and I think she is much better for it. Maybe not so nice for the nurses, but that is what we are paying them for. We are most fortunate to have a great staff of nurses. Her main day nurse is a darling and is more of a companion to Dolly than nurse. She is darling to her. I see her everyday and we have guards on duty and her household staff is excellent too-all wanting to give her the best possible care, which she deserves.

Sorry this couldn't be a more UP letter. I will be pleased to keep you informed of any changes, and feel free to call me any time.

Apparently Steve is no longer with the bank and you have ventured into a new business? I presume Tim is a grown young man by now. I visit in Denver some as all my relatives are there. Dr. Dean and Betty Yates (Betty is my first cousin) I believe have known Steve's parents. I had mentioned the name at the time Dolly flew over for your wedding and I believe they said they were members of the same Country Club or ???

Thank you again Diane for your letter. We will keep in touch.

Sincerely,
Elinor Logan,
Secretary to Dolly Green

CHAPTER SIXTY-SEVEN

Author's Notes:

In 1989 our own lives were plunged into amazing turmoil. The company that had seemed just the solution for Steve and me did a death spiral under the partnership with Arthur M.

Arthur saw one way to run it and Steve saw it as a completely different situation, a business not a personal bank account for his desires.

Steve bowed out and let Arthur deal with the company we thought would have been the rest of our lives.

To clear our heads, we took a cross-country trip.

At the end of the journey, we stopped at Steve's parent's home for the night in Vail, Colorado. A pause that would also change the course of our lives.

On that fateful evening, we discovered through an advertisement in the Vail Daily that our favorite kitchen store, Krismar, was for sale.

Weeks later we bought the business and moved permanently to the mountain town.

So to say our situation was tumultuous while everything changed around us is an understatement.

In addition to that, Tim was at a formative age of an early teen. He was horribly unhappy about the move and made sure we were suffering every step of his extraction from his beloved town.

Despite that, we moved lock stock and parakeet to Vail in the fall of 1989.

It was a turbulent time in our lives. Getting our entire world moved, Tim settled in a new school environment and just generally switching complete gears.

Little wonder that the Dolly situation was put on the back burner. There was nothing we could do but move

*forward with our own lives at that point so proceed
with that we did with great verve.*

*We embraced the change from city life to the rural
mountain community and once there, Tim managed to
fit in to a certain extent. But decided at eighteen, he
needed to go his own way and moved to Boulder to go
to school there.*

*Empty nesters for the first time in our lives, we forged
ahead with the business of Krismar and monitored the
Green situation as we could. But little seemed to
change.*

*However, I continued to have frequent updates with
Maria. The last conversation follows in this chapter.*

*Intriguingly enough, Maria never mentioned the
chauffeur's name. She referred to him as 'that chauffeur'
in all her conversations that I recorded. So that is how
I refer to him as well.*

Fall of 1989

BUENOS DIAS SEÑORA BEAU

I had not heard from Maria for a while. She knew
we were busy with our new business and said she
would keep me informed, but I had heard little from
her recently.

Maria was on the line, whispering very low, "Beau?
It is Maria, can you hear me alright?"

I was instantly alarmed. "Maria, what's wrong?"

"I can't stay long on the phone. I afraid with all
these calls to Colorado, Mrs. Logan will be furious
with me, talking to you."

I immediately offered, "I'll call you right back."

"If I don't answer, say you are my cousin Elaina and
try to sound Spanish if you can."

"Como esta, Chica?" I voiced, "Good enough Señora,
Rivera?"

332

"Si, Beau. I get off and you call right back."

I shook my head with bewilderment as I rapidly dialed the number I'd known for so many years.

It rang two times and was answered, curtly, by a man.

"Green's." his gruff response.

"Maria Rivera, por favor, um...thees is her cousin, Elaina. I'm calling long distance from Puerto Rico. Please hurry, Señor, I no can afford to pay too long a phone bill."My spotty English was incredibly well feigned.

"One moment," he sighed impatiently. His reply was less than pleasant.

I wondered if this was THE chauffeur I had heard all about when Maria and I had last spoken. It surely had to be him, because the last house-man, Julio, had drowned in Puerto Rico some years ago. This had to be the chauffeur that Maria so despised. He certainly sounded unpleasant enough to convince me he was a rough character.

It was some moments before Maria came on the line.

We chatted randomly for quite a while in Spanish. Both were unwilling to say anything until we heard a disconnecting click on the other line.

Finally, the other phone was hung up and we resumed in English.

Maria complimented me on my Spanish, not realizing that I spoke so fluently.

"Gracias," I thanked, then inquired again, "Is anything horribly wrong? You sound really upset."

"Mrs. Green has been so bad lately they have had to tie her to the bed with restraints. It's been horrible, Beau. The doctor came and gave her heavy sedation. They have hired another nurse. She is a very large, black woman named Marti. She lifts 'my Mrs.' like a feather. She restrains 'my Mrs.' when she goes berserk, which lately is almost every night. Oh, Beau, things are very bad here."

I interrupted, "Maria, you sound horribly alarmed. What has happened to upset you so much?"

"After Mrs. Logan find out I let you into the house, she yell at me that I was a 'stupid Mexican Cow'! 'Cook' tell me that she accidentally tell Mrs. Logan that I let you in and Mrs. Logan tell 'Cook' she gonna fire me. She no do that, she no fire me, I too valuable to her with 'my Mrs.'! But she plenty mad. I never seen Mrs. Logan so furious over something that I make judgment must be done. I let you in because you came all the way from Colorado to see your god-mommy. I no think I cause this kind of reaction. I can't understand what I did so wrong."

I offered concern, "Oh, Maria, I hoped you wouldn't get in trouble over letting us in. I thought we were there alone and no one would ever find out. When did 'Cook' get back that she saw us at the house?"

"She come back from church and even I not know she was home. She say nothing to me, but she tell Mrs. Logan. 'Cook' no think Mrs. Logan mind so much, either. She was happy for 'our Mrs.' you finally come to see your godmother, even though she so sick. Whooh, 'Cook' say she never say nothing again to Mrs. Logan, if it cause her to react like that."

"I am so, sorry. What do you think Mrs. Logan will do?"

"Well, I don't think she is going to fire me. She always has been mostly wind, little harm. But, 'that chauffeur' scare me to death. I no trust her or this horrible man. Since you were here, he watches my every move. I think he is evil. I'm beginning to be afraid of him. I overhear them talk some funny conversation the other day. I no could hear the words real clear but I did catch them say, 'they have to eliminate someone'. I think he's gonna arrange for someone to get rid of your mother."

334

I felt the hair raise on my arms, a cold wind seemed to blow at my back. "Maria, you need to get away from there! It sounds to me like things might be getting completely out of hand."

Maria quickly picked up, "Beau, I no can pick up and go just like that. I have ties I would have to break here in Los Angeles, I have many friends I make over the years. Some of whom I am making arrangements to talk to and tell about these things that are going wrong. If they know I have talked to people outside, they no ever think to bother with me."

I interjected, "Well you should at least think about resigning, especially if the chauffeur has you this scared. After all, maybe she will fire you, then you will be forced to leave."

The maid continued to confide, "I no think she get rid of me so easily. I help her with 'my Mrs.' far too much. She tell that to 'Cook' because she so mad at me. The other day, though, Mrs. Elinor, talk to 'that chauffeur' awful about you. She say how much she hate you. She say you better not stand in her way over Mrs. Green's will or she get rid of you. Mrs. Elinor has become like a woman possessed over 'my Mrs.' money! You better watch yourself, Beau."

"Maria, she wouldn't recognize me if I walked into a deserted room. And, how on earth can she possibly dislike anyone she doesn't know? I think you are probably just over reacting to a situation that is finally grating on your nerves."

"All I know is your mother is failing fast. I don't think Mrs. Logan is going to have to wait long before 'my Mrs." go all together. But listen to me, I think you need to be careful, Beau. Mrs. Elinor, she got nothing out of any of the other Greens' estates. Your mommy is her last and only hope for any money at all."

"But Maria, if they have been messing with her will, we can contest it and you will be my witness that things were going amiss."

"You can bet she has been playing funny business with 'my Mrs.' will. Remember I tell you about that meeting with those lawyers where she get 'my Mrs.' all dressed up? Well I know Mr. Van Vleet, 'my Mrs.' attorney. He was there as was Mrs. Logan, some banker, and another lawyer. They were asked to witness 'my Mrs.' sign something. Mrs. Logan helped 'my Mrs.' sign the documents. I was hiding in the hall. Logan, she no see me. They made changes, all right, maybe changes, harming you. But your mommy no have any idea what she was doing that day. As blind as a bat and crazy, she only do what Mrs. Logan tell her to do."

I moaned, "I'm sure Elinor increased her ante during that signing. But we have no way of getting to the papers until Dolly dies."

"It's no matter if you think I am coming up with silly talk, I am not. I am worried for you, your mama and even myself if she find out we have talked. You don't know these people. They will stop at nothing to get money! I begin more and more everyday to believe this is so. They gonna get things, and won't let no one stand in their way."

I sensed the terror in Maria's voice. "Maria, if you are this scared, then you should definitely get away. Tell them since they hired a new nurse, that you feel you've done what you can for your mistress and return to Puerto Rico and lay low. Don't you still have quite a lot of family there?"

"Oh, yes. My mother and father are still alive. Bless them, they are both ninety-five. The Riveras live forever, thank the saints. All my cousins, my aunts, they want me to come back. In fact, they have begged me."

"Then go, Maria. Dolly does not know who you are anymore. Your loyalty has far surpassed the call of duty in your love and devotion, unlike someone else who thinks she should be martyred, for service to my mother."

Maria expressed relief at my suggestion. "I sometimes do feel like I just sitting in the mouth of the tornado by staying here. Beau, you really think I should resign?"

"It's the eye of the hurricane, Maria." It made me inadvertently laugh. So far, it was the only levity in the conversation. "I do think you should quit. Especially if you are afraid. Do it, Maria. Maybe not tomorrow, at your own time frame. Get yourself organized, and tender your resignation to Elinor. Then, on your way to Puerto Rico, stop here in Gypsum. We have direct flights from L.A. to Eagle. I'll drive over and get you. You can stay with us and we'll go over our strategy away from prying ears."

"Oh, Beau, you have helped me make up my mind. Like I say, I have many loose ends to tie up, but in a few weeks or so, I will resign. I'll let you know when I come."

I insisted, "Resign as soon as you can. This stress of living this way with the unpleasantness overshadowing everything you do, cannot possibly make you feel well. Pressure and anxiety always tend to be physically wearing on people. Are you holding up, all right?"

"Oh, Beau. You know me. I never been sick in my life. I like a horse. I never let anything get me down. No, things like this no affect me. You see. I'll be fine. As soon as I get things in order, you be the first to know. I'll be seeing you after Thanksgiving, no later, maybe even before."

We signed off the phone. I was comfortable that Maria would take my advice and I would have a houseguest soon.

****

337

I never spoke with Maria again.

I then received a letter from Elinor Logan saying how tragic it was to relate the news of Maria's death.

I could not believe it. However, I also believe that they realized that Maria was talking to me and that she needed to be eliminated.

This is the final poison pen I received from dear Elinor. It was dated December 9th, 1989:

Dear Diane,

I have horrible and shocking news. Our darling, faithful, Maria is dead. November 19th, she was stricken by a massive cardiac arrest. We rushed her to the hospital where she survived the day but not the night. By dawn our darling was gone.

There was little warning of her poor health, though the doctor suspected she had been hiding her illness, all along.

Lately, I had noticed that she tired easily and seemed to have a shortness of breath. A few days before her death, I noticed she looked listless, older, and her color was not good. I chalked it up to stress over Dolly's increasing downhill, battle. I assumed Maria was just reflecting stress in the anticipation of Dolly's loss.

Never would I have anticipated Maria would pre-decease Dolly. We all are filled with enormous shock over her death.

Her parents flew in from Puerto Rico but did not arrive in time to bid her farewell.

Her parents took her body and asked us to send personal belongings, along later. They had services for her in Puerto Rico, just the other day.

This has been truly a horrible month.

Soon after Maria's shocking departure, dearest Dolly refused to eat again and we were forced to hospitalize her. They discovered she had lumps of cancer in her breasts, so performed surgery, right away. She is recovering well and is still at Cedars of Sinai. They are trying to build up her weight as she has become so frail.

I hope that my news has not too unduly disturbed to you. I called but the operator said your home phone was unlisted in the directory. I called the shop, but some young woman refused to give me your private line, which in my absent-minded state, I seem to have misplaced. So I had to tell you this way.

We still pray daily that Dolly will be her old self. I doubt, however, that will happen, yet they always say there is hope.

I'm afraid the Christmas season will be a sad, lonely one, for me without my dearest Maria, and with dearest Dolly off in the hospital, I feel as if I have lost my two very best friends.

I expect your Holiday will be wonderful with your dear family around you. I just know you have made the right move for all of you.

I apologize about our rather terse conversation the other day. I have been so-over loaded with all my responsibilities that I have not been quite myself. I guess we both got a little out of line. Certainly I accept your kind apology, as I feel perhaps I caught you off guard.

Sincerely,
Elinor Logan
Personal Secretary to Mrs. Green

I remember getting the letter and reading it in the back area of Krismar. I was doing a Christmas display when Steve rushed into the store and handed me the letter and waited for me to read it. Wordlessly, I handed it to him and dissolved into tears. I simply could not believe that my worst nightmare had just come true. Maria was dead! I had warned her but she refused to believe anything could happen to her.

That day, my entire focus shifted to my own peril. We immediately contacted an attorney and began discussing the situation with him.

He advised that we retain counsel in Los Angeles and promised to investigate who was an estate litigator there. That we certainly needed to be ready in the event Dolly subsequently suddenly died.

Sadly for Dolly, she lingered for almost another year.

But at this point in time, Steve insisted I get my sister on board with this dilemma. Now that Maria was deceased, our ace in the hole gone, Penny needed to be entirely brought up to speed.

CHAPTER SIXTY-EIGHT

Author's Notes:

The entire process of finding a qualified estate litigator seemed to go well as there were plenty to pick from in LA. That being a town that seemed to routinely be rocked by familial suit disputes.

I am choosing not to mention the Attorneys that we retained because the litigation was rocky and to the greater extent, fruitless.

Also, because I firmly believe that in the end, our chosen counsel was bribed to go away with an undisclosed amount by the legal representation for the Green's estate.

I do not want to get into a legal pissing contest with them twenty years later. All are still actively practicing law at the time I am writing this tome.

SPRING 1990

SISTERS REUNITED AGAIN

I drove hurriedly on my way to Glenwood Springs where I was to pick up my arriving sister,
I seemed to pace the train in my urgency to be at the station by the time she actually arrived.

Penny Clark was on board and it had been almost ten years since we had seen one another. That last reuniting of us sisters was for our Dad's funeral in 1981.

Unfortunately over the passage of the past twenty years, we had not been rejoined for very many happy times. Soon after Steve and I were married, Marie Hunt developed heart problems which eventually claimed her life. Penny and I were only in our twenties when Mom passed away.

So we lost our mother early in our lives, a risk of parents adopting so late in life. Their children will not be enjoying them very long into their own adulthood unless the adoptive parents lead a very long life.

So the reasons Penny and I had been together over the past few times, had been ones of sadness and grievous unhappiness over the loss of a loved one. Not exactly conducive to reviving old sisterhood friendship.

Plus, Penny always hated to fly. Growing up she hated it. As an adult she refused to do it, making travel and times together for us hard to accomplish.

With me living in Colorado, the distance loomed an obstacle that seemingly promoted keeping us apart.

For many years we had been in contact only occasionally, by the telephone and then, usually only mandatory, because of holidays. Because of the distance we lived from one another, we never had the time to be adult sisters to one another.

With Steve's urging, I determined to get back together again with my sister. Steve thought that with all that was happening with Dolly Green, the reunion was imperative.

After I had seen Dolly in her state of deterioration, I decided that the years were fleeting away before I could stop them. It was high time to re-unite and reacquaint with my sister, Penny Clark.

It had been my fault that so much time had slipped away. I rued the fact that because of my own busy life and the pursuit of what seemed so much more important, things like my own family had been put on the back burner.

Life was passing by and if I did not take some matters in my own hands, Penny and I would be in nursing homes together, not able to go off on shopping jaunts.

I got it in my head that we should see if we could spend some fun time with one another again as adults. We had been very good buddies as kids, why not try it now.

I called Penny and insisted that she come out to Colorado so we could spend some quality time together after all these years. In that phone conversation, I got an update of what was going on in my sister's life.

Penny and her former husband Bill, had moved to Elko, Nevada some years ago to buy up property and build. Elko at the time they moved there was a booming mining town.

Penny and Bill took the inheritance from Dad's estate and built several warehouses in the city outskirts which provided them with a nice income while they lived at the foot of the Ruby Mountains in what was voted 'Americas Friendliest Little Town'.

They had the urge to get away from it all just like we had done when we moved to Vail. However, Bill had become dissatisfied as the town grew so rapidly. He wanted to move to a further isolated spot at which point, Penny drew the line. She liked her home in Elko, liked her friends and refused to move.

Subsequently, Bill alone moved to a remote coastal Oregon town named Glide. The couple then divorced.

Penny agreed that a trip to Colorado sounded like a wonderful break in her routine.

So March 12th had rolled around which was the designated day for Penny to travel to Colorado. She would be with me for two glorious weeks of just 'girl stuff'.

Glenwood Springs is home to one of the older train depots in Colorado. The Colorado River runs swift and turbulent beside the approaching trains almost as if the water dares the train to race.

The sky was winter blue, dotted with puffs of marshmallow clouds, scudding across the horizon like ships on a turquoise sea.

The Super Chief chugged into the station just as I drove into the parking lot and made a dash for the platform. I watched as Penny descended the stairs.

We rushed into one another's arms and hugged. We looked one another over. I told Penny she looked tired and run down, scolding my sister who was normally so beautifully kempt. I told her that she needed to take better care of herself. Dark circles were under her eyes, she was semi-gaunt and her hair lacked its normal healthy glow. In short, I was taken aback by Penny's appearance, but chalked it up to the ravages of the recent divorce. Hopefully the trip to Vail would put the peaches back into my sisters sallow cheeks.

I helped Penny carry her bags to the car and once loaded, we boarded the Suburban and headed off to Vail to spend two glorious weeks together catching up on the passage of time.

The first night we were together, Steve had a Lionshead Merchant's Association meeting he couldn't miss. He had been recently elected the Association President and he needed to conduct the important meeting. So Penny and I were alone.

We dined on a sumptuous dinner that I prepared. Veal chops smothered in caramelized onions, a side of pan flashed polenta and a crisp garden salad with blue cheese dressing fit our bill of fare to a tee.

In the food-stuffed-aftermath, we were sitting by the fire, relaxing and sipping a glass of Chardonnay.

Penny asked, "Do you remember when we were little kids? I always dressed up as a bride and you were the flashy Spanish dancer? Boy," she snorted a sarcastic laugh, "I sure had no idea when I was small how many times I'd repeat the marital act. I certainly had enough dress rehearsals as a kid."

I nodded in recollection of the long past years. "We were both good at the 'pretend' game. We perfected it to art form. It's too bad that childish masquerades don't always turn out to be real. You were a beautiful bride, but I guess, we forgot to practice the happy endings, riding off into the sunsets and what not."

Penny looked reflectively into the fire, wistfully finishing the train of her thoughts, "We both certainly grew up in the midst of a fairy tale world."

I nodded in agreement, "That's for damn sure."

We both reflected silently for some moments on those introspective words.

This lull in the conversation prompted me to pour us both another glass of wine.

When I settled myself down in front of the fire, Penny tentatively ventured, "Do you remember much about when we were growing up?"

"Everything!"I looked into the gold wine as I watched the flames from the fire shimmer through the amber liquid. "I recall everything even back to when I was one and my life revolved around Dolly Green!"

Penny sat up stiff in her chair. "You little creep! You did remember living with Dolly. I knew you did. A kid with a memory like yours could never have forgotten those early years. You faked it, not remembering about your past when Dolly decided to blast back into your life? Didn't you?"

I nodded my head affirmatively. "Unfortunately or not, I recall everything as if it were an album of photographs. I can recall my circus tent room, my toys, but the hardest of all was to be without Dolly and Maria, whom I truly adored. I never did figure out exactly what I did that was so wrong that Dolly would send me away.

"Of course I knew 'Uncle Neil' did not want me there. And if he would not marry Dolly she would not keep me because I was a disgrace to the Greens. I learned all that from overhearing conversations in the

Mountain Drive house. You know I listened at doors at Dolly's house, as much as we both did at the Hunt's."

Penny chuckled richly and said, "Yes but it's unbelievable to me that you could have fooled everyone into thinking you did not remember. You even kept the secret from me till now. Why didn't you tell me?"

"You may or may not remember, Sissy dear, but your temper was pretty extraordinary and tattling was one of your main strengths. I was afraid if you got mad and knew I still recalled my past, in anger you might tell Mother and Dad. When they finally decided to let me be with Dolly again, I was not about to jeopardize that privileged right."

"Tell me, do you recollect the day you came to live with us or was that so traumatic that you blocked it out?"

"I must have a reverse memory ability because instead of blocking, I recall things verbatim. It's kind of spooky, but it sure comes in handy sometimes when I have to figure out what Steve has done with a bronze he put in a safe place, or even a set of keys." I took another sip of wine. "No, I can remember every detail of the day I came to stay, as if it was yesterday. I had been so excited to go to play with you, I did not recognize the emotional distress the servants were undergoing. They were all sad to see me go, even crying. I had no clue what was going on. When you said I was there to stay, I couldn't believe my ears. I thought I was dreaming but it was more of a nightmare, not one of the good dreams."

Penny shook her head in disbelief. "I can hardly believe you never let on till now. But go on tell me more. This is fascinating to me!"

"You know when I was there in Dolly's home, she and Neil were always fighting. Of course it was over me. Dolly screamed, she cajoled, she made love to him all in the living room and I would sneak down the stairs and listen for hours behind the Chinese lacquer screen.

"I didn't know any better that people argued, so as I grew more to understand, I realized my name was mentioned a lot. That is why I thought Dolly sent me away. Because Uncle Neil always said, it didn't matter a wit that she'd had the child! 'Beau-Beau' meant nothing to him! I remember one time he even said he did not know for sure who the father was and doubted Dolly did as well. I remember that made Dolly really mad because she threw a valuable vase at him and the next day cried a lot and tried to glue the pieces back.

"When her father noticed the porcelain gone, Dolly said I overturned it and it shattered. I got the blame. Burton was angry but said nothing to me."

Penny shook her head in disbelief. "Should we get a tape recorder and be getting this down? I mean this should go into your book you have been promising to write about the Greens."

I negatively responded, "No need, it's all in my steel-trap-brain. But we probably ought to go over some of the grey areas. If I forget some things, maybe you could recall them. We should collaborate on the book. After all, you are quite a character in the telling of the tale."

"Sis, I'd love to work on the book with you. I've been so at loose ends since Bill split, it would give me something to concentrate on, rather than what a three time failure I am."

I inserted, "Penny you just need to find the right companion. I can fix you up with one of my pals."

"Don't bother to make blind dates for me that you are so famous for. I'm in no hurry at all to resume any relationships except with you. But you said something about Maria being worried about things going on with Dolly. Now that Maria is dead, how are you going to prove her worries were valid facts?"

"Well, Sis, you may have to be a witness for me if my mother's captors are doing what Maria suspected they are doing to her will. You may have to testify on my behalf as knowing I am Dolly's daughter. Maria definitely thought the secretary and chauffeur messed with Dolly's will. Now with her gone, you are my last real hope. Maria did send a diary of Dolly's, but Steve thinks though it will be very helpful, a person who was involved with the whole deal would even be better yet."

Penny nodded, "I have no qualms with that. I am positive Dolly is your birth mother. I remember all the conversations she and Mom had over the six months we were trying to adopt you. You may think you have a corner on recall memory, but mine is pretty sharp as well. Mom and Dolly schemed for hours on the phone over how to fool Daddy. Dolly is your birth mother, there is no doubt in my mind. I'll swear to it in court."

"Thanks, Sis. If the will is manipulated, I'll need you there for me. Meanwhile, we can begin the book in the spring, when things die down for us at Krismar, and you can clear your slate."

"Great plan." Penny stood and stretched. She went to sit near the fire. "I've been so cold lately. I can't seem to stay warm. I sure hope I'm not coming down with anything. I wanted to come here and do nothing but lunch, shop and catch up on sister stuff, not be sick."

"I have a good internist here. If you get ill, Tom will fix you up." I handed Penny a shawl that was draped over the back of the couch and urged her to put it on for added warmth.

"Thanks, but doctors and I are not best friends."Penny adjusted the wrap and asked, "Does Steve know all about the adoption?"

"Yes. I told him everything while we were still in college. We never have had any unshared secrets."

"You have led a very charmed married life, unlike the three-time-failure here. Steve is a wonderful man. He reminds me a lot of Daddy. So loyal, so kind. He treats you like a queen. I never in all my three attempts seemed to find a man who did anything but end up treating me mean."

"I'm so sorry. Maybe here we'll find you a good guy. I know some fellows you might like."

"No, thanks. I have no interest in men right now. Maybe the next trip. Meanwhile, let's continue on this Dolly thing. Did you ever get your adoption papers? Or did you give up on those?"

"I actually did get them. Boy did they throw me for a loop until I had a conversation with Maria. She told me that I was born at Dolly's home assisted by a midwife. Maria confided that she was in attendance at my birth. Apparently, when Dolly decided to get rid of me, she chose first to send me to an orphanage. Burton had to get papers of birth to get me into the orphanage so he got them from a friend whose son had gotten a show girl preggers and the little baby died. The certificate Burton procured caused all kinds of trouble in my adoption for the Hunts. At one point, the show girl was so belligerent to sign off on the papers that the Hunts almost gave up adopting me. Then on top of that, there was some deal with the father paying Dolly off. The balance of the money was to be transferred for my Westlake schooling, and that almost shot the deal down as well."

"I know. If Mom had not been like a dog on a bone, the adoption would have blown away like smoke. Daddy was ready to walk away but Mother persevered!"

I agreed. "From the letters I read, at one point Dolly was getting very bored with the whole thing. There are letters in the adoption file regarding 'how restless the woman in custody of the child was getting and how anxious she was to be rid of the child'. Those letters would be from Neil McCarthy, my real father, directed to Elmo Conley. He was the attorney for Mom and Dad who were handling the adoption. Neil seemed more anxious to get rid of me than anyone else, just to get Dolly off his back."

"How lovely. But our dad never knew you were Dolly's child. You know that, don't you?"

"Oh, of course. He remained fooled to the day he died. According to Maria, that was some part of Dolly and Mother's bargain. Mom realized if Dad knew Dolly was my mother and disposing of me, he'd adopt me, but the 'godmother' role would have been nixed. And, I know for a fact, that Mother felt Dolly's input in my life was important and of course, she was right."

"Exactly! Mother and Dolly always plotted your life when they spent hours on the telephone."

I laughed at the memory."I swear I thought for the longest time Marie Hunt had a phone attached permanently to her head."

Penny yawned and said, "I'm still tired from that train ride, I think I'll turn in. I'll take a few aspirin and hope I feel better tomorrow. Beau, I'm so glad we are having this time together. It's really important to me." We hugged and both went to bed.

As I got ready to retire, I was thinking how unhappy I was with the way Penny seemed so run down. Her color was not good, something about her just did not ring as healthy. I would try to get her to my doctor and see what Tom Steinburg had to say. But I knew Penny had an aversion to physicians and I doubted I would get my sister to pay the clinic a call. I had an oppressive feeling about the way my sister looked. In all actuality, she seemed horribly run down and ill.

But I rationalized to myself that if I had been through the rigors of three divorces, perhaps I would not look like I stepped out of a beauty salon.

This trip to Colorado would surely put my sister on the mend!

CHAPTER SIXTY-NINE

Author's Notes:

It was an amazing visit. I felt a lot like we both stepped back in time. Going over the recollected memories of our combined childhood, was like tripping the 'dark fantastic' all over again.

So vivid were our remembrances, that it almost seemed we were just little girls again.

It was a wonderful two weeks of bonding that neither of us knew would be the last.

It should be noted that Penny and I came up with the title to the Dolly Green fictional novel and that is still what it is today...

Dark Side of a Fairy Tale!

BACK IN THE SISTERHOOD GROOVE

For two days, Penny complained that she did not feel all that well. Symptoms of listlessness, headaches and muscle cramps kept us from any major outings. It sounded like the flu to me, so I hauled my doctor-hating-sister, off to my physician, Tom Steinburg.

He did quite a few tests that failed to prove anything except that she probably was suffering the influenza that was going around. Her white count was elevated but that was a part of the current flu. Proper medication was prescribed and after a few days, Penny felt much better.

We proceeded to continue with our anticipated shopping and lunching spree. Catching up daily on old times, we resumed the sisterhood groove.

It was amazing how Penny recalled many details that I had spaced. So day by precious day, things remembered by both of us were committed to my computer. Little by little the core of the novel was in the memory disc. With our simple childhood recollections, we had already logged close to forty thousand words.

Always the clinician when it came to my books, I surmised, *"Reservations for One in Hell* was eighty thousand plus words. My gosh! We are already half way there and we have hardly even begun."

Penny chuckled, "You know it has been so long since I even thought about this stuff, it is causing me to revisit the whole scenario all over again."

I groaned, "Man, you and me both! I have always had an overactive dream situation but now I am reliving being in Dolly's mansion and doing so many things that I had thought I had put to rest. The mind is an incredibly complex thing. Some people have so little recall. Sometimes, I just don't know where I pull things from my mind."

Penny snorted a laugh, "Part of the reason I decided my marriage to what's his name was over was that he accused me of pulling things out of my ass one too many times, not my brain. It is refreshing that you think that is where your ideas hail from, not the other aforementioned anatomical part!"

I guffawed, "If anyone tried to say that to me, they would be having a conversation with someone down in the region where I titled my first book."

And so things went.

CHAPTER SEVENTY

Author's Notes:

Steve had been busy finding an attorney in L.A. that was reputed to be a high level estate litigator.

During the time Penny was with us, the attorney made the trip out to interview us regarding the possibility of a Green will contest.

When he saw the wedding picture of me with Dolly and Burtie, his comment was "it was like looking in a mirror twice!"

The good old Green schnozzle ruled that day!

SUMMIT TALKS

In the middle of Penny's visit, Steve arranged a summit meeting with 'the attorney' that he had retained.

The lawyer was astounded at Penny's memories regarding the early years and after picking her brain for four hours commented on her recollections. "The two of you are amazing! I have trouble recalling what I had for breakfast and you ladies remember what color party dresses you wore to your tea parties. Shocking! This law suit will be a damn slam dunk!"

Steve quipped, "Now Penny, don't go doing anything foolish like getting hit with a runaway bus. We really will be relying heavily on your testimony and that is the fact."

We wrapped up the meeting and Steve went back to work.

Penny and I headed out to lunch at the Uptown Grill.

Penny was first to ask, "Do you trust that man?"

I hesitantly replied, "He came highly recommended by someone Steve trusts. I think we'll be okay. He is reputed to be a real snake when it comes to will contests."

So it was left at that, but I chewed on my sister's worry the entire time. Penny was amazingly intuitive. If she had asked the question, there was a reason why.

Two evenings before Penny was to return to Elko, Steve was again away on business. We continued to rehash more memories from the past.

I watched my sister's animated chatter, feeling more at ease about how much better Penny seemed after the past few weeks. Her color was better, she was more relaxed, and in general she was more the person I had anticipated seeing. It relieved me because I wanted my sister to have a good life!

Inspired by our recent bonding, I insisted, "Penny, move here in the fall. What do you say? Get your loose ends picked up in Nevada, and move out here then."

Penny sat quietly for a moment, reflecting on my words.

She responded within seconds, "You know I think I will. I have fallen in love with Colorado. I could help you with your books and also work in Krismar if you'd like. I just need to get my ducks in order and I'll motivate out here next September before the snows fly."

I stood and walked over to Penny and gave her a big hug. "That's just what I hoped you'd say. I'll drive out when you're organized, we'll pack up the Suburban and drive back together. This is going to be so great!"

We spent the remainder of the evening making moving plans. We mapped out the strategy of the move and exactly when it should take place.

CHAPTER SEVENTY-ONE

Author's Notes:

I am so thankful I had that time with my sister, had I not, it would have been a regret all the rest of my life.

The things we had discussed were logged, the gaps between our lengthily separations bridged. I was sad to see her going off again but looking forward to our plans of her moving here in the fall.

Time always passed quickly, Steve and I had a busy summer schedule ahead and I knew the months would simply fly till Sis and I were back together again.

TILL WE MEET AGAIN

March 25th was a snowy day as Penny and I traveled through Glenwood Canyon to meet the west bound train to Salt Lake. The weather reflected our mood, glum and sad. We had not allocated enough time together, but were assuaged by the prospect of the upcoming eventual move.

Philosophical to the bitter end, I hugged Penny and said, "September will be here before we know it. I love you Penny, you know I always did."

We hugged each other hard. It seemed Penny would not let me go. I gently pushed her away and urged her to board the train. I stood watching the giant engine huff and puff my sister away.

I drove back to Vail, intermittently quietly weeping over the parting. I kept wishing we had allotted a little more time because so much was still unsaid. But I dried my tears as I neared our home, placating myself with the exciting thoughts of the upcoming spring and then the major summer season that I knew would just fly by.

September would be around the corner and Penny would be here in Vail for good. Sisters reunited once again. Nico and Billy Bob ride again. High Ho, Buck. I began to laugh at myself over how silly I was being, acting like a God-damned kid again.

I was still chuckling to myself when Steve greeted me as I walked in the door. "Hi, love. You and your sister have that much fun?"

"Yes, we did. And it really did feel good to remember what good friends we were and could become again. It felt neat."

When Penny got home she called me to say she was safely there. Still feeling a little under the weather, she vowed to go see her doctor for further tests to figure out what exactly was wrong with her.

****

A week later a Dr. Hall called. We were at home about to get ready for bed.

Steve heard me ask, "Is Penny very ill?"

Steve, sitting in his leather wing-hair by the fire, looked up at my words. He had been very concerned over Penny's appearance, but had not said a great deal to me. He watched as my face froze with horror of the notification. I stared at the phone with utter disbelief!

Steve sensing that something horrendous was being disclosed, rushed to my side as I dropped the receiver.

I raced to our bedroom crying while Steve picked up the dangling headpiece and talked to the person on the other line. "What on earth did you just say to my wife?" he commanded, his voice harsh with uncertainty.

"Mr. Stockmar?"

"Yes." he affirmed, still terse.

"I'm Dr. Frank Hall. I was Penny Clark's physician and close personal friend. I'm afraid Mrs. Clark has just passed away."

Steve needed to comfort me but barked terse instructions. He then thanked the doctor and hung up the offensive phone.

He hurried to our bedroom and grasped me in his arms trying to console me.

It was some time before I could halt my tears. "Why, Steve? Why? She was too damn young to die?"

"Honey, the doctor asked to do an autopsy. I gave him the consent. We really should know. I mean she was sick when she was here, but we thought it was just the flu."

****

Ten days later, we had our answer. Though the cause of death was a blood clot to the brain, Penny was completely riddled with deadly cancer. The liver had huge lesions and probably threw off the fatal clot.

I was devastated over the findings. My sister had such an aversion to doctors, she probably avoided going until the very last.

In Vail, she'd insisted that the doctor do only the cursory tests. She promised to have a complete physical when she returned home.

A neighbor had been worried not seeing Penny for two days, knowing she just returned from a trip. The neighbor broke into Penny's house and found her lying almost dead in her den.

According to Dr. Hall, she had been transported by ambulance in an unconscious state.

They had done all they could, but it had been by far too late to save her life.

CHAPTER SEVENTY-TWO

Author's Notes:

I needed to go out to Elko and deal with Penny's home and belongings. The dogs and cats and everything about her life, needed to be resolved.

Her daughter Kathy was a wreck but was mentally challenged as well. Kathy had been under psychiatric care for years and we had never been very close.

I managed to get Penny's house packed, while the animals were all taken by a former friend. The family belongings I wanted were packed in my trusty Suburban and I managed to rent Penny's home to her former veterinarian. He later bought it from us.

It took me a long time to get over my sister's death but I needed to proceed with my life. The second I got back from dealing with the issues in Elko, I was back at Krismar's helm.

FALL OF 1990

BEARER OF TIDINGS ILL

When the phone rang in the private offices of Krismar, the speaker phone was quickly answered because we were anticipating an important conference call.

We were expecting a Ma Bell, tête-à-tête with someone that we were courting. We were trying to acquire The Lodge at Vail as a new client, we were awaiting the important call.

This was the first day that I had been back in the store since my sister died and I was still struggling with the loss.

Closest to the phone, I answered on the first ring. "Krismar."

Unexpectedly, a female voice hesitantly began, "Diane, is that you?"Undaunted by the mute end of the phone the caller continued, "It's Elinor Logan, dear? I'm sorry I'm the bearer of sad news, again. We lost our dear, Dolly a few days ago. She simply died in her sleep. Because you were not close over the past years, I don't think you should even bother to attend Dolly's funeral. It's scheduled for tomorrow at two o'clock." The voice continued with almost a jovial lilt, "Sorry I wasn't able to call sooner, but I had so much to arrange on such short notice. It will be staged at the Church of the Good Shepherd and the choir will be singing her favorite song, 'Hello Dolly', did you know she loved that so?"

"Mrs. Logan?"I finally managed to intercede.

But the voice on the speaker raced on to interrupt and continued in an almost jubilant rhetoric, "Poor dear, Dolly! But she is finally with God after all her years of struggle and pain!"

There was a hugely audible sigh."Oh, and Diane, I hate to further bear bad tidings, but as I forewarned, your god-mommy did not even mention you in her will. As I guessed, as she got older, she reevaluated what she wanted to do with her money. She left almost all of her estate to her beloved, Catholic Church."

I finally managed to speak, "Mrs. Logan," my voice was a study in calm."Who else but the Church did she remember? You?"

The woman crooned back, "Oh, Diane, our dear Dolly was wonderful to me and the other staff, but mostly she left her estate to Good Shepherd Catholic

Church in Beverly Hills. The Archbishop is *so* pleased."

"I should say!" I articulated carefully. My hands were clenched in front of me, my knuckles straining white, bloodless with effort to control an outburst I might regret.

"So, Diane, sad but true, if I were you, I'd wash my hands of this whole chapter in your life. After all, Dolly knew you didn't need anything after you married Steve. She knew you were taken care of. She took care of the little people in her life who needed her things more than you do. Remember the good times you had with your god-mommy. Don't be angry that she didn't leave you a 'little this or that'. I told you, she probably never intended to leave you anything anyway since over the last few years you were not close. And, after all, for as long as I can remember, the Church was her whole life."

That comment made me flat furious and I spat, "The Church? The Church was her life? Oh, good Lord, what a travesty you are!"

"Well, Diane, I've scads to do. I am so pleased with the service arrangements. I so hope everything is well with you, dear. Take care."

The phone went dead.

Steve stood, moved and drew me into in his arms, as I burst into racking sobs. Through my tears I managed to voice, "I just knew that bitch would do this to me. Steve, what are we going to be able to do?"

Steve spoke in his deep resonate voice, anger was evident as he spoke, "We knew they were manipulating things. We knew Dolly was in a state of dementia for the past years. We were in full realization that Logan and the chauffeur were plotting to alter her will. So, here we are! Dolly is dead and they God-damned well did exactly what we expected and our hands were tied to prevent!"

I collected myself before replying, "I know. But why take me completely out of her will? Dolly told me once she would leave me everything. I'm not greedy about her money. I just want to be able to go through her things and pick certain items that may have meant memories to me. Like her diamond necklace she always urged me to wear, she wanted me to have her furs and many of her personal things. The Hurd painting would mean nothing to anyone but me. All her personal things mean a lot to me and to no one else."

Steve was smoldering with building rage. "Dolly Green was your mother, not your godmother. That was just nothing but a sham dreamed up by your adoptive parents and her, long ago. Jesus Christ, 'not even mentioned in her will'. Bull shit, on that crap! We're giving our lawyer the go ahead right away. That Logan bitch needs to be taken out. She got way too greedy on this one!"

Dejectedly, I shook my head with resignation, "Steve with Maria dead and Penny as well, I don't stand a chance if I contest the will."

Steve's eyes smoldered with fury. "Even if we don't stand a snowflakes chance in hell of winning, we'll at least hold them up a while on spending her ill gotten dough. Five will get you ten they have already spent half her money. If we can delay them for even a while, piss in their Cheerio's, it would be worth it just to make them furious, even if there is no chance of a win."

He rapidly dialed the phone, advising, "I'm calling the legal eagles now. Maybe we can get an injunction. Stop them from burying your mother so we can get a sample that can be tested for DNA. If we don't move on this fast, we won't be able to prove a thing. Especially if we need to go for a DNA."

Steve was on the phone to counsel, who promised to move immediately. They advised the Stockmars to sit tight while the attorneys made phone calls.

Logan was way ahead of them in all respects. Immediately after the funeral, Dolly was interned at Forest Lawn.

Even though the Stockmars filed a contest to the will within twenty-four hours, it was too late to perform a DNA.

****

The Los Angeles Times Obituary section, September 05, 1990, stated:

Philanthropist 'Dolly' Green; Heiress Owned Thoroughbreds
September 05, 1990/ Myrna Oliver/ Times Staff Writer:

'Dorothy Wellborn Green-better known as Dolly Green, the socialite, philanthropist and racing stable owner-died at her Bel Air home after a long illness. An aide said Miss Green had requested that her age not be disclosed.

Miss Green, the last surviving child of Beverly Hills founder and oil magnate, Burton E. Green, bought into thoroughbred horse racing in an attention-getting way in 1980 when she spent 2.2 million for five yearlings at the Keeneland sale in Lexington, Ky.

"Oh, it was the most exciting thing," the irrepressible Miss Green later said of the auction, "I couldn't believe after all these years I was actually bidding on a horse...then to bid that kind of money for a horse. My, I did have some trepidations."

Conceding that her only involvement with horse racing before that auction was attending races, Miss Green was initially considered a "mystery woman" in horse-racing circles.

363

But she worked at her new interest, spending part of her profits from the $3.6 billion sale of her father's Belridge Oil Co. to Shell Oil Co. in 1979 to build her stable of horses and hire top trainers and jockeys. At one point, she owned 74 Thoroughbreds.

In 1986, Miss Green's filly, Brave Raj, won the $1 million Breeder's Cup race for juvenile fillies at Santa Anita and was voted the Eclipse Award as champion 2 year old.

"It was quick, short and wonderful, wasn't it?" was her reaction to the victory run.

In 1984, Miss Green established the Dolly Green Equine Research Lab of the Southern California Equine foundation in Hollywood Park.

Miss Green had served as trustee of the Burton E. Green Foundation, which was set up in her father's name after his death in 1965 at the age of 96.

Her own charities included endowment of the Dolly Green Scholars Award at UCLA, Jules Stein Eye Institute. She was a former member of the Los Angeles Junior League and the advisory board of the Los Angeles Orphanage Guild.

A popular socialite and hostess for six decades, Miss Green reportedly startled her socially prominent parents in her youth by refusing to be presented at a formal coming out party.

"I wish to perfect myself in several studies, I would rather study languages even law, if I could do so in preference to a life of parties and dinners and teas." She said.

Miss Green was an alumina of Marlborough School. Her late sister, Liliore Green Rains who had no college education, left $240 million to Pomona College, Stanford University, Loyola Marymount University, Caltech and two hospitals, when she died in 1985.

Her other sister, Burton Bettingen, died in 1986.

Miss Green is survived by a niece and nephew'.

CHAPTER SEVENTY-THREE

Author's Notes:

The will contest was launched by our attorneys in the first part of January of 1991.

As previously noted, because the lawsuit was very rocky and we suspected that there was subterfuge regarding the final settlement, 'counsel' will remain unmentioned. Let them squirm, they know who they are. So they will only be referred to as 'the lawyers', 'attorneys' or 'counsel', not the legal jackals we believed they became in the end.

SLUGGING OUT FOR THE GREEN

In the long, drawn out days that followed the will contest, I spent hours with 'my attorneys' going over every minute detail of accounts that might lead to anyone knowing of my true identity as the child of Dolly Green. To say they came up with dead ends was an understatement! Everyone who might have been involved, literally was deceased.

The conspirators had done their job well. Even though they had not been aware of the threat from the 'purported' daughter, so much time had elapsed since my birth that there was no one left to testify as to my legitimacy.

Luck, bluff, timing? No one could say what guided these criminals so successfully to work their wiles. But nothing, not a single pawn, king, knight or queen, fell to the winner's side of the Stockmar's chess board.

With Burton Green building the cover-up with my adoption papers, the smoke screen with the birth certificate was a perfect ruse, because it completely contradicted what I alleged. My adoption papers said I was living with Mrs. Walker (her married name at the time I was born) at the time of my adoption, but did not claim Dolly as my mother. They simply stated that 'the child' was in residence with a Mrs. Walker at the time the Hunt's adoption was made.

It seemed to completely elude the opposing attorneys that I was the spitting image of my mother, Dolly Green.

It seemed to totally go against everyone's grain to exhume the body to prove DNA. Due to some alleged religious conviction of the deceased, Sandi, the niece and Barry, the nephew, firmly insisted their 'dearest Dolly' be left alone.

EVERYONE was dead who could attest to my blood relationship to Dolly Green.

My surviving aunts and uncles were clueless to any solid facts.

Elinor Logan's attorneys all said that any evidence from my relatives was hearsay anyway, at the very best and mostly third or fourth hand.

Dolly had been buried rapidly after her death, so if a DNA was to be expedited, the body would have to be exhumed.

There was nothing but resistance and defeat around every corner.

Both my adoptive parents had died in the early eighties and my step-mother was clueless to any story except for what Ralph had told her. The lie that Dolly was not really my mother had been what she had been told by Ralph Hunt and believed.

My real father, Neil McCarthy, had died in the early seventies. Certainly his family was never privy to his little indiscrete affairs. If they were, they refused to admit any claims against the revered, deceased man.

Dolly's sisters were both gone, although they would surely not have admitted the truth regarding the scandalous affair's results.

Dolly had never chosen to have close women friends. She was far too jealous to share the limelight with anyone. So no one who had seemingly vaguely known Dolly in her younger years, had a clue about my true relationship to Dolly Green.

So, the contriving chauffeur and secretary had moved their chess pieces far better than they could ever have imagined. The timing of everything simply played to their advantage and it was looking more and more everyday that they would be able to shout the victory cry of the final checkmate.

Elinor Logan held steadfast to her now altered position that I had indeed been mentioned in Dolly's will! Stating that the 'Grand Dame' had become so angry with the badgering god-child's extortive ways, that Logan maintained she had told me the other information to soften the blow of 'not even being mentioned in the will'!

Dolly's attorneys were required to divulge the legal documents to the opposing team.

I had not only been 'mentioned', but I'd been left three million and any personal effects of Dolly's that the 'godchild' had desired, explicitly leaving me the Peter Hurd.

The records showed that in 1987, there had been a little incident where Dolly had a fall down the marble stairs late one night.

Shortly after that, Dolly had called a little meeting with key witnesses. At that meeting, Dolly struck me from that will with a single pencil line through my name. The pencil strikes were supposedly executed and signed by Dolly's own shaky hand. Also signing as witnesses on that fateful day, were a banker, a lawyer and Dolly's doctor.

The doctor had reported in an interview, that 'Mrs. Green had been quite bruised but as to her mental capabilities...she was as sharp as a tack and as charming as she had ever been. Mentally impaired...heavens no! She was on her game as well as he had ever seen his patient'.

At that point in the disclosure, Logan muttered to the Green attorneys, that she had only been trying to 'spare Diane the hurt of Dolly striking her from the will'.

There was evidence of Dolly's flux of adding and subtracting me over the years. But in 1985, I was in the will for three million and by 1986 I was back down to $300,000, still a substantial amount. Then in 1987 I was stricken completely, how odd!

The fact that Maria told me that in 1987 Dolly was legally blind and mentally gone, completely surprised everyone. They were so sure Dolly looked the picture of health that day. They all concurred over the fact that Dolly had expressed anger over all the numerous extortive letters her godchild, Diane, had been barraging her with over the passage of the years.

They relayed that when Elinor Logan reminded dear Dolly of what she wished to do with Diane, willingly Dolly had aggressively stricken the bothersome godchild from the will.

The fact that Maria was no longer alive to attest to the things I alleged, I believed was nothing but a horrendous detriment to our case. Not to mention the fact that Penny had died with all her knowledge of the matters of my real parentage.

Our 'counsel' ran into nothing but insurmountable brick walls. Week after grueling week passed.

Finally, subtle threats began from the opposing attorney's side.

****

On a bright spring day, the Green attorney called to chat with the Stockmar's attorney.

"Ya, know, this Green will contest is just the bunk. I think your client should give some serious thought as to some of the potential problems with this will contest."

Our 'counsel' asked, "Such as what?"

"Well," a wheedling tone was employed."You know, sometimes some people get really annoyed. I mean," again, he cleared he throat, "People have been known to get extremely pissed off over something like this."

"How pissed is that?" he wanted to keep it strictly impersonal. He no more wanted to be this legal shark's confidant than he wanted to place a Luger to his head.

"Well," the wheedling tone prevailed, "Ya know all about that U-haul heiress who was found over in Telluride? They believe that was a hit kill!"

"I see," was his gelid reply. But he did not feel cool. He'd been to Diane and Steve's home enough times to see how isolated they were. Though they had dogs and alarms to warn them of harm, it would be a matter of a high powered scope and good eyesight from the woods and all the Stockmars would be history. No one would ever find the killer, so isolated was their home. Someone could be in and out without ever being seen. Hop on that I-70 corridor and be half way back to LA before the bodies were even cool. That was exactly what had happened to the U-Haul heiress, Eva Shoen.

Green's talent asked, "You still there, old pal?"

"Are you making a threat to my clients or is this just a fireside chat?"

"Threat? What's a threat? I'm simply pointing out similarities in a case. Mega bucks. Impatient inheritors may equal dead 'pretermitted' heiresses. I'm just telling you things can get tense! Your client has kept these people on tender hooks for well over a year, for Christ sake, with no God-damned proof!

Give it a rest, already. The woman just happens to look like the dead broad, that's all. Big deal! I look like Frank Sinatra! Ya' think I'm gonna sue his estate when old Blue Eyes is gone because I look like the son-of-a-bitch, for Christ sake?"

Our attorney spoke firmly into the phone, "We want Dolly's fucking DNA!"

"My clients won't dig Dolly up! They sob at me all day long. It was against her religion. You dig her out of the ground and she'll be damned for all eternity. You can't go and consecrate a Catholic's grave, for Christ sake. They say the freaking religion was the old broad's whole life, she was that devout, my boy."

Our counsel was furious. He was beyond mere frustration. He so believed in his clients legitimacy that if he could figure a way to dig a core sample into Dolly's grave, he'd have done it himself to get the God-damned denied DNA. But, he was worried! Green's attorney said no threats, but he considered Diane at huge risk. He needed to talk it over with her, again. He needed to warn her that these people were getting antsy and the Stockmar side was getting nowhere fast.

Anger laced our counsel's voice when he reiterated, "We want a God-damned DNA!"

Green's attorney cajoled, "What about a little settlement?"

"Like what are we talking here?"

"One hundred grand."

"When she was originally in for three million and then cut to three hundred grand. I really think you are kidding about this being a legitimate settlement."

"How about one-seventy five, cash!"

"I'll consult my client, but don't hold your fucking breath."He then slammed down the phone.

CHAPTER SEVENTY-FOUR

Author's Notes:

This was an incredible time for me with all the negativity swirling around. I sometimes felt as if I was invisible.

I guess it did teach me another life lesson! You should always cover your bases better than we did and never assume that things will work out okay.

They did not!

When it comes to an enormous amount of money, mercenaries will always prevail! They have all the money in the world on their sides and don't hesitate to spend it to defend themselves to their own cause.

However, since the sum total of Dolly's estate eventually was reported in the four-hundred-millions, it is my belief that it was not just greed that prevailed.

The three million Dolly had originally left me would have been a drop in the bucket in light of the magnitude of the Green estate!

According to Maria, the retaliation on Elinor Logan's part was justifiable because I snubbed her all those years ago at the Mexican Gala.

Logan swore to pay me back over that and indeed her final payback to me proved to be a minor dose of hell!

BETWEEN A ROCK AND A BRUISED HEART

Who are you and what have you done with 'Beau-Beau' Hunt was something that kept running around in my head.

I was struggling with the day-to-day of the dragging investigation of the will contest discovery and the constant barrage of accusations and lies that were being hurled from the opposing legal team.

Their clients were howling at the moon over the injustice, malice, absurdity and flat duplicity of the entire allegations that the 'Stockmar woman' was anything more that the impostor of the century. She was making the world's most notorious liars look like princes among men, compared to 'Stockmar's fraudulent claims'.

The Green's attorneys intended to prove beyond a shadow of a doubt that the pretender be dragged through the slime for her absurd contentions and be exposed hands down for the charlatan that they would eventually prove her to be.

Barb after insults were being heaved in all directions and they were causing me to seriously debate the prudence of the retaliatory case.

I absolutely knew I was in the right, but the opposition was death on proving that I was the biggest impostor to ever stand forward in a will contest as a true, 'pretermitted heir'.

After great effort, my own 'legal beagles' were able to contact Dolly Green's niece, Sandi. She had been avoiding phone calls from either side like the proverbial plague. She flat denied that she had ever met Diane or Penny Hunt and was beyond being a bitch, calling Diane Stockmar everything from a "charlatan" to "a money grubbing 'hoe'!"

I was beginning to wonder who I had been and what had they done with my sister Penny. I clearly recalled all those fun trips with Sandi while we rode around in her little sporty top-down Nash Rambler, cruising the city and having a blast. Who on earth did Sandi recall that we were all those years ago, 'Peter Pan' and 'Tinkerbelle'?

It was getting downright scary the amount of people that had just "forgotten" not only Dolly Green's 'child', but her 'godchild' relationship with La Señora Green, as well.

To say that I was feeling caught between a rock and a bruised heart was the place where I was residing at this particular time.

I had been warned by everyone that this will contest would be atrocious. But to have suddenly become 'invisible' or conveniently 'forgotten' by all who were interviewed, was completely beyond my belief. I was feeling moderately pulverized, to say the very least.

Almost two years into the contest, when the phone rang in my office, I picked up immediately. When I realized it was my 'attorney', I flipped it to speaker phone. Steve was due any moment and I expected him to soon walk through our office door.

Our attorney sounded exhausted. I knew him well enough to know this conversation would not be full of good news.

"Diane," he began with a sigh, "There is no justice in what these people have done to you. But, the fact your mother was senile and blind when she struck you from the will, is alleged only by you and the deceased maid.

Maria is gone, your sister is gone. They were your only aces in the hole that could attest to the fact that you have any blood relationship to Dolly Green. And even their testimonies might have not been strong enough. The little red diary is a wonderful tool, but Logan is alleging that Dolly wrote it purely as a fantasy. That it was well known to all her friends that the 'Grand Dame' had always had delusions of grandeur.

"Though she refers to you as 'her beloved this and that' and in that last passage of the mother of the bride it seems she feels cheated by giving you away. She never actually does admit you were physically born to her. It seems as if you were delivered by the infamous 'Stork'. Schazam! Abra kadabra! One day not there, the next fine day you appear! Logan is saying that Dolly adopted you then realized you were too much trouble and arranged with the Hunts to adopt you away."

"My God!" I moaned. "This woman should audition to be a White House Aid. She lies far better than anyone in the hot seat there."

"Well anyway, Logan had built a strong case for herself." He sighed again, continuing, "The Greens' attorneys told us they have credible witnesses that say you were stricken from Dolly's will when she was in perfect health. They all say she grew to detest you and your continuous badgering for funds. When Dolly decided to strike you from her will of the three million, Dolly's words were and I quote, 'I think I have done quite enough over the years for Diane!' She then proceeded to strike a pen-mark through your name and all the other things that she left you. There were several witnesses to that whole execution."

I sighed, "Dolly was under Logan's influence. She was brainwashed by Elinor from the second she became so very ill. Maria told me of a conversation that she and Dolly had after Dolly had just gotten off the phone with me. The one that would have been my last conversation with Dolly ever. Maria said when Dolly got off the phone with me she asked, "who was that young woman? She asked me about my horses and all sorts of things. But for the life of me, I have no idea who she was!" Then she asked Maria, "Who on earth was Brave Raj and who on earth is Steve"? Maria said that she was completely stunned by Dolly's confusion. Dolly was already a Stockholm Syndrome victim by then. She was completely under Elinor Logan's carefully crafted spell."

"Makes sense. That is probably why there is no memorabilia of you at the house. Logan says Dolly ordered your pictures all to be destroyed. Further, Logan insists you hounded your 'godmother' mercilessly for money in the last few years. She swears Dolly grew to despise your extortive ways. She has stacks of letters that you wrote month after month where Logan says you begged and begged for money from Dolly. She got sick to death of your driving her nuts asking for additional funds. Some letter on blue stationary in particular where she alludes that Dolly waived it frantically and said, "What am I going to do about this girl?"

I interrupted, "This is all trumped up lies. Steve and I have pulled our financial weight all our married lives. We have done absolutely everything on our own. Has Elinor been asked to show those threatening letters? All I ever wrote were chatty newsy missives that I though Dolly might enjoy. I was giving her a running update of our lives, not begging for unnecessary funds."

My attorney replied, his voice flat, "She's not required to turn them over unless we take this to a jury trial. And in all honesty, Diane, I highly advise you against further proceedings."

"Why?" I was shocked that he was going to drop the issues without a greater fight. So convinced was I that we could sway a jury to my side, I was flabbergasted by this sudden tact. "We all agreed that we could string these people out for years."

"Their attorneys told me today that they would never exhume the body and that was our only last hope. It was against the firm Catholic beliefs of the entire family. The niece and nephew are death against exhumation. Something about Catholics and the consecration of Dolly's grave. They swear by all that is holy that they will fight you to the death on this. Diane, without a DNA to establish your parentage, this issue is moot.

"Diane, I'm sorry, but the crooks have won! You guys might as well wave the white flag. They have all agreed that if you guys don't toss in the towel, they will litigate you into the ground. It's not my nickel, it's yours and Steve's. But in all honestly, I wouldn't waste the dough. I think no matter what, you'll end up with a loss. I mean, we can continue, if you feel strongly that you want to drag this through the courts. We can go to trial. It will make wonderful fodder for the media. They will have a fricking field day with all this. As it is, we have managed to keep you out of the limelight as per your requests. I guess I felt that your own lives and continued privacy meant a lot to you guys. I got the impression from my long run conversations with Steve, that the reason you moved to Vail in the first place was to get out of the fish-bowl. If we continue to litigate this, you both will jump right back into the waters you so stalwartly fled.

"Diane, it's up to you! But as your attorney, from a fiduciary sense, I don't advise that you continue with this any further than we have. I think you'd just be pissing more money down the drain. I believe you are her daughter so strongly, I believe we could convince a jury as well. But they have offered a pretty fair settlement. It is not what you hoped for, but it is better than a kick in the ass."

"I don't want to just settle! It means they have won. I think we should continue with this suit. We all stand to gain a lot if we can get it leveraged up into the mega million bucks."

"Diane, there is another angle that I have hesitated to talk to you about because I did not want you to be overly paranoid."

I was silent for so long, the attorney wondered if the connection had gone dead.

"Diane?" he questioned. "Are you still there?"

"Yes. What have you hesitated to discuss?"

"Today, the Green attorney brought up the U-Haul heiress murder over in your neighborhood in 1990, which still remains under investigation to this date. Telluride is right out your very back door. Everyone

376

I've had conversation with in legal land, believes Eva Berg Shoen was a hit kill. They think the kids got greedy and hired someone to take her out. Her case is not so unlike yours as far as money is concerned. Eva did not need to prove who she was, but someone believed she did not deserve the dough. This is a lot like your case. I think we need to think about this as well. I'm truly worried for all of your lives."

I responded immediately, "I read every word of the articles. When I read the story, I put myself in her place. It chilled me to the bone. It was an unbelievably grizzly killing and still they have no clue who was behind that actual kill. This happens way too much in real life. Lies built on lies. Duplicity rules the day. I spent all my life playing by someone else's rules only to have it shattered this way by a pack of conspiring thieves."

Counsel contradicted, "I guess it all depends on how you look at things. You and Steve have a wonderful life. You've a strong marriage, a fine, upstanding son. You have a beautiful business and a luxurious home. I think it speaks quite well for you regarding your personal achievements. You did it all on your own. Diane, you and Steve have come by that life by constructing it with building blocks of honesty. On the other hand, the rest of Logan and the chauffeur's lives are going to be spent wondering if they will ever get caught in the fabric of lies they have woven over the passing years. At the very worst, they will have to live with what they have done. How comfortable would you feel winding down your years, as Elinor is doing already, facing the great beyond having been responsible for what she has orchestrated? They both have to endure the formidable shadow of a heinous murder wrap. We all are convinced beyond a doubt, that Maria was murdered because she knew too much for her own good. Maria did the unthinkable, she crossed over orders that Elinor laid down as law by letting you see Dolly at the very last."

I voiced, "Maria was assassinated by those crooks because she cared enough about me to allow me to see Dolly at her end. I will always have to live with that."

"Yes, and then they perpetuated Dolly Green to their own gain. You know darn well they kept her alive long beyond when the poor woman should have died. Anyone with a shred of human compassion would have allowed her to pass away. But they needed more time to work their wiles. No, they as in your words, created the prisoner of Bellagio Road."

"This is so Hollywood movie script. I can't believe this could happen in real life."

"Those connivers will have to live with robbing you of your rightful estate. Maybe when you were just a godchild, it was okay. But no, it turns out you were Dolly's daughter. If they weren't afraid to establish that you are not her child, they would be turning handsprings to dig Dolly out of the ground and produce DNA! They know as well as I do that you are Dolly Green's child. They have seen a recent photograph of you. We sprung one on Logan the other day. Christ, you should have seen her face. Diane, anyone would have to be blind to not see you as the mirror image of Dolly by looking straight at you. You have the damn Green family beak which you so often have complained about. But, Diane, though it seems there is little justice, think of all those mentioned positive things. I think we need to drop this case."

I already knew all the logic in his words, but still was reluctant to give the winning nod. "I just wish there was someone out there who knew the story that we can't seem to turn up."

Counsel answered, "We're grasping at all straws. Maria and Penny were our only real hopes, and now I am even questioning Penny's convenient death. Then there is the butler's drowning as well."

There was silence on the line.

"Diane? Are you still with me?"

"Penny died of cancer. She was ill when she was here with me and she was not diagnosed in time."

"Right. And Maria was a healthy early seventies and died of a massive cardiac arrest. Julio was a championship swimmer and he drowned, it was blamed on drugs. I'm not so sure! How well do you know that doctor of Penny's?"

"I don't know him at all!" My tone was remarkably flat.

"We think Penny may have been murdered, as well."

"Christ! Steve and I were afraid of that but did not want to even believe they would take it that far."

"I believe they did and paid the doctor to lie. I think you should drop the will contest. The opposition swears they will litigate us into the ground before they will exhume Dolly's body to do a DNA. That Diane, was our last and only hope."

"What is their offered settlement?"

They are willing to do cash of one-hundred-seventy-five-thousand, if you walk away from this will contest today."

I did not respond.

"Diane? I think it is entirely more than we could expect. They want us to go away. They want this concluded. I think if we go forward with this litigation, we could lose everything not to mention the threats on your precious lives."

I sighed, "I need to talk this over with Steve. He may not be good with this." I added. "I swear, someday, somehow, I'll fix Elinor Logan in the end. She was at the helm of this mutiny and someday I will expose this to the world."

Counsel added, "Look. They did discover that you are a novelist, they want you to sign a gag order and we flat assed refused. Write this in a book a la Dominick Dunne. He gets away with it, so can you.

You've got a good start because of that little red diary you showed me that she partially wrote. Use that material and all the facts Maria told you that we have documented, and you've got yourself a bestselling book. We need to wrap this whole thing up. As I've told you before, I'm still plenty worried that they may get so frustrated over this contest dragging out, they will try to kill you off just to get you out of their way. I told you, if they can 'off' Maria, you would be just as easy a shot. Keep in mind that business in Telluride. They still haven't found that woman's killer. Hit men are out there, that's for sure. I'd sleep a lot better tonight if I know you are safe. Let's give up the fight today. I can call Green's counsel and tell him we are dropping the contest.

"I know you want the Hurd painting but it seems that so far, no one can find that piece. It would mean little to anyone but you. I'll continue to try to ferret it out. I know you hate to do this, Diane, because you are the rightful heir. You always knew it, but now they do too.

"Now, all it boils down to is this principal. We're not going to completely win, why keep pissing money away on a losing fight. Take the money they are offering and go out and buy yourself a bunch of horses, that's a much better way of spending money than on some God-damn attorney fees that are getting you nowhere. You can get more mileage for your money out of putting it into horseflesh, than my bank account. I think it's time to get on with your lives. What do you say, Diane?"

Steve had walked in and caught the last part of the conversation. He stood silent, waiting for me to speak.

"Steve just walked in catching the last of your advice. I'll fill him in later but here's my decision on this."

I stood and moved to face my husband. I grasped his hands and squeezed them tightly then clasped him around his waist and looked him in his eyes. "All our lives we've known who my real mother was and just lived with the facts. We've been through a lot together on this one. But, we've been through a lot in life together as well. I think we have done what we needed to do. We held them up and frustrated them for a few years. Elinor and the chauffeur know we know what they did. If they did in fact murder Maria, Julio and Penny, as we all firmly believe, they have to live with the fear someday someone may squeal. Someday this travesty may consume them after all.

"You can't live forever with a lie. Look how my beautiful mother, Dolly, spent her last years of life. The raven haired princess, who all her life lied and made it all better by batting her eyes, finally went stark raving mad. She sat consumed by the demon's of deception while she lived her remaining days, imprisoned in the shell that became her shriveled body. If that was not hell on earth, I know not what is. I am the product of a lie. All my life I was made to pretend I did not know the truth. I was made to fib and I too became a victim, because I could not prove she was my mother. So I will lose everything that meant fond memories to me. I don't want to continue this. I know she was my mother. I have nothing to prove to my family or myself.

"Let the criminals go off with the spoils, they deserve the offal like jackals. Let them tear at one another like the vultures they are. I believe in the end, they will have to answer to someone. Who knows who that is when their end will eventually come?"

Steve nodded for me to conclude, "Honey, I completely agree, but finish your thoughts now."

I continued to stare at my husband and softly spoke sotto voce, so only Steve could hear. "He is saying these people are making noises about death threats. I am not willing to do a repeat performance of the

Marvin Davis days, no matter how well we are body-guarded for the rest of our lives!"

Then in a normal voice I concluded so that my attorney could clearly hear, "So they apparently have offered a small settlement. Our counsel is going to try to push further on the Peter Hurd."

Steve's eyes had gone to slits of anger. Obviously he had certainly known that our entire family safety had constantly been a clear and present danger while he'd been President at the helm of Davis's bank. "And?" he calmly asked.

I concluded, "Let's drop it today. We trust you will do the best for us in the end. Thank you for all your help. Sorry it did not turn out the way we hoped. Just settle with the slimy cads."

Steve grasped me and added, "I guess that wraps it up. Tell the bastards to 'divide up the spoils'. They win this one, but tell them from me, to never, not ever once let down their guard! I will have my people shadowing them twenty-four hours a day. If they make one false move, they're discovered. When they chose to mess with the Stockmars, they picked the 'wrong team' to double cross."

Counsel replied, "Will do, Steve old pal."

Signed, sealed, and paid a mere pittance to go away, the will contest was dropped.

EPILOGUE

Author's Final Notes:

IN SUMMATION OF THIS NOVEL

It was twenty years exactly to the day that Dolly Green died and I began the final draught of this book. That was when Michael Gross contacted me regarding my relationship to Dolly Green.

Remember, Dolly died 9/5/1990, or so 'they' said. Gross emailed me first on September third, 2010 and the reissued email came though on September sixth, 2010. We spoke at great length over two weeks during which time he coaxed far retreated memories from my mind.

Twenty years and one day after Dolly Wellborn Green died, I began to dust off the cobwebs on the rough draft of this novel.

How serendipitous was that?

Michael Gross calling at just the right time and his perseverance, his general enthusiasm over my 'amazing' story, finally prompted me into revealing this fascinating saga of a seemingly 'forgotten' little child.

His documentation and his own exposé regarding me in Unreal Estate, spurred me on to finally complete my own telling of this revealing exposé!

So I have documented my own story in a way that I hope the reader has enjoyed.

This book was written to present evidence of the true facts behind the 'mysterious woman' called, Dolly Green.

You can interpret it any way you wish. But I will admit, it was written with more sadness for Dolly, than with angst regarding my own past.

There is always the question of what would my life have been like had Dolly not given me away. I've thought about it many times. I can't see how living full time with Dolly would have been anything but a very sad ordeal.

I am certain that I would have been raised by Maria to the greater extent had I been allowed to remain in the Green household.

But on top of being 'a bother' in her life, I developed asthma, which was very misunderstood in those days. Told by specialists to get rid of the possible cause of the affliction, the boxer and the cat, Dolly preferred to replace me rather than her beloved pets!

Dolly was a very selfish woman who felt she was the one who deserved to have an unencumbered life and chose to dispose of her child! It was too much trouble to deal with the day to day, but seeing me frequently was perfectly fine. Once I was properly trained to be a 'nice little companion', she allowed me back into her life.

Wow! I bet she never would have been given the Mother-of-the-Year award over that!

I never, ever, saw Neil McCarthy again after my adoption. Not even once when I was constantly back in Dolly's home did we lay eyes on one another.

It has been documented very clearly by other sources, that Dolly proclaimed Neil McCarthy was the 'love of her life'. She did not give up on Neil until Heinie came into her scope and replaced Neil.

My real father, Neil McCarthy, consciously must have avoided me and I think that is very harsh.

I truly grew to love the Hunts for all their conservative ways. Marie, my adoptive mother, was Ralph's guiding force. I remember them both with eternal love and devotion to this day!

Daddy was wonderful. I would never wish to have been denied his adoration of me.

My sister, Penny was a guiding factor in my early life. I so regret her premature, mysterious passing as we were just getting back together as sisters once again.

The fact that my adoptive father, Ralph Hunt was a graduate of Colorado College was paramount in my decision to study there. As a family, we went there when I was only thirteen. I fell in love with Colorado as a state and when I viewed the Colorado College campus, I truly fell in love with the beautiful college at the base of Pikes Peak.

Who knows what college I would have attended if I had been kept by Dolly Green. My guess is that Westlake would have been the college preparatory school choice, but more than likely I would have ultimately ended up at UCLA.

Therefore, I never would have met Steve and I am amazed by the thought of that. After forty-one years of marriage, I simply can't fathom having been without my husband and my best friend.

So can I honestly fault Dolly Green for giving me away? No, I really cannot do that, as I do not regret one thing that happened in my early life.

I loved the Hunts and my sister Penny implicitly and would never give that experience away for all the money in the world.

So instead, I became a child of two worlds.

I was gifted with the stability of my dearest family the Hunts.

Then, I was a frequent visitor with my birth mother Dolly, who lived a life of a fairy tale princess. She just wanted nothing more than 'to have her cake and eat it too'.

What I vehemently resent are the people that held Dolly captive in her mansion on Bellagio Road. Doing this under the guise of 'keeping the poor dear in her own home till she died'.

I resent the fact that Elinor Logan needed so badly to 'pay me back', that she took me completely out of Dolly's will. Considering Dolly's net worth of over four-hundred-million dollars, any amount that I had gotten would have been considered chicken feed!

I was thankful that we did go through the litigation to the point that we did in the end. At least I had the satisfaction of knowing that Dolly had not lied to me all my life regarding her bequests. She had remembered me nicely in her will after all. Just not quite as generously as she promised. But then what could I have expected from the 'Queen of the Little White Lies'?

The people who conspired against me, are the ones that will need to come to terms with their own consciences. Including my attorneys, as it is our belief that there was egregious financial deception on the final Green settlement that even my own counsel represented to me.

But as my dearest Maria would probably have said, 'It is water through the viaduct, or don't weep over dribbled cream'!

****

So what have we been doing the last twenty years?

Early in our marriage, Steve and I both shared a passion for collecting, restoring and racing British cars. We restored several Austin Healeys and XKEs.

For years we were involved with car racing with the Jaguar Club of Denver.

I still drive a Jaguar XK which was one of both of our favorite cars.

I am now a member of the Jaguar Owners Club of Oregon and participate in events with them.

One favorite is the Oregon Coast Exotic Car Show that is orchestrated by Kurt Shanaman and his wife, Leilani.

Gourmet cooking was always a passion for both Steve and me and I continue that pastime still. I love to experiment in the kitchen with new recipes, and am always trying out different culinary delights at Pot Lucks with my group of friends.

We were working on a cookbook that I someday hope to finish, but for now I content myself with writing my novels and that keeps me plenty busy, to say the least.

In the mid-nineties, we closed our kitchen store, Krismar as Vail's seasonal economy could not support the business.

So we both moved on to different careers.

I reveled in several years of managing two very prominent Art galleries in Vail.

Then, in 2000, we conceptualized and owned one of our own Art Galleries, called Dragonfly.

During that time, I was blessed with the lasting friendship of Sharon Doll who helped me manage our beautiful Gallery.

Sharon was a member of one of the founding families of Gypsum Valley and lives there still today.

Sharon remains a constant support and long distance friend that I miss a great deal with my being so far away in Oregon. But she and I are able to visit occasionally, and we weekly keep in touch by phone.

Other cherished, lasting friendships we established through Dragonfly's brief flight were Kate Palmer and Robb Habbersett, a wonderful married couple that lives in Santa Fe.

Kate was my most prominent, talented and rising star of artists. Her husband, Robb and Steve were great buddies. As a couple, we were very close friends.

I still keep in constant touch with them, phone often and try to get to Santa Fe as frequently as possible to enjoy their company, when I can.

Sadly, though the Dragonfly Gallery venture could have been one of supreme glory, it ended up in a partnership disaster because of another situation spawned of jealousy.

There was finally a positive resolution in our favor of that legal travesty; with a minor court compensation to the wronged artists. The District Attorney unequivocally dismissed the case as being one that simply was not trial worthy at all.

With that finally resolved, we decided to call it quits with Vail.

The town simply grew too large, too uncaring, too commercial for our tastes. We saw such extreme changes in the Vail Valley and frankly they were not positive in our eyes. Vail went from a little, mountain, family-oriented ski town to a commercial industry beyond Disneyland.

We decided to get out of Dodge and move to Oregon where we are still happily here on our rural property.

There is no true finale to this story as I am whole and healthy and doing well on our beautiful property, our lives march forward in a positive manner.

Our son Timothy and our daughter-in-law, Jennifer, moved here to be with us as well. They live on our shared property with their wonderful twins, Austin and Alexander. They live in a beautiful home across the way from our main house. I feel privileged to have my family all together with me here on our ranch.

Timothy manages our eight acres of property in addition to both parents raising and nurturing their two adorable sons.

We have six gorgeous Paso Fino horses that are enjoying their lives as pasture ornaments until the twins are old enough to ride. I get out occasionally, but have been so busy producing my books that riding has not been my main sport.

2010 finally brought about the publication of Reservations for One in Hell. I have produced its sequel, Pale Diamonds. I have recently released my Merlin Trilogy, Merlin's Ring, Merlin's Quest and Merlin's Triumph. They are all available now.

I am working on the sequel to Pale Diamonds, called, The Dark Side of a Fairy Tale. 'Dark Side' will be the fictitious rendition of, All that Glittered Was Not Told. Don't miss this when it is released, sometime in 2012.

We have good friends who have traveled along with us on this interesting road and plenty who did not choose to follow our path. They know who they are and know also that they are loved and missed but only a phone call away.

I was blessed that when Reservations for One in Hell was published in 2010, a dear friend jumped on board and began to help edit my literary endeavors. Through our editing, Pale Diamonds and All That Glitters Is Not Told, Marsha Logan Campbell and I have been able to renew our very dear friendship. Our editing partnership works well even though it is by cell phone.

We get an occasional trip to see one another, but not nearly enough to satisfy us both!

Hopefully, someday that will change for the better in that stead.

We have a wonderful group of Oregon friends who over the past seven years have become close as well.

So our move to this beautiful State was perceived as a positive and good choice for us all.

I travel a fair amount with my novel distributions being paramount right now as I am getting my books out in the marketplace more every day.

I have been fortunate to have a literary associate in Jean Kellogg who became a good friend in 2010. She and I became acquainted with one another through an Art Show I organized for her mother, the talented artist, Flora Bolstad.

Jean now travels with me, commiserates with me and has been added to my editing team, as of 'All That Glittered Was Not Told'.

My editors, Marsha Campbell and Jean Kellogg deserve medals for their tenacity, as no one but an editor and an author comprehensively realize how grueling the final edits in any novel truly can be to complete!

So a heartfelt thanks to both my gals!

Steve had a home office on our ranch where he ran his Commercial Real Estate company. He was as happy as I had ever seen him in his life to be able to sit in his beautiful home office and look out as the rural, Oregon countryside.

Oregon embodies a great deal of the wonderful ranch experience that both of us had hoped to enjoy for the rest of our lives.

So from my own home office on our ranch, I continue to produce my novels and intend to persist for as long as I can pound keys and keep the ideas flowing.

'All That Glittered' was cathartic for me and a story that needed to finally be told. It had its highs and lows, but it simply needed to be committed to a book so my family and I could put the untold tale to rest.

Now I can proceed with happier pursuits in the more uplifting realm of fiction.

Long and short, I am and always will be the natural child of Dolly Green and the granddaughter of Burton Green who was the primary founding father of fabled, Beverly Hills. I am proud of that heritage and am glad to have finally gotten this story out.

I was robbed of my inheritance by those who professed to be the keepers of the Castle Green while Dolly was in a severe mental decline.

They deprived me of my rightful inheritance and my ultimate payback to them is that I have finally written this exposé as I swore to do, twenty years ago, today!

After all this time... All that glittered finally has been told!

****

I had been married to Steve, my love and best friend for almost forty-two years and we both cherished that.

A tragic note to end on, he died on May 18th of this year 2012, from the side effects of a drug called Avalox. It is a dangerous medicine that should be taken off the market. It robbed me of my truest love and I am certain that the drug company, Bayer, will never pay us a dime for his untimely death.

Despite his heartbreaking loss at sixty-four, I continue to write my novels, and that is in itself a full time job.

Steve would have wanted me to continue with my career and highly endorsed all my most current works.

It is largely that in the weeks after his death, I pushed myself to finish this journal as a tribute to him and our long, challenging yet mostly happy lives together.

He will always be a monumental influence in my life as well as a continuously missed companion. I feel him by my side, always and with undying love, he will remain forever in my heart!

SOURCES:

Beverly Hills: An Illustrated history by Geneveve Davis

Early Beverly Hills: by Marc Wanamaker

Beverly Hills: Portrait of a Fabled City by Fred E. Basten

Letters from the Edge: Letters from Hunt's attorneys

Letters from Dolly's Attorney, Neil McCarthy, Esq.

Letters from Ralph V. Hunt's attorney's, Frank Mallory and Elmo Conley that orchestrated the Green baby hand off to the Hunts

Portions from: Documents from Superior Court of California, County of Los Angeles in regard to the Ralph V. Hunt adoption matter

Westlake School for Girls senior quotes: Westlake School for Girls 1963 Yearbook. Senior Quotes from Westlake 1965 *Vox Puellarum* yearbook

Articles from the *LA Times* and *The Wall Street Journal*

Letters in Diane Hunt Stockmar's archives

Quotes from Dolly Green as recalled by Diane Hunt Stockmar and Penelope Vee Hunt

Quotes from Maria Rivera: Documented journals and recorded tapes

Taped phone conversations with Maria Rivera from the Green mansion on Bellagio Rd.

Quotes from Penelope Hunt Clark: Private documentation taken during conversations with Penelope Hunt Clark

Other sources: Diane Stockmar's life-long journal documentation of this amazing journey

Letters from Elinor Logan to Diane Hunt Stockmar

Letters and notes from Dolly Green

Several quotes from *Los Angeles Times* Jody Jacob's columns and other staff writers articles

Obituary: Los Angeles Times September 05, 1990

Documents from Superior Court of California, County of Los Angeles, Court documentation from litigation against Dolly Green estate filed in January of 1991

Quotes from printed emails from Michael Gross to Diane Hunt Stockmar

Quotes from conversations between Michael Gross and Diane Hunt Stockmar

Quotes from the Michael Gross novel, *Unreal Estate* published in November, 2011

Made in the USA
Middletown, DE
25 May 2015